Europe's Growth Challenge

Europe's Growth Challenge

Anders Åslund and Simeon Djankov

OXFORD
UNIVERSITY PRESS

OXFORD
UNIVERSITY PRESS

Oxford University Press is a department of the University of Oxford. It furthers
the University's objective of excellence in research, scholarship, and education
by publishing worldwide. Oxford is a registered trade mark of Oxford University
Press in the UK and certain other countries.

Published in the United States of America by Oxford University Press
198 Madison Avenue, New York, NY 10016, United States of America.

Library of Congress Cataloging-in-Publication Data
ISBN 978–0–19–049920–4
Printed by Sheridan Books, Inc., United States of America

Contents

List of Tables and Figures

TABLES

FIGURES

Acknowledgements

Table: Date of Entry to European Union

1957: Original six members: Belgium, France, Germany, Italy, Luxembourg, and the Netherlands

1973: Denmark, Ireland and the United Kingdom;

1981: Greece;

1986: Spain and Portugal;

1995: Austria, Finland and Sweden;

2004: Czech Republic, Estonia, Cyprus, Latvia, Lithuania, Hungary, Malta, Poland, Slovakia and Slovenia;

2007: Bulgaria and Romania (completing the fifth wave of enlargement that started in May 2004); and

2013: Croatia.

Source: http://ec.europa.eu/economy_finance/international/enlargement/index_en.htm

Abbreviations

EBRD	European Bank for Reconstruction and Development
ECB	European Central Bank
Ecofin	Economic and Financial Affairs Council
ECSC	European Coal and Steel Community
EIB	European Investment Bank
EPO	European Patent Office
EU	European Union
EU-15	The 15 countries that were members of the EU in 1995
EURES	European Job Mobility Portal
Euratom	European Atomic Energy Community
GDP	Gross domestic product
GNI	Gross national income
GNP	Gross national product
IMF	International Monetary Fund
OECD	Organization of Economic Cooperation and Development
PISA	Program for International Student Assessment
PPP	Purchasing Power Parity
VAT	Value-added tax
WIPO	World Intellectual Property Organization
WTO	World Trade Organization

MAP

[To be added by OUP: We would like a map of Europe with EU members marked in a color different from other countries; label the names of the countries; add the below text as a table]

TABLE: YEAR OF ADMISSION TO THE EUROPEAN UNION

1957: Original six members: Belgium, France, Germany, Italy, Luxembourg, and the Netherlands
1973: Denmark, Ireland and the United Kingdom;
1981: Greece;
1986: Spain and Portugal;

1995: Austria, Finland and Sweden;

2004: Czech Republic, Estonia, Cyprus, Latvia, Lithuania, Hungary, Malta, Poland, Slovakia and Slovenia;

2007: Bulgaria and Romania (completing the fifth wave of enlargement that started in May 2004); and

2013: Croatia.

Source: http://ec.europa.eu/economy_finance/international/enlargement/index_en.htm

Introduction

Europe is a wonderful continent. International surveys recognize that Europeans enjoy the highest quality of life in the world. European society also benefits from equality in income, excellent healthcare and basic education, good infrastructure, and developed institutions for the rule of law. The United Nations Human Development Index 2015 ranks 26 of the 28 EU countries among the top 50 countries in the world.[1]

But the European Union (EU) has problems as well. It has entered a period of stagnation. Its GDP in 2015 did not reach its level of 2008—before the Eurozone crisis—and it is losing market share in the global economy. In some sectors like chemicals and telecommunication technology, it is falling behind to competition from North America, East Asia and other emerging markets. Productivity growth has dwindled and is close to zero. Europe stopped catching up with the United States in the mid-1970s, but Europe's lagging behind has grown worse in recent years.

Non-economic threats are also gaining momentum. The conflict in Ukraine has exposed weaknesses in the European Union Eastern Partnership and neighborhood policy and the absence of an EU security policy. In 2014 and 2015, the continent was overwhelmed by the flow of refugees from North Africa and the Middle East, which threatened the abolition of border controls in the Schengen zone. One of the largest members, the United Kingdom, has opted for a decision referendum about leaving the EU. Fundamental questions are being raised. Is the European Union politically sustainable? Can it reform? Can it survive?

Our view is that Europe is in a serious crisis but that it can face up to these challenges. The European Union can only be successful if it carries out substantial changes in the European economic system. The aim of this book is to set a reform agenda suggesting what European policymakers can do to secure Europe's long-term economic growth.

We focus on a few big questions and suggest correspondingly big answers. How can Europe develop a strategy for higher economic growth? Which should be its main components? What measures are relatively easy to carry out and can deliver improvements relatively fast? Our approach is empirical. We want to establish what works and does not work in Europe on the basis of statistical analysis.

WHY WE ARE WRITING THIS BOOK

The literature on the European economy is immense and the obvious question is what we can add. Both of us have worked extensively on the economic transformation in Eastern Europe. Since Europe is experiencing a serious growth crisis and needs a profound rethinking of its economic policy, our previous study of economic transformation appears relevant.

Today Europeans need to pose fundamental questions, whose answers are usually taken for granted. That was the case also in the post-communist transition, where both of us were involved as advisors and policy makers. For example, how large a fiscal burden is reasonable? How can social welfare best be organized?[2] How can red tape be cut?[3] In previous work we have both analyzed the fiscal role of the state, public expenditures and taxation, as well as pension reform. We have used such analyses to deal with the big policy questions and assess what really matters for economic success.

We are both cosmopolitan Europeans, who have visited all EU countries, lived in several and follow the economic debate in Europe closely. We have written plenty about European economic affairs as well.[4] Most of the time, Europeans become irritated when outsiders tell them what to do. We have the advantage of being European and looking to success in Europe to find solutions to European problems.

Much of the European economic discussion has been North vs. South. Our aspiration is to be more nuanced. In several areas, such as taxation and public finance, Eastern Europe offers viable alternatives usually ignored in the European debate. Rather than comparing Germany and Greece, we are inclined to compare Greece with nearby Bulgaria. Coming from small European countries, we see the advantageous solutions in countries such as Denmark, Estonia, Ireland and the Netherlands.

A red thread throughout this book is that variations between European countries are often vast and not well justified. Countries have developed in one way or the other accidentally. For example, public expenditures have risen because more taxation was possible, not because of a deliberate policy based on clear objectives. Countries have changed course when crisis has struck, not because they changed their viewpoint.

We focus on successes in various European countries and suggest what could be applied to other European countries. Ireland and five East European countries have sensibly limited public expenditures. Bulgaria and Estonia take pride in some of the best tax systems in the world in terms of simplicity and collection. The Netherlands nurtures an outstanding pension system. Denmark runs a highly sophisticated but liberal state regulation. Ireland and Britain have excellent labor markets, which is also true of Germany and Denmark. Scandinavia has well-functioning energy markets. The United Kingdom harbor as good elite universities as the US. The Netherlands, Estonia, Finland and Poland possess excellent high school education. Germany and Austria excel with outstanding vocational training through apprenticeships. Sweden, Finland, Estonia and the Netherlands are doing well in hi-tech development.

Three objections are frequently raised against an attempt to formulate a reform agenda for the European Union as a whole. The first objection is that everybody knows what to do, but current problems prevent the focus on long-term economic growth issues. The second is that a European reform agenda is not feasible because the problems vary too much from country to country. A third objection is that reform is all about politics and therefore one should focus on political economy. Let us dissect these three arguments.

In 2007, Jean-Claude Juncker, then Prime Minister of Luxembourg and President of the Eurogroup, was quoted as saying: "We all know what to do, but we don't know how to get re-elected once we have done it."[5] The idea that policymakers have a broad consensus about the desired reform agenda has been widely accepted but having gone through the literature we have found no broad updated reform agenda for the European Union.

Each new European Commission presents its program, as the current commission has done in *The Five Presidents' Report*, which outlines the most-needed reforms of European institutions.[6] The Brussels-based think tanks interact closely with the commission. Bruegel has published books with memos to all relevant commissioners.[7] The Centre for European Policy Studies and The European Policy Centre also present their alternatives, in sufficient detail. These policy proposals are highly useful but they tend to be incremental and tactical, rather than principled.

We strive to present a broader policy perspective. Arguably, the European Union has not formulated a plan with clear daring targets since the Lisbon Agenda of 2000, which set concrete goals for the next decade.[8] It failed in implementation so miserably that the EU has become afraid of strategic thinking. The problem was that the sound goals were accompanied neither by means nor agents of change. The time has come to once again set a daring reform agenda for the EU, and such agenda needs to clarify how the change can be accomplished and who the reformers would be.

We propose policies for the European Union as a whole because it comprises one policy area. Europeans do discuss it as such and the EU has a single market for goods and the four freedoms, that is, the free movement of goods, services, people and capital. The European Commission has far-reaching competences, notably in competition policy and trade policy and the European Court of Justice has jurisdiction for the whole of the EU. The European Central Bank reigns over 19 of the 28 EU members. Furthermore, most European countries suffer from similar ailments, while others have shown how they can be resolved.

The other idea in Juncker's above-cited comment is that electorates punish politicians that carry out serious reforms that may lead to short-term suffering. Even before the eurocrisis a group of senior economists at the European Commission argued against this thesis on the basis of the available empirical evidence.[9] This became all the more evident during the eurocrisis. Two of the three Baltic governments that carried out severe fiscal adjustments in 2009 were re-elected, while none of the many Greek governments that resisted fiscal adjustment and structural reforms was re-elected. More reformist governments than anti-reform governments have been re-elected during the crisis, for example in Germany, Finland and Poland.[10] People prefer responsible politicians who solve serious problems at a time of crisis.

Many economists call for a focus on political economy, and so a large European studies literature deals with the politics, political economy and institutional development of the EU. We stay out of that well-researched sphere, which primarily pertains to political science, and we leave the discussion on the restructuring of European institutions to better-qualified scholars.

MACROECONOMIC STIMULUS IS NOT THE CURE

Since the global financial crisis hit in the fall of 2008, the EU has been preoccupied with macroeconomics, fiscal stimulus, monetary stimulus, the survival of the euro and the burden of public debt. This preoccupation has brought about some positive developments, but they have been late in coming, and policymakers have been so absorbed by macroeconomic issues that they have done little else.

Overwhelmingly, the literature about the European economy in recent years has dealt with the euro, the eurocrisis and macroeconomics. Most economists have advocated fiscal and monetary stimulus, but at present Europe's main economic problems do not lie primarily in demand but in poor supply, calling for structural reform, which is the focus of this book. We have dealt extensively with the macroeconomic aspects of the eurocrisis elsewhere. One of us was minister of finance of Bulgaria, 2009-13, and wrote about the eurocrisis.[11] The other wrote two books about the impact of the global financial crisis in Eastern EU countries.[12]

Today, few EU countries have any fiscal space left for fiscal stimulus. In 2014 their average public debt ratio was 87 percent of GDP and 92 percent of GDP for the 19 euro countries.[13] Therefore, most EU countries cannot be advised to pursue any further fiscal stimulus. The empirical evidence is ambiguous with regard to smaller public debt, but when it exceeds 90 percent of GDP, it depresses economic growth and consumption for years to come.[14] As the World Bank noted in 2012: "Fiscal consolidation should be a top priority in Europe during the next decade and controlling the public expenses related to aging will remain the policy imperative over the next 20 years."[15]

Nor has the empirical evidence been kind to attempts at fiscal stimulus.[16] Alan Auerbach concluded for the US: "There is little evidence that discretionary fiscal policy has played an important stabilization role during recent decades."[17] An econometric study of stimulus policies in 91 countries after World War II found that "governments that use fiscal policy aggressively induce significant macroeconomic instability."[18]

In the face of a global crisis, the IMF committed itself fully to fiscal stimulus from the fall of 2008. In January 2013, IMF chief economist Olivier Blanchard and his colleague Daniel Leigh published a working paper, arguing that fiscal multipliers—the change in output induced by a change in the government's budget deficit—were larger than previously thought. Tight fiscal policy, in other words, would squeeze output more than economic modelers had typically supposed. The implication was that fiscal adjustment should be delayed, but important questions were not answered in the study. It presumed continuous access to international financial markets without major hikes in interest rates; and it was entirely short-term, focused on the next year.[19] The medium-term evidence contradicts its single-year findings: the EU crisis countries that have achieved the highest economic growth since 2008 are the three Baltic countries and Ireland, which all pursued early and substantial fiscal adjustment.

Moreover, failed attempts at fiscal stimulus have proven dangerous to financial stability. No less than eight EU countries had to resort to IMF programs. In 2008-9, the EU and IMF argued that all countries should pursue fiscal stimulus. Countries that were perceived to have fiscal space included Spain, Cyprus, and Slovenia, which soon ended up in financial distress. The fiscal stimulus in 2009 was not the cause of their problems, but it aggravated their fiscal jeopardy. The countries that could claim success from fiscal stimulus in 2009 were those that had a sound fiscal situation before the crisis, notably Poland and Sweden.

The EU and IMF flooded Greece with credits, which had negative consequences because the credits postponed crisis resolution and structural reforms, thus aggravating the crisis. The initial Greek fiscal adjustment in 2010 was tiny, and the country's public expenditures have stayed among the highest in Europe as a share of GDP. As a consequence, Greece's public debt became overwhelming, driving the country into a messy default. The pressure on Greece to carry out badly needed structural changes was limited.

Monetary policy has already been deployed extensively. The European Central Bank (ECB) has pursued soft monetary policy ever since 2008. It and some other central banks have even opted for negative interest rates. So far the apparent stimulus on the European economy has been slight. The euro has fallen sharply in relation to the US dollar, and independent currencies of EU countries even more, so the problem can hardly be the exchange rate.

In spite of all fiscal and monetary stimulus European output has stagnated since 2008, and several countries have suffered from prolonged recessions. Cheap credits were supposed to stimulate investment but investment has stayed low. The large fiscal deficits were intended to promote consumption but that has not happened either. The prime source of growth has been rising net exports spearheaded by low exchange rates. As one observer noted: "Monetary stimulus alone cannot fix debt overhangs low productivity, persistent unemployment, stagnant demographics and a lack of reforms. . ."[20]

The EU has made some progress, reinforcing its rules for fiscal discipline. It has found out how to manage a sovereign default within the Eurozone, and it has attempted the development of a banking union with a common bank regulator and a single resolution mechanism for failing banks. On the whole, however, surprisingly little structural reform ensued.

One explanation is that the EU was overwhelmed managing the Greek financial crisis, which consumed most policymaking capacity both at European and national levels.[21] Neither the EU nor EU member countries have carried out much structural reforms, save for Ireland and perhaps Portugal and Spain. Ambitions to raise the potential growth after the crisis have come up short.[22]

Funding from the EU and the ECB was abundant and kept the sense of crisis at bay. It eased the pressure to undertake necessary growth-promoting structural changes. Therefore the right appreciation of political urgency has not evolved. In hindsight, economists realize that the worst problem with the Eurozone was not that it did not allow countries to devalue but that it kept countries away from the necessary sense of crisis. The dean of Swedish economics, Assar Lindbeck, reported that during the midst of the Swedish financial crisis in 1993 journalists asked him, "Can Sweden be saved?"[23] During the euro crisis, on the contrary, the argument ran that Brussels, Berlin and Frankfurt "had to" provide more funding to the suffering crisis countries, which were not supposed to save themselves as Sweden was in 1993.

Leszek Balcerowicz noted that "far too often the European response to crisis has consisted of policies that were either designed to avoid or postpone the deeper repairs so many economies need."[24] Some countries did carry out successful structural reforms but largely during severe fiscal consolidation as in Ireland, the Netherlands, Finland and Sweden before 2008 and in the three Baltic countries and Ireland after 2008. In the end, some of the over-stimulated countries pursued significant reforms, but none was comprehensive.

Since the solution of Europe's growth crisis lies elsewhere, macroeconomics is not the topic of this book. Neither is the European banking union, another much-discussed topic. The key to long-term growth lies in structural transformation and the opening of markets to facilitate competition to boost efficiency and welfare.

In 2015, the four EU presidents observed: "The crisis in the euro area, triggered by the global financial turmoil, can also be said to have been a *competitiveness crisis*, with several weaknesses predating the crisis. While there had been some catching up with the U.S. in terms of productivity until the 1990s, this process has stopped over time." As the EU pursued macroeconomic stimulus deep-rooted vulnerabilities did not allow the supply side to catch up with demand.[25] These views seem to have become mainstream. A widely-held opinion is now that monetary policy can only do so much, when there is limited fiscal space. Therefore "supply-side improvements to enhance productivity growth are essential if the economy is to generate sustained, faster growth."[26]

THE URGENCY OF CHANGE IS RISING
WITH STAGNATION AND CRISIS

How can Europe change? One issue is whether a clear idea exists of what changes are needed. The other question is whether these are politically possible. Little can be accomplished without clear ideas, as John Maynard Keynes observed his *General Theory*:

> the ideas of economists and political philosophers, both when they are right and when they are wrong, are more powerful than is commonly understood. Indeed the world is ruled by little else. Practical men, who believe themselves to be quite exempt from any intellectual influences, are usually the slaves of

some defunct economist . . . I am sure that the power of vested interests is vastly exaggerated compared with the gradual encroachment of ideas.[27]

Our ambition in this book is to draw on ideas that have been developed over time, and currently represent a broad economic policy consensus. Our endeavor is to be clear and focus on the most essential shortcomings and fixes, because such a framework is necessary for a major change, and at the same time present ideas that can be widely understood and appreciated.

Are beneficial changes politically possible? In his volume *The Political Economy of Policy Reform*, John Williamson has shown that crises usually precede major reforms.[28] Margaret Thatcher won her elections in May 1979, when everybody had written off Britain after years of stagnation. Poland's reformer Leszek Balcerowicz called the period of extreme crisis "extraordinary politics," when many policies could be implemented that were otherwise politically impossible.[29] In 1999, *The Economist* magazine had a cover story about Germany with the title "The Sick Man of the Euro."[30] Four years later, Social Democratic Chancellor Gerhard Schröder carried out important labor market reforms. The conclusion is that economic change becomes politically possible when it is vital.

As the global financial crisis hit, President Barack Obama's chief of staff Rahm Emmanuel stated: "A crisis is a terrible thing to waste." In academia, Drazen and Grilli have made the case that a fiscal crisis breaks up old vested interests.[31] Famously, the father of the EU, Jean Monnet wrote in his memoires: "Europe will be forged in crises, and will be the sum of the solutions adopted for those crises."[32] The point has been made that the eurocrisis since 2010 has proven Monnet wrong, because this was a time of divergence among the EU members rather than convergence. Few structural changes took place,[33] but as we have argued above the problem was that Europe was flooded in fiscal and monetary stimulus, which can no longer continue. Therefore, the time for reform has hopefully arrived.

The current situation is sufficiently bad to spur major reforms to promote economic growth. The EU's GDP grew merely by 1 percent during the seven years from 2007 to 2014.[34] In that period the EU-28 population grew slightly more from 498 million to 508 million,[35] so Europe experienced a decline in real GDP per capita of 1 percent. These seven years of stagnation are forecast to be followed by a decade of minimal growth. Europe should be able to stand up and deliver change sooner than that.

Sensibly, the four EU presidents conclude that in the short run, it is important to implement a consistent strategy around the virtuous triangle of structural reforms, investment and fiscal responsibility so as to "move towards more effective commitments to growth-enhancing structural reforms in the euro area." They continue, "the functioning of the Single Market needs to be improved. . . Enhancing labor mobility is key. . . Further initiatives to complete the Single Market for example in the areas of the digital economy and energy are essential to strengthen growth prospects."[36]

THE REFUGEE CRISIS CAN BE A CATALYST FOR CHANGE

One of the factors forcing Europe to reform is migration. In 2015, more than a million and a half refugees from North Africa and the Middle East fled to Europe. This is unlikely to be a single event. The United Nations High Commissioner for Refugees counted 60 million refugees in the world, more than at any time after World War II. Modern transportation renders travel easy, and information crosses the globe in real time through contemporary telecommunications and social networks. Economists have long argued that the easiest way for an individual to raise her standard of living is to move from a poor to a rich country.[37] It is the most effective way of raising global welfare too.

Migration flows are likely to increase over time. Tens of millions of people in Africa, the Middle East and parts of Asia could greatly benefit from moving to Europe. Migration can be regulated, but it cannot be stopped. As long as Europe remains so much richer than Africa and the Middle East and has so low birth rates, immigration is bound to replenish Europe's labor force. Eleven EU countries already have an immigration population of more than one-tenth, and five EU countries—Luxembourg, Estonia, Belgium, Sweden, and Austria--have a larger foreign-born population than the US.[38] European countries have to handle large-scale immigration as traditional immigration countries, such as the United States, Canada and Australia, have learned to do. Europe needs to offer appropriate work incentives through taxes and social benefits as well as the labor regulation through issuance of work and residence permits.

The current immigration wave is among the most serious crises Europe has faced after World War II. At the end of 2015 Carl Bildt observed: "As the European Union prepared to enter the new year, it faces an almost perfect storm of political challenges. The strategy it has used in the past—barely muddling through a series of calamities—may no longer be enough. . . .. The situation is far more demanding than anything the EU has seen so far."[39]

Dealing with past European crises offers valuable lessons. Waiting for the storm to pass is usually a poor option. For too long, Europe's policymakers did not face up to the Eurozone crisis, hoping to muddle through. As a consequence, all decision-making took place in slow motion, which increased the costs and the suffering in many crisis countries.[40] The successful crisis management in the three Baltic countries in 2008-9 offer a sobering contrast, indicating what the EU could do.[41] It needs to speed up its policymaking, which would be much easier if the European Commission gained more power.

The refugee crisis requires urgent funding, which demands savings elsewhere. It may compel EU countries to reduce labor taxes so that more people can be employed in the formal economy. In the absence of conducive labor regulations, many new migrants are forced either to live on social welfare or work in the underground economy, which deprives the host countries of tax revenue, while the new arrivals suffer. A sufficient number of labor permits need to be issued in an orderly manner to satisfy national labor markets.

The economic impact of migration is not a given but depends on the policies pursued. In a 2016 report, IMF experts summarize the lessons: "The impact of refugees on medium and long-term growth depends on how they will be integrated in the labor market. International experience with economic migrants suggests that migrants have lower employment rates and wages than natives, though these differences diminish over time."[42] Europe needs to integrate refugees much more efficiently than currently is the case.

Immigration is both a challenge and an opportunity. Without it, Europe might be condemned to the economic stagnation Japan is experiencing in the past two decades. Immigration can bring large economic benefits. For a country with sizeable immigration such as Sweden it expands the population in spite of low birth rates and a healthier age pyramid, rendering the future financing of the social welfare system more sustainable. Most developed countries suffer from a shortage of specific kinds of highly-skilled labor that immigrants often can offer. Many immigrants bring with them desired skills, from which a nation can benefit if it allows them to work.

If the labor market is opened up, the European service market could finally be freed as well because trade in services usually involves the movement of labor, which would be a great positive contribution from migration. Labor market regulations, social benefits and taxation need to be adjusted to accommodate immigrants and make them accepted.

Citizens are reluctant to pay higher taxes for social benefits for immigrants not allowed to work because of stringent labor market regulations. Migrants are mobile and often move on. European social welfare systems need to be adjusted so that earned social benefits can be used in another country, but also so that citizens feel that both they and migrants get a fair deal. In particular, pension savings should be personalized. Increased movement of population is also an argument to trim social transfers.

TTIP CAN HELP EUROPE OPEN UP VITAL MARKETS

The biggest present Western integration project is the Transatlantic Trade and Investment Partnership (TTIP), which is an attempt to form a free trade area between the US and the EU. It could be a catalyst of positive change in Europe.

The Eastern European EU members offer two good examples of the positive impact of economic integration. In the early 1990s, the EU opened its vast market to the post-communist countries, offering them excellent incentives to turn their economies around to become competitive.

When eight East European countries acceded to the EU in 2004, they obtained another impetus to high economic growth from 2004-7. Their economic integration also boosted the old EU economies, as the East European economies integrated into the European supply chain. Outsourcing to the East reinvigorated high-cost EU companies, while Eastern Europe grew faster than the old EU countries thanks to foreign direct investment. Germany and Sweden would have been far worse off if they had not benefited from outsourcing to their eastern neighbors.

A substantial free trade agreement within TTIP could have major impact on Europe. Presumably, the greatest and most beneficial effects would be if TTIP opens up the European and US service trade and digital trade. The benefits would be mutual, but they would be the greatest within the EU because of its failure to liberalize service trade on its own.

The US has already opened up for exports of LNG and crude oil to Europe, which should help Europe to develop its energy market. TTIP would lead to far greater foreign direct investment and greater market integration in the whole of Europe. New companies would promote innovations and new technologies, and Europe could accelerated its hi-tech development.

REINFORCING INTERNATIONAL ECONOMIC FREEDOM

In his book *The World America Made*, Robert Kagan emphasized how Britain and then the US have developed essential global public goods, such as free markets and free shipping. "The global free-market economy we know today was created by British power in the nineteenth century, and when Britain faltered between the two world wars, that liberal economic order. . .collapsed." It was absent in the interwar period. "It was only when the United States took on the task of creating and sustaining a liberal economic order after World War II that it took hold, and then only in those parts of the world not controlled by the Soviet Union or China. The liberal economic order is a choice, not the inevitable product of evolution."[43]

In the 20th century, the alternative to economic freedom was central planning under communism. Today, the main alternative is state capitalism. It is represented by large emerging economies neighboring Europe, such as Russia, and Turkey. By most measures, the emerging economies now account for half the global economy, and the developed Western economies for the other half. The ultimate question, as it was put during discussions of the new Transpacific Partnership (TPP), is whether the West or the East will set the standards.

In recent years, the US has been reluctant to engage in its traditional postwar role of global policeman. It took years before the Somali pirates were subdued by international action. In Libya, some European countries wanted to stand up against President Muammar Gadhafi's mass killings of opposition. When they finally did, they lacked the necessary air force to be effective and they were salvaged by US air support. In Syria, the Western nations hesitated and largely stayed out. Instead international support from more dubious parties was given to extremists on both sides, which led to the mass flow of refugees to Europe in 2015. Ukraine suffered the loss of Crimea and endured a protracted bloody war in its east because the new nation had given up its plentiful nuclear arms in return for insubstantial security "assurances" in the Budapest Memorandum of 1994, but the West did very little.

These examples show how military disorder easily evolves if the US chooses to stay out. As Germany's long-time Foreign Minister Joschka Fischer stated: "Europe must recognize that if it doesn't take care of its geopolitical interests, sooner or later crises in its neighboring regions will arrive on its doorstep."[44] And yet, that has already happened.

United Nations peacekeeping is precluded if Russia or China vetoes it. Heinous forces may gain the upper hand as in Syria, which is reminiscent of the Spanish Civil War 1936-39, when Stalin, Hitler and Mussolini provided military support to their sides, while the democratic West kept out. Alternatively, armed conflicts may just linger on at great cost to many.

The US could have intervened in these recent international dramas, but it chose not to do so. Many worry that the US will not be sufficiently strong to play as great a military role in the future. At present, US military expenditures account for 34 percent of global military expenditures at current exchange rates, but this share is falling and the US GDP is only one-fifth of global GDP.[45] Can the US military strength hold up if rising economies turn militaristic? The answer is uncertain, and the US would be greatly helped if the EU that accounts for another fifth of the global GDP stood up for Western values with military strength.

Another question is whether Europe will act as a serious strategic partner. In 2003, the EU issued its first European Security Strategy. It stated bluntly: "Europe has never been so prosperous, so secure or so free. The violence of the first half of the 20th century has given way to a period of peace and stability in European history."[46] Peace and security were considered self-evident and eternal. As a consequence of such sentiments, in 2014 Europe spent only 1.3 percent of its GDP on defense to compare with 3.5 percent of GDP in the US. Europe has long enjoyed its peace dividend after the end of the Cold War, ignoring NATO demands for minimum defense expenditures of 2 percent of GDP.

Europe's strength and commitment is questioned: "The key question in assessing Europe's power resources is whether the EU will retain enough cohesion to speak with a single voice on a wide range of international issues." He continued: "In 1900, Europe accounted for a quarter of the world's population. By the middle of this century, it may account for just 6 percent—and almost a third will be older than 65."[47]

The restrained US policy in Syria and elsewhere in recent year has shown Europeans that they can no longer live as free riders on US security. NATO as a military organization has hardly been real while the US has allowed its members to rely on its bilateral security guarantees based on Article 5 of the NATO charter. Europe needs to be able to defend itself, forming a security policy and gathering more and real military resources.

Russia's aggression against Ukraine has been a wakeup call for Eastern Europe, and the war in the Syria is shaking up the whole of Europe. The US has a major interest in Europe becoming an effective ally once again. As Robert Kagan wrote: "What has been true since the time of Rome remains true today: there can be no world order without power to preserve it, to shape its norms, uphold its institutions, defend the sinews of its economic system, and keep the peace."[48]

To be able to defend itself Europe needs sufficient economic means. Europe is in a prolonged economic stagnation. One of the foremost European thinkers, Estonia's President Toomas Hendrik Ilves, has put the challenge of the EU in all clarity: "Either we do things better or, if we don't, the EU is going to lose its ability, as an entity, to act in the world."[49] Our hope is that this book provides some answers for Europe on how to continue being a leading actor.

STATISTICS

The extensive statistics we use throughout this book require a note. The leading organization for the study of structural shortcomings and required reforms in developed economies is the Paris-based Organization for Economic Cooperation and Development (OECD). It produces regular country studies, cross-country sectoral studies and overall studies on economic growth.[50] The OECD is an excellent source for objective analysis and statistics on structural reforms, while its ability to pass clear judgments is checked by the political control of its members. Its studies are admirable, detailed and extensive, though their recommendations tend to be extensive lists noticing everything that is wrong and should be amended. Our aim is rather to select the key issues and raise their significance to render them strategic, but in doing so we are most of all drawing from OECD studies. Unfortunately, the OECD has recently been more interested in big countries than in small countries with great governance standards, so it has not admitted the latest EU members, Latvia, Lithuania, Bulgaria, Romania, and Croatia.

Because of this lacuna in the OECD statistics, we are largely using Eurostat statistics, which have the great advantage of including all the 28 EU countries in standardized comparable statistics. Eurostat generates excellent statistical studies but unfortunately the EU is pursuing much les of sectoral studies than the OECD. The EU entity that seems to display the greatest independence of judgment is the European Parliamentary Research Service.[51]

For the world as the whole, the World Bank is the great source of studies on sectoral reforms. Alas as a development bank the World Bank has done little work on Europe. It did one big study published in 2012, which is highly useful and clear in its judgments, but it is one of its kind.[52] World Bank statistics and individual studies, however, are often useful. In particular, the World Bank Ease of Doing Business Index is highly useful for this study and the basis of one of our chapters.[53] Given that we do not focus on macroeconomics, the International Monetary Fund (IMF) is not all too important for our study as a source of data.

Increasingly, international consulting companies are producing studies on how to improve efficiency of public services, and McKinsey Global Institute has a number of interesting studies of sectors, countries and Europe as a whole.[54] The 2010 McKinsey Global Institute summarizes three broad growth opportunities that should be the priority, namely pursuing further labor market reform, unlocking productivity and growth in services, and aligning policies to growth and innovation.[55] This conclusion represents a broad consensus, which we are happy to join.

Given that our interest is comparative economic performance of various countries, we do not used weighted averages, in which the big countries dominate. We prefer unweighted averages giving all countries equal importance.

THE STRUCTURE OF THIS BOOK: EUROPE'S GREATEST ECONOMIC CONCERNS

This book analyses Europe's greatest economic concerns and offers some proposals for how these problems can be resolved in nine chapters.

Chapter 1 provides an exploratory overview of the European economy in comparison with the US to identify the roots of Europe's growth problem. The overall conclusions are that the fiscal and regulatory burden of the state is excessive, that Europe can do much more to create jobs, that Europe needs to open up several markets, notably the service and digital markets, and that Europe is not keeping up in innovative development, while basic human capital, infrastructure and rule of law are sound.

We devote Chapter 2 to the need to reduce the fiscal burden of the state by eliminating unjustified public expenditures. We review volumes and kinds of public spending and pass judgments on what volume and structure of public expenditures that are desirable. Predominantly the suggested cuts pertain to social transfers.

The companion Chapter 3 discusses how the excessive tax burden could best be trimmed. We focus on the four major taxes—corporate profit tax, value-added tax (VAT), personal income tax, and the payroll tax. The corporate profit tax yields similarly limited revenue regardless of tax rate. Tax competition has driven down tax rates and led to simplified tax administration. The VAT administration and rates have converged through EU harmonization. The two taxes on labor, the personal income tax and the payroll tax, on the contrary, have not converged and are harmfully large, restricting labor input and investment in human capital. The taxes on labor should be reduced.

The key to reduction of the fiscal burden lies in pension reform, which is the topic of Chapter 4. Pension reform should aim to develop substantial private pension savings, which enhance personal security and stimulate financial markets and investment. Such a reform will also improve incentives to work more. The Netherlands has developed the seemingly most successful pension system.

Chapter 5 focuses on the need for a common European service market. The single European market is widely seen as the greatest success of the EU, but it is limited to goods, whereas an all-European service market is conspicuously absent, although services account for about 70 percent of EU GDP. In the US, fast-expanding and well-paid business services drive hi-tech development offering well-paid new jobs.[56] Europe is losing out because of overregulated markets and excessive taxation. In 2006, the EU issued an important services directive that aimed to ease freedom of establishment for providers and the freedom of provision of services in the EU.[57] As of yet, it has not been properly implemented.

The dysfunction of the EU labor market is discussed in Chapter 6. EU unemployment has stabilized at the tragically high level of over 10 percent of the active labor force. Youth unemployment has exceeded 50 percent in Greece and Spain. Labor force participation is low and incentives to invest in education are limited. Many reforms are required to create more jobs, including more vocational training, incentives for women to join the labor force, better absorption of immigrants, reduction of labor tax wedges, and more flexible labor market regulations.

Excessive or flawed state regulation remains a problem, and Chapter 7 considers how to cut red tape. Some EU countries do well, but improvements are relatively easy to accomplish and can reap great benefits. The four EU presidents have noted: "In the World Bank rankings on the ease of doing business, there is only one euro area country (Finland) in the top 10, and several countries are not even in the top 50."[58] Europe can do better and we suggest how.

So far, Europe has failed to develop a single market in energy, notably natural gas and electricity, which is discussed in Chapter 8. Europe has fallen behind the American energy revolutions in shale gas and tight oil, while Europe has partaken in the liquid natural gas, solar power and wind power developments. The EU has attempted to create the missing energy markets through its Third Energy Package of 2009 and the energy union proposed in 2015. The question is whether these projects will be properly implemented.

Europe is lagging behind most in innovation, research and development, which we analyze in Chapter 9. Europe used to be innovative, but it is increasingly falling behind not only the United States but also some East Asian countries, notably China. We discuss various elements needed to help Europe gain momentum in innovative activities, such as more venture capital, less rigid legislation, improved quality of higher education, and more business research and development.

In the brief conclusions, we sum up our seven key proposals for change.

1. European countries need to cut their public expenditures by 10 percent of GDP.
2. Pension reform is the most important means to reduce public expenditures.
3. Reduce taxes on labor.
4. Reduce the burdens on labor to combat unemployment.
5. Open up services and digital trade.
6. Complete the European Energy Union.
7. Improve higher education and create better conditions for hi-tech development.

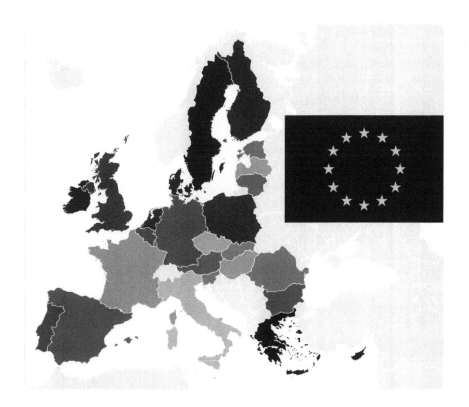

MAP 1 MAP 1

1

What Is Right and Wrong with Europe?

Europe is home to the richest country in the world (Luxembourg), the current World Cup champions (Germany), the most-recognized painter (Picasso) and music band (The Beatles), and the best-selling living artist (Adele). These achievements are manifestations of a single observation: Europe is a good place to work and live in. Its standard of living is the highest in the world, as is average life expectancy. Europe is by far the most equal continent, and has remained so in the past decade when inequality has risen in both the United States and most of Asia. European art, history, fashion and gastronomy attract customers from around the globe. Basic education is free and of high quality. Democratically elected governments have guided the development of all EU countries for at least the past 25 years.

There are problems to be sure. Financial stability remains a worry after an exhausting Eurozone crisis that left some European countries with significant unemployment. Greece in particular continues to be in tatters, with GDP having fallen down by 23 percent of the last 7 years and youth unemployment of over 50 percent. The conflict in Ukraine has exposed weaknesses in the European Union's neighborhood policy and resulted in thousands of deaths. The ongoing immigrant wave is testing the boundaries of European solidarity and the free movement of people.

The goal of this book is to formulate an economic growth proposal for Europe and offer a convincing justification for its need. In order to do so, we first present an overview of what is right and wrong in Europe. The achievements of Europe are well-documented and hence briefly summarized here. The problems are also well known but change has been timid and political action requires convincing analysis.

Section one discusses the dialectical development of the EU. Section two reviews the recent growth record, and section three considers population and migration. Section four observes that Europe does not employ its labor force sufficiently, while section five points to the high quality of human capital. Section six is devoted to the importance of the rule of law in increasing economic activity. Section seven summarizes Europe's economic strengths and weaknesses.

A DIALECTICAL DEVELOPMENT

Since its foundation in 1957, the EU has gradually expanded from the original six members to the current 28 members[1] and its cooperation has deepened. Its evolution has occurred in steps, usually unleashed by crisis. A key battle has stood between market and state power.

The European Coal and Steel Community (ECSC) was the origin of the European Union. Its treaty was ratified in 1952 and it aimed at the establishment of a common market for coal and steel between the six founding members,[2] to achieve "economic expansion, growth of employment and a rising standard of living" (Article 2).[3]

In the 1950s, nuclear energy was the new promise. When the six original EU members signing the Treaty of the European Union in Rome in 1957, they also signed a parallel agreement on Euratom, a European Atomic Energy Community. It was inspired by industrial policy, aiming to pool nuclear energy assets to "ensure security of supply," since "the costs of investing in nuclear energy could not be met by individual States."[4] The Coal and Steel Community and Euratom represent two opposing ideas in the European integration process, market competition versus centralizing resources for large-scale investment, and this tension has persisted.

A permanent bone of contention has been whether, when and how to expand the EU. Enlargement has always occurred at the request of the applicants and never by EU design. Usually, the neighboring countries of the applicants have been most positive on EU expansion. Applicants have been admitted after having fulfilled rigorous legal, democratic and economic criteria. The latest major enlargements occurred in 2004 and 2007, when 12 mainly East European countries joined. At present, no further EU expansion is expected for several years, although several former Yugoslav countries are proceeding with their applications, as is Georgia.

At various times, Europe has tried to stand up to the American challenge. Most famously, the French politician Jean-Jacques Servan-Schreiber did so with his best-selling book *Le Défi Américan* in 1968.[5] Servan-Schreiber's idea was that Europe and the United States were engaged in an economic war, and that the United States won on all fronts, including management techniques, technology and research and development. He called for greater European cooperation. This occurred at a time when Europe was still catching up with America.

The European banking crises in the 1980s and early 1990s combined with the new US hi-tech challenge led to the Lisbon Agenda of 2000, which set concrete targets for the EU for the next decade. Its language was strong and upbeat, focusing on knowledge and innovation: "The Union has today set itself *a new strategic goal* for the next decade: to become the most competitive and dynamic knowledge-based economy in the world capable of sustainable economic growth with more and better jobs and greater social cohesion."[6]

The EU had formulated the targets, but member governments had to form the policies to achieve the targets, and few did so. As the dotcom bubble collapsed in the US, the US hi-tech challenge looked less daunting to European politicians and bureaucrats. In the end the verbally ambitious Lisbon Agenda achieved little.

A decade later, the European Commission made a comprehensive evaluation of why the Lisbon Strategy had failed. This document highlights the ardors of EU bureaucracy: the original strategy gradually developed into an overly complex structure with multiple goals and actions and an unclear division of responsibilities and tasks, particularly between the EU and national levels. The Lisbon Strategy was therefore re-launched in 2005 following a mid-term review. In order to provide a greater sense of prioritization, the relaunched Strategy was focused on growth and jobs.[7]

In this evaluation, Europe's excessive bureaucratization and obstacles to innovation were not highlighted. Instead the failure was blamed on poor coordination among European institutions and governments. The word "coordination" appears 13 times in this evaluation. "The governance structure of the re-launched Lisbon strategy was complemented by the Open method of coordination—an intergovernmental method of soft coordination by which Member States are evaluated by one another, with the Commission's role being one of surveillance." The main conclusion was the need for procedural improvement in addressing competitiveness issues, showing that all serious substance had evaporated.

EUROPE'S ECONOMIC GROWTH PATH

In the immediate post-war period, Europe was in a terrible state of devastation. The Marshall Plan of 1948 brought new hope, and so did Ludwig Erhard's currency reform and social market economy of 1948. The Coal and Steel Union of 1951 offered a new beginning and the great step forward was the foundation of the EU in Rome in 1957. Europe experienced 30 "glorious years" of economic growth, fueled by the reconstruction effort and the ideological competition during the Cold War, reaching 4.5 percent annually between 1945 and 1975.

Growth slowed down considerably in the period 1976-1995, the "difficult" years, and a number of European countries experienced banking and financial crises. The opening up of Eastern Europe and its integration with the rest of Europe brought about renewed growth in the period 1996-2008 (figure 1.1). Still, total productivity growth was trailing that in the United States and Asia. From 2009 to today, the "crisis years," Europe went through a deep recession, and has only just started to recover.

Since the mid-1970s, Europe has not fared well relative to its chief competitors the United States and increasingly Asia. Slow economic growth has been the key concern of many European politicians. In the 1970s and 1980s, a protracted discussion about Eurosclerosis evolved. This term was coined by the German economist Herbert Giersch. The idea was that excessive government regulation and too generous social benefits could result in economic stagnation. The Eurosclerosis debate did not lead to many concrete reforms, but it prepared the ground for new economic thinking.

Around 1980, things changed. In the 1970s, the United Kingdom stood out for its British disease of substandard growth and a disruptive labor market with frequent wildcat strikes. The break came with the election of Margaret Thatcher as prime minister in 1979, which was followed by a decade of market economic reforms. In the late 1980s and early 1990s, most North European economies went into banking and financial crises because of an excessive expansion of the public

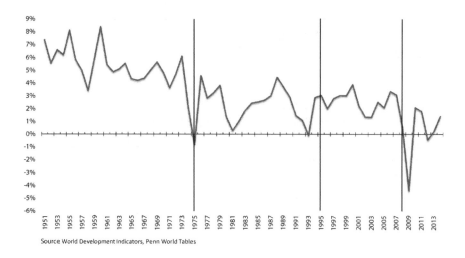

Source World Development Indicators, Penn World Tables

Figure 1.1 The Four Periods in Europe's Postwar History
Source: World Development Indicators, Penn World Tables

sector. The response was deregulation, cuts in public expenditures, tax reforms, and privatization. The outstanding example of a commission of economists that composed a program in the midst of such a crisis and changed policy for the next two decades is the Lindbeck Commission in Sweden.[8]

In 1989, one after the other of the communist regimes in Eastern Europe collapsed. They were all in serious economic crisis. They responded with far-reaching market reforms and privatization. For a few years, these economies contracted, but beginning with Poland in 1992 they started growing faster than the West European economies. In 2004, eight of them became members of the EU and in 2007 also Bulgaria and Romania. Their economic integration and convergence with the EU-15 boosted EU growth as well. This new growth spurt started around 1995 and it lasted until 2007. From 2000 until 2007 the whole of Europe thrived on a global credit boom. This period was cut short with the advent of the global financial crisis in 2008 and the Eurozone crisis starting in 2010, which exposed weakness in economic governance in a number of EU countries.

To offer an international perspective, we compare with the United States and focus on the EU-15, the countries that had become members of the EU by 1995.[9] Greece, Ireland, Portugal and Spain were rather poor countries in the 1970s and grew fast, so Europe should have gained on the US in this period. Instead the total GDP of EU-15 declined from 130 percent of US GDP at constant GDP dollars in 1970 to 96 percent in 2014 (figure 1.2). The World Bank summarized the outcome: "Aging Europeans are being squeezed between innovative Americans and efficient Asians."[10]

This is a troubling result, though the main reason for the US overtaking the EU-15 in total GDP is that the US population has grown much faster than in Europe. A more relevant GDP measure is GDP per capita in purchasing power parity (PPP).

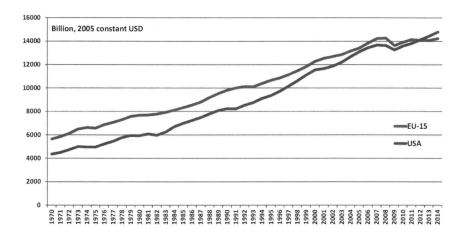

Figure 1.2 GDP EU-15 vs US, **1976-2015**
Source: the World Bank, http://data.worldbank.org/indicator/NY.GDP.MKTP.KD, Retrieved
2015-07-20

By this standard, the US has all along been superior to the EU-15, and Europe has
never caught up. No convergence is apparent. In 1975, the GDP per capita in PPP of
the EU-15 was 79 percent of the US level, and by 2007 it had increased marginally
to 80 percent. After the global financial crisis, the gap between the EU-15 and the
US has increased significantly. In 2014, the EU-15 GDP per capita in PPP was only
74 percent of the US level (figure 1.3).

   These divergences may appear minor. After all, Europeans are living better than
ever. Do we really need to worry? Yes, because new markets, technology and products
develop all the time. If Europe does not keep up, it may be hopelessly behind soon.

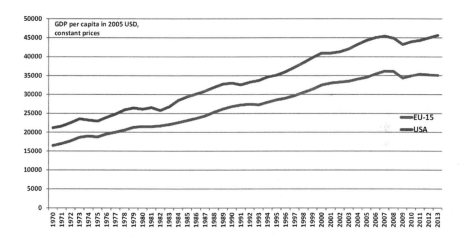

Figure 1.3 GDP per capita in PPP, EU-15 vs US, **1970-2013**
Source: the World Bank, http://data.worldbank.org/indicator/NY.GDP.PCAP.KD, Retrieved
2015-07-20

Throughout the world, creative destruction is proceeding ever faster. The recent American hi-tech startups Apple, Google and Amazon rule the world of information technology, while the dominance of Finland's Nokia and Sweden's Ericsson in mobile phones in the 1990s is a distant memory. Only South Korea's Samsung and China's Alibaba stand as competitors to these American hi-tech companies.

The problem is not only past growth, but also forecast future growth. The Organization for Economic Cooperation and Development (OECD) puts the growth prospects for 2014-2030 at an annual average of 1.9 percent for EU-15 and 2.4 percent for the United States. These averages hide large variations within Europe. Whereas the United Kingdom and Sweden have a respectable expected growth of 2.6 percent a year, Germany, Portugal, Spain, and Italy have anticipated growth rates of only 1.1-1.5 percent.

Even these numbers look too rosy for Europe. In their analytical note of 2015, the four EU presidents included an assessment of the potential growth in the EU for 2015-19 with an average of 1.2 percent for the euro area, with Italy at 0.4 percent.[11]

Ultimately, the issue is Europe's economic, political and social sustenance. As Alberto Alesina and Francesco Giavazzi have put it:

> Without serious, deep, and comprehensive reforms Europe will inexorably decline, both economically and politically. Absent profound change, in twenty or thirty years the share of Europe will be significantly lower than it is today, and perhaps more important its political influence will be much trimmed. Europeans seem to be living in the dream that their past splendor and their current prosperity cannot be lost. This is a mistake. A major European decline is indeed a serious possibility.[12]

These words were written a decade ago, and so far the development has proceeded as feared. Yet the recent Eurozone crisis has focused politicians' minds on this challenge. The need for higher economic growth is no longer questioned. "Europeans are starting to forge a broad social consensus that economic growth will be needed to provide a better life for our children and retain our much-vaunted 'social cohesion'."[13]

According to standard economic theory, growth depends on labor, capital, and technology.[14] We leave capital aside because Europe has persistently had higher capital investment ratios than the US, although it has been far surpassed by Asia. The gap in per capita GDP between the EU-15 and the US can be explained by differences in employment, productivity and technological development. Between 1995 and 2009, for example, labor productivity in the US grew at 1.6 percent annually, but just by 1 percent in the EU-15.[15]

Also in the supply of labor, Europe is lagging behind both America and Asia. Labor force participation is lower than in both its competitors, though even so young workers have difficulties in finding jobs. The recent immigration wave can address the lack of supply to some extent, but even with current inflows Europe is expected to lose between 10 and 12 million workers in the next quarter century. Policies to expand the labor force are urgently needed.

Another big challenge in Europe is innovation. The theory of endogenous growth holds that investment in human capital, innovation, and institutions contribute significantly to economic growth.[16] While Europe leads innovation in a number of sectors, from fashion to biotechnology, European companies are strikingly absent from many hi-tech fields. This phenomenon has many explanations, such as the fragmented European digital market and the lack of venture capital to support such companies during the early formative stages. The largely missing link between research at universities and development by business is also a deterrent to innovation.

In its attempt at "Mapping the Cost of Non-Europe, 2014-19," the European Parliamentary Research Service found that the biggest losses of lacking EU cooperation are found in the digital single market (€340 billion) and single market for consumers and citizens (mainly for services €330 billion), while integrated energy markets would yield €50 billion.[17]

MIGRATION: BIG WAVES

Europe's population has gone through radical shifts, which have been accompanied by major changes in economic growth rates. In the immediate aftermath of World War II, 11 million Europeans were forced to move to their national home countries. Germans in Eastern Europe were expelled to Germany and Poles left lost territories in the east to new Polish territories in the west and north. As the European economy caught speed, emigration started from the poor south to the north, mainly Germany, but also from Finland to Sweden and all the time from Ireland to England. The colonial powers, the United Kingdom, France, the Netherlands and Belgium saw substantial immigration from their soon-to-be former colonies. In the early 1970s, Germany attracted a large number of "guest workers" from Turkey and Yugoslavia.

To this labor migration came political refugees in waves from the political conflict of the day: Hungary in 1956, Poland in 1968 and after 1981, Iran after 1979, Afghanistan in the 1980s, Ethiopia, Eritrea and Somalia during long periods.

After the big eastern enlargement of the EU in 2004, many skilled workers went from the new member states to the flourishing British and Irish economies, making the French coin the term "Polish plumber." Austria and Germany also became favorite destinations for East Europeans seeking better job opportunities, as did Sweden.

The changes in migration have been most striking in Spain. From 1850 until 1950, approximately 3.5 million Spaniards emigrated to Latin America, and in the 1960s and 1970s Spaniards emigrated to wealthier European countries. As Spain grew richer, the direction of migrants turned. From 2002 to 2014, Spain received a net inflow of 4.1 million immigrants. Its total foreign population rose from 2 percent in 2000 to 14 percent in 2014.[18] Something similar is happening on a smaller scale in Poland and the Czech Republic, which have received large Ukrainian populations in the last half-decade.

The slowdown in European economic growth that occurred around 1990 coincided with a reduction in population growth because of low birth rates. In order to maintain a stable population, a country needs a birth rate of an average of 2.1 children born per woman, but in 2013, the EU average was 1.55. France that historically had very low birth rates has now the highest rate at 1.99. Also Ireland, the United Kingdom, Scandinavia and Benelux have reasonably high birth rates, while they range from 1.2-1.4 in Germany and Southern and Eastern Europe.[19]

Many analysts have forecast an implosion of Europe's population, but that is unlikely because Europe is so open to immigration. No less than eleven EU countries have a foreign-born population comprising more than 10 percent of their population.[20] Large flows of immigrants emerge quickly, for example half a million Ukrainians in the Czech Republic.[21] The challenge is to integrate such large inflows into society and the labor force.

The European country that seems to have done so most successfully is Ireland. In the 1990s it became a major destination of labor immigration for two decades, which greatly contributed to its superior economic growth. When the Eurozone crisis hit the economy hard in 2008-2010, emigration ensued to the United Kingdom and the United States. It has since stopped and turned into large-scale immigration.[22] Ireland favors immigration of labor by offering adequate social support. It appears the model for other European countries to follow.

FAR FROM FULL EMPLOYMENT

To a surprising extent Europe's available labor force is idle. The two measures that best demonstrate this phenomenon are the employment rate and the average hours worked per employee. The overall picture is striking and we shall discuss the details in Chapter 6 on creating jobs.

The European employment rate is much smaller than in the US. In 2015, the US employment rate was 68.6 percent of the population of the age 15-64, as compared with an average of 64.3 percent in the European Union. This is a large difference of 4.3 percent of the labor force. Furthermore, the hours worked during 2014 averaged 1,706 hours in the EU, as compared with 1,789 hours in the US, that is, 4.9 percent more than in Europe, once again a stark difference.

It might appear perplexing that Europeans work so little, and this phenomenon has been carefully studied. Comparative studies between the US and Sweden have shown that the difference is only a matter of formal work. Including domestic work, Swedes work longer hours than Americans.[23] The official decline in working hours reflects reduced specialization in the work place, as Swedes repair their houses and pursue other domestic chores, for which Americans hire craftsmen. This misallocation of labor results in lower productivity in Europe. It is caused by high marginal taxes on labor and the strict regulation of the labor markets and work hours in Europe. The most extreme case is France with its 35-hour work week, six weeks of holidays, and a retirement age of 60.

The trade-off between the employment rate and working hours is striking in Southern Europe. Because of strict labor market regulation those who are already employed can hardly be laid off, which may compel them to work long hours, while employers are reluctant to hire more workers because they cannot lay them off. [24] Thus, Greece has both the lowest employment rate and the longest working hours.

Some Northern countries, such as Germany, the Netherlands and Denmark, display another pattern, with high employment rates but short working hours. These countries have opened up their labor markets somewhat, but they have not offered sufficient incentives to work more because their taxes on labor remain high, in particular their marginal income taxes. As a consequence, workers limit their official work time. Nobel-Prize winning economist Edward Prescott has argued that the difference in hours worked between the US and Europe can be explained entirely by taxes.[25]

If Europe had as large an employment rate as the US, and Europeans worked as long hours as Americans, the addition to the European labor force would be 9.4 percent. Presuming that these additional workers would be as productive as the average workers, this would imply a corresponding increase in GDP, recovering one-third of Europe's lag behind the US in terms of GDP. This change depends primarily on two policies, a reduction of the high marginal tax on labor in most European countries and the opening up of the most strictly regulated labor markets, notably in Southern Europe.

GREAT HUMAN CAPITAL

One of Europe's greatest prides is its excellent human capital nurtured by supportive educational and career environment and living conditions. Europe stands out when it comes to its health standards.

Europe's record is at its most stellar when it comes to health standards. All old EU countries have longer life expectancy at birth than the US, with Spain, Italy and France taking the lead. The formerly communist countries reduce the EU average, as it takes time to eliminate their inheritance of communism. But these countries are catching up, registering the fastest increases in life expectancy. Spain, Italy and France take the lead (figure 1.4).

Europe's low infant mortality is even more outstanding. Apart from five new EU members, all EU countries have lower infant mortality than the US, reflecting the high quality of health care services. Here the European leaders are Cyprus, Finland, Estonia and the Czech Republic (figure 1.5). The improvements in Estonia and the Czech Republic are nothing but outstanding. In these areas, the US needs to learn from Europe.[26]

Comprehensive public education is another great European pride. The US used to be the global leader in the share of the population that has graduated from high school, but that is no longer true. Eighty-eight percent of the US adult population has completed high school, but six East European countries supersede that level. Yet, the South Europeans are lagging seriously behind. Only 42 percent of the

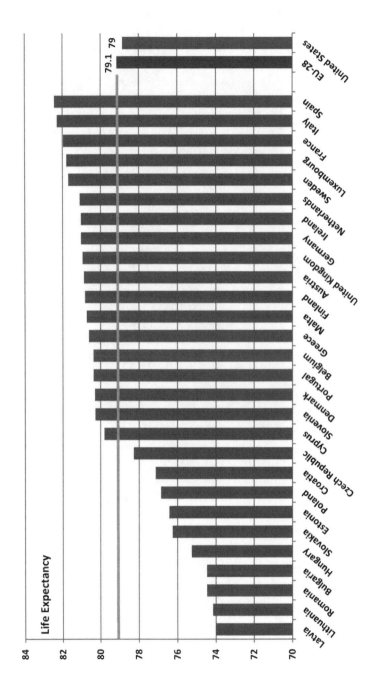

Figure 1.4 Life Expectance at Birth

Source: The World Bank, http://data.worldbank.org/indicator/SP.DYN.LE00.IN, Retrieved 2015-07-10

Figure 1.5: Infant mortality, 2013

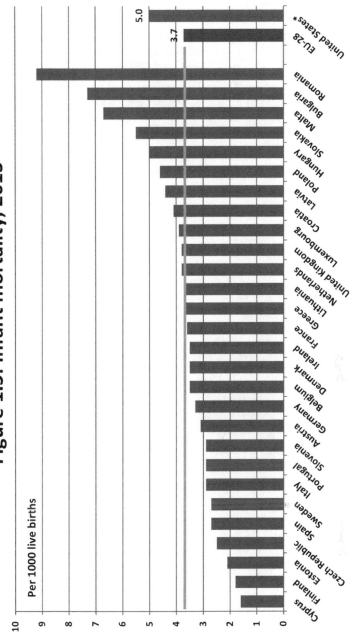

Per 1000 live births

Figure 1.5 Infant Mortality

*Data from 2012Source: For EU-28: http://ec.europa.eu/eurostat and for the US: http://stats.oecd.org/, Both retrieved 2015-07-07

Portuguese have completed high school, and Spain, Italy and Greece are also suffering from limited secondary education.[27]

The achievement in tertiary education is similar. The picture varies somewhat with the choice of measurement, but the completion of higher education for the age cohort of 25-34 appears most relevant. In 2011, Europe fell into two large categories divided between North and South with Ireland leading the successful North, and the South headed by Italy. In 16 EU countries 35-50 percent of the young have completed higher education, and nine surpass the US. In the remaining 12 EU countries only 20-30 percent of the youth had completed higher education. This group includes Germany and Austria, but these two countries have extensive apprenticeships delivering vocational achievement, which are not considered higher education.[28]

The best measure of the quality of school education is the OECD Program for International Student Assessment (PISA) scores and mathematics probably offers the most objective measure. In general, Europe does well. The US is just below the EU average, but four EU countries lag far behind, namely Bulgaria, Cyprus, Romania and Greece.[29]

The most difficult challenge for Europe in further improving its human capital is to catch up in university education, research and development, and innovation. In no other areas is the US so dominant, and this is arguably the most important factor for future economic growth. To resolve them will require significant resources, especially in Southern and Eastern Europe.

INSTITUTIONS SUPPORTING THE RULE OF LAW

"The great gift to the Western world of law from the Magna Carta in 1214 was the notion that no person, including the sovereign, is above the law and that all persons are secure from the arbitrary exercise of the powers of government. The Magna Carta is the spiritual and legal ancestor of the concept of rule of law" writes legal historian John Kelly.[30] The origins of the protection of citizens and investors from government or other private actors come from Europe. First in England and then in other European countries, judges were expected to apply the law equally and fairly.

Initially, the focus of laws was to discourage or punish government expropriation of private property. With the development of private commerce, the rule of law evolved to safeguard property and contracts against business competitors or partners. In both its variations, the rule of law was increasingly seen as a determinant of business and financial activity in the 19th and 20th centuries.[31]

During the last two decades a large number of indexes have been developed on the state of economic and legal governance. Our preferred index is the Fraser Institute index, because it is broad, empirical, and exists for many countries for a relatively long time period. In its overall index for economic freedom the US ranks close to the top of the world, but Finland, the United Kingdom and Ireland are at approximately the same level. The EU countries do well by this measure, but four countries fall far behind the rest, namely Slovenia, Greece, Italy and Croatia (figure 1.6).

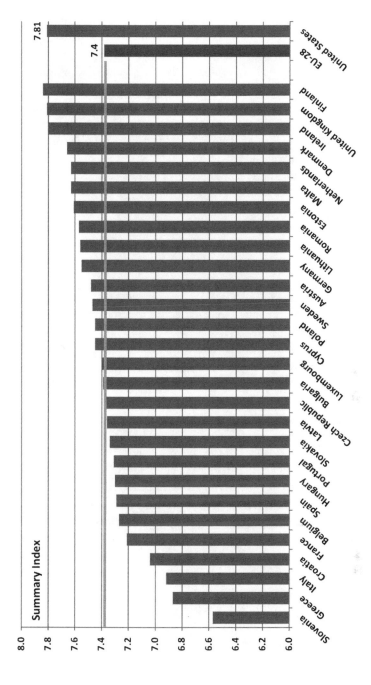

Figure 1.6 Economic Freedom, 2014

Source: Fraser Economic Freedom Index, http://www.freetheworld.com/release.html, retrieved 08/07/15.

Since the 1980s, the rule of law is increasingly recognized as the main ingredient of economic growth, as argued by Nobel Prize winner Douglass North and his disciples.[32] A large empirical literature has followed, measuring the effects of the rule of law on entrepreneurship, access to finance, innovation, and economic growth.[33] A number of think tanks and international institutions have designed indicators capturing changes to the rule of law across the world.

The Fraser Institute provides a broad measure of the rule of law. Europe dominates the top positions. The US has gradually declined from taking the top space in the world in 1991 to the 38th place in 2015. Finland's legal system ranks as the best in the world and half the EU members have a legal order superior to that in the United States. The EU countries judged to have the worst legal order are Bulgaria, Greece, Romania, Slovakia and Croatia (figure 1.7).

A second measure of the rule of law is the corruption perception index composed by the non-governmental organization Transparency International. Its results are quite similar, but it puts Bulgaria, Greece, Romania, and Italy at the bottom.[34] Thus, with a few Southern exceptions Europe is the global leader in upholding the rule of law.

A third measure is the enforcing contracts indicator in the World Bank's Doing Business index. There, too, one-third of European countries, including Austria, France, Estonia, Germany and Lithuania, are more efficient than the United States. However, several Asian economies are even better at resolving commercial disputes, including Singapore, Korea, Australia and China. This suggests that Europe fear increasing competition from Asia in attracting entrepreneurs and investors.[35]

The strength of the rule of law is seen both at the EU level, and the individual countries' level. In EU law, there are established mechanisms for individuals to challenge regulatory measures before national courts and have them referred to the European Court of Justice. The European Commission can bring infringement proceedings against national governments to enforce EU law. The Commission has dealt with several such challenges to the rule of law in recent years, for instance against Hungary on cases like the early retirement of judges; or on the violation of the data protection supervisory authority's independence. Another example is the case on the equal treatment of Roma children in schools in Slovakia.

If fundamental values are disrespected in a EU country outside the scope of EU law, a special mechanism in Article 7 of the EU Treaty can be applied and lead to the suspension of the country's rights, including its voting rights. This is a measure of last resort, introduced after Jörg Haider's party joined the Austrian government in 2000. In 2011, the European Commission considered imposing such suspension over the Hungarian government's decision to reassign three radio frequencies, taking one of them from the country's largest opposition radio station, Klubradio. The case was resolved before activating Article 7 with changes in the Hungarian media law.

The spread of democracy across Southern Europe in the 1970s and Eastern Europe in 1989 also ensures that growth-promoting laws and regulations are more likely to be put in place. A 2014 research paper shows that democracy is conducive

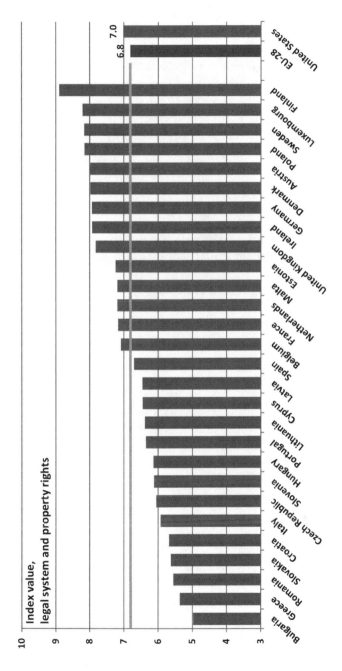

Figure 1.7 Rule of Law, 2012

Note: Rule of law, is decomposed into factors assessing the functioning and independence of the legal system, how well property rights and contracts are enforced as well as the reliability of the police and business costs of crime.

Source: Fraser Economic Freedom Index, http://www.freetheworld.com/release.html, retrieved 08/07/15.

to reform, as politicians embrace growth-enhancing reforms to win elections.[36] In particular, moving from the lowest to the highest value on the democracy scale increases the probability of economic reform by 8 to 21 percentage points, where the reforms taken into account are part of the World Bank's Doing Business index. Using an alternative measure of political rights and civil liberties, democracy increases the likelihood of growth-enhancing reform by a high of 25.2 percentage points and a low of 7.2 percentage points. Research by Daron Acemoglu and others at MIT also points to the beneficial effect of democracy on growth.[37] The study finds that the long-term effect of democracy is 20 percent higher economic growth.

In sum, institutions of the rule of law both at the national and union level make Europe a preferred place to do business. The spread of democracy ensures that regulatory changes that foster economic activity are more likely to take place.

CONCLUSIONS: ECONOMIC STRENGTHS AND WEAKNESSES

Europe has many advantages that make it a good place to live in and to start and run a business. It has a well-educated workforce, excellent health standards and superior institutions that uphold the rule of law.

However, since 1975 Europe has been unable to catch up with the United States economically. The economic convergence stopped. One reason is very low birth rates, resulting in a near stagnant population. Thanks to the attractions of Europe, the continent is enticing the interest of immigrants who can reverse the demographic decline most European countries face, but Europe can only benefit if it takes good care of the immigrants.

Another concern is that the average European employment is 5 percentage points lower than in the United States, and the number of working hours of the average European worker are a further 5 percentage points lower than her American comparator. Both factors reduce economic output. The causes are rigidities in labor markets and high tax wedges on labor discourage economic activity despite these beneficial starting conditions. Steps towards eliminating these gaps would increase the outlook of European growth.

Other causes of low productivity growth we shall discuss in ensuing chapters, notably fiscal burden, structure of public expenditures, taxes on labor, absence of markets for services and digital trade, shortcomings in various regulations, and insufficient stimulation of innovations, which is the most complex and difficult issue.

2

Limit the Fiscal Role of the State

"Like many societies, we went too far in our welfare-state ambitions," says Anders Borg, Swedish finance minister between 2006 and 2014.[1]

According to the World Bank, Europe has 8 percent of the world's population, 25 percent of its GDP, but half of its social expenditures,[2] which shows how high EU public expenditures are by international standards. As an average share of GDP, they reached 50.3 percent during the global financial crisis in 2009. By 2014, they had declined slightly to 46 percent of GDP, still above the 45 percent of GDP before the Eurozone crisis in 2007. In contrast, they were 35 percent in the United States and 34 percent in Switzerland in 2015.

In 2014, public expenditures in various EU countries ranged from 35 to 59 percent of GDP. The highest public expenditures as a share of GDP were to be found in Finland (59 percent), Denmark and France (57 percent), Belgium (54 percent), Sweden (53 percent), Austria (52 percent) and Italy (51 percent) (figure 2.1).[3] On the other extreme, Lithuania and Romania had public expenditures of 35 percent of GDP in 2014.[4]

Some European countries, notably in Scandinavia, have shown that they can manage high public expenditures without increasing the debt burden on future generations. But they did so only after having experienced severe financial crisis in the early1990s when their public expenditures skyrocketed. The record is held by Sweden where public expenditures peaked at 71 percent of GDP in 1993.[5] Other countries, such as Hungary and Greece, both with public spending of 50 percent of GDP in 2015, appear to have ended up in a "premature social welfare state."[6]

The aim of this chapter is to consider what a modern welfare state can reasonably finance. This task involves finding a stable balance between security and economic dynamism. We start by discussing the great expansion in public expenditures in Europe in section one. Section two examines the backlash against too high public expenditures. The questions we explore in the following three sections are: What is the right level of public expenditures? What can the state do and how much does it really cost? How can public expenditures be kept at affordable levels? Section six discusses the Maastricht criteria. The seventh and concluding section sums up what balanced approach to public expenditures would amount to.

Usually, public expenditures and state revenues are discussed in the same context, because they go together rising tax revenues are a precondition for higher

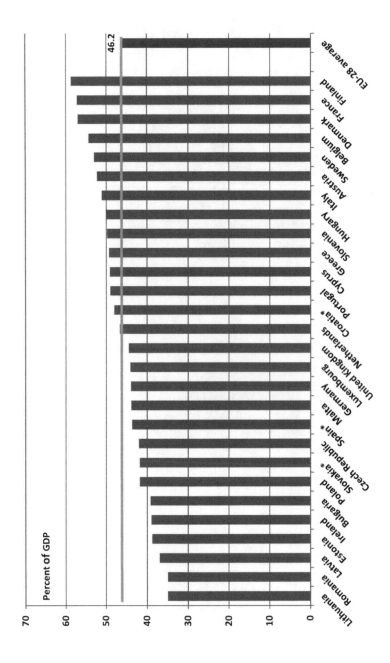

Figure 2.1 Total Public Expenditure, 2014

*Provisional value

Source: Eurostat, available at: http://appsso.eurostat.ec.europa.eu/nui/show.do

public expenditures. Our aim, however, is to assess what expenses are justifiable, which we do in this chapter. In the next chapter, we discuss how those expenditures can be financed most efficiently.

THE GREAT EXPANSION

Vito Tanzi, legendary head of the Fiscal Affairs Department of the International Monetary Fund for two decades, has examined how public expenditures have evolved over time in his books, *Public Spending in the 20th Century,* written with Ludger Schuknecht[7] and *Government Versus Market: The Changing Economic Role of the State.*[8] He concludes: "The role of the state in the economy changed enormously from the beginning to the end of the 20th century."[9] Public expenditures were small until World War I because European states focused on half a dozen basic institutions: the army, police and courts, state administration, building and maintaining basic infrastructure, elementary education, health care, and pensions.[10]

In 1876, a German economist Adolph Wagner argued that the share of public expenditures in national income would rise with the increasing national income. This relationship has become known as Wagner's law and it became widely accepted because by and large public expenditures have risen with national income. This could be explained by rising social obligations of a wealthier social welfare state. Wagner was also one of the early strong voices for redistribution through taxes and social benefits.[11]

However, Tanzi and Schuknecht argue that "the growth in public spending resulted from changing views on the role of the government in the economy."[12] Between 1870 and 1913, its ratio as a share of GDP barely grew, rising from an average in developed countries of 11 percent to 13 percent.[13] Yet, Wagner's law has been important as a rule of thumb telling European politicians that it is acceptable that public expenditures rise with GDP.

The emerging socialist thinking concurred with Wagner, advocating that the state should pursue broader social objectives, and use its redistributive power to achieve those. John Maynard Keynes' publication of the book, *The End of Laissez-Faire*[14] in 1926 marked a turning point. Keynes' insight was that the market did not necessarily grant macroeconomic balance. He argued that the government should increase expenditures and reduce taxes in order to stimulate demand to pull the economy out of depression.[15] The previous strict limits to state action were soon abandoned, and Europe gradually extended the role of the state in economic and social activity. Politicians found this to be popular, and embraced larger public spending. In Tanzi's words, it "was always politically easier to increase spending or reduce taxes than to do the opposite."[16]

During World War II the economic role of the state grew greater than ever. All governments spent as much as they could on defense regardless of state revenues, allowing public debt to rise to previously unprecedented levels. Governments took over enterprises and mobilized or interned citizens as they pleased. Prices were widely controlled below market levels and goods rationed. The economic role of the state was greater than ever.

People got used to the state doing everything. After the war, the dominant view in Europe was that central state planning was superior to private enterprise, which was seen as unable to meet social goals. The social democratic parties grew strong in the aftermath of the war, and they had been radicalized, pursuing debates on the need for nationalization and central planning. Communist parties surged in France, Italy and Finland. Although not able to join governments in Western Europe, their ideological impact was palpable. In Eastern Europe, the Soviet Union imposed its state-controlled economic system.

Postwar governments nationalized "strategic industries," such as steelworks, railways, energy companies and mines in the United Kingdom, France and Italy. The last major wave of nationalization of industry and finance occurred in France in 1981 after the election of the socialist Francois Mitterand as president, as French socialists and communists "agreed that nationalization was necessary to dispossess private capital of its power."[17] At that time, Sweden adopted con-fiscatory tax laws that compelled some of the wealthiest businesspeople to leave the country.[18] In a book from that era, *The Sleeping People*, future conservative Prime Minister Fredrik Reinfeldt, compared the effects of Sweden's welfare state to the plague.

Many arguments were used to justify a larger role for the state. An old socialist idea was that natural resources were national assets, which should not contribute to private enrichment. Another idea was that natural monopolies should be state-owned. Radio and television were also perceived as natural national monopolies because they were financed with license fees rather than advertisements. Certain projects required so much long-term capital that only the state was considered ca-pable of financing them. The same argument was applied to technical development.

The role of the state increased greatly in the social sphere. During the war, a British government committee chaired by Sir William Beveridge authored the so-called Beveridge report, whose proposals were largely implemented by the Labor government after World War II. It expanded the role of the state in the social sector. The National Health Service Act of 1946 introduced a fully state-owned health care system and the Landlord and Tenant Act of 1949 led to far-reaching interference in the rent market in the United Kingdom.[19]

Fortunately, Western Europe never turned communist. The big countervail-ing economic event was Economy Minister Ludwig Erhard's currency reform in West German in 1948, which was accompanied with a freeing of prices and mar-kets.[20] Also in the rest of Europe, prices and markets were gradually liberalized. International trade was opened through the two parallel processes of European in-tegration and World Trade Organization (WTO) rounds.

In the 1960s and 1970s, social democracy with its ideas of a far-reaching social welfare state dominated Europe. The belief in the benefits of government inter-vention reached an all-time high in the 1970s. Many ideas coalesced demanding higher public expenditures. Richard Musgrave, who was the most influential public finance economist, saw a vast and beneficial role for public finance, which should have allocative, stabilizing and redistributive functions.[21]

The perceived need for more social transfers and services required ever higher public expenditures. Risks were increasingly socialized. The dominant view during the glorious 30 was that the government should reduce unemployment through demand management by increasing inflation. Economists claimed that fine-tuning of fiscal stabilization policy could abolish the business cycle.[22] Market failures, for example pollution, were invoked in calls for more government intervention.[23] The possibly pernicious effects of state intervention were much less discussed.

The big expansion of public expenditures occurred from 1960 to 1980, when they surged from 28 percent of GDP to 43 percent of GDP in the Western world. This surge was not caused by war or any major calamity but by a changed attitude to the state. Governments allocated and redistributed ever more funds, while trying to stabilize the economy. After 1980, this expansion slowed down and stopped at 45 percent of GDP in 1990.[24]

The central cause of public spending in Europe was the social democratic belief in the good state that could stabilize the economy and provide an extensive social welfare state. Still, most understood that private enterprise drove economic development, and it was forced to survive in severe competition on open world markets. Europe had opted for a combination of capitalism and social welfare state. For the period 1945 to 1975, the two co-existed in harmony, but in the mid-1970s the two would collide.

THE PENDULUM SWINGS BACK

The big expansion of public expenditures occurred from 1945 to 1975, when they surged from 28 percent of GDP to 43 percent of GDP in Western Europe (figure 2.2). This surge was not caused by war but by a changed attitude towards the role of the state. Governments allocated and redistributed ever more funds, while trying to stabilize the economy. After 1975, this expansion slowed down and stopped at 45 percent of GDP in 1989.[25]

In the 1980s, the ideas of the all-embracing social welfare state in Europe were challenged by a combination of poor economic performance and globalization. Many kinds of public expenditures were questioned and new ideas evolved about how to manage the public sector. Economists such as Friedrich Hayek[26] and Milton Friedman[27] complained about state failures. They pointed out the limitations of government and their work started influencing European politicians.

Keynes had promised economic stability with low inflation and unemployment combined with steady economic growth. At the end of the 1970s, Keynesian policies had instead produced stagflation (that is, stagnation and high inflation) and high unemployment. When these ideas had failed to deliver, a political reaction followed. In May 1979, the tory party won the British parliamentary elections and Margret Thatcher became prime minister. Thatcher focused her energies on opening up of the overregulated British labor market. The continuous expansion of the

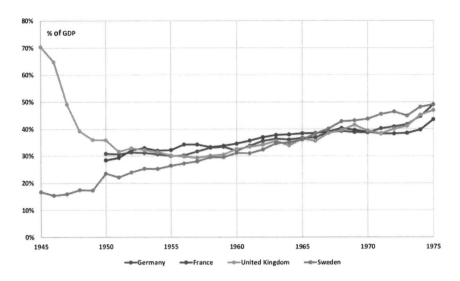

Figure 2.2 The Glorious 30 in Public Expenditures, **1945-75**
Source: Flora, Peter et al. 1983. State, Economy and Society in Western Europe, 1815-1975

state no longer appeared desirable. "The larger the slice taken by government, the smaller the cake available for everyone," was one of Thatcher's favorite quotes. Her course was supported by the election of Ronald Reagan as US President with similar views in 1980.

In the 1980s, financial crises erupted in one European country after the other, typically with a combination of large budget deficits, high inflation, large unemployment, exchange rate crisis, and banking crisis. Such crises hit Europe's richest social welfare states, Denmark in 1982, the Netherlands in 1987, Norway, Sweden and Finland in 1989-92. These crises transformed their economic thinking towards more disciplined public spending and multiple structural reforms.

The second turning point was the collapse of communism in Eastern Europe in 1989. The early East European economic policymakers, Leszek Balcerowicz in Poland and Vaclav Klaus in Czechoslovakia had lived through the excesses of indulgent communist states. They opted for disciplined public finances and a diminishing role of the state and were soon followed by the rest of Eastern Europe.[28] The pendulum had swung towards fiscal responsibility throughout most of Europe.

WHAT IS THE RIGHT LEVEL OF PUBLIC EXPENDITURES?

It is a difficult empirical question to establish how large public expenditures are preferable. Two questions need to be answered first. How have various levels of public expenditures influenced economic growth and which kind of state spending has benefitted or harmed economic growth? These have been extensively studied in the economic growth literature from the late 1980s onward.

Robert Barro published a seminal paper on public expenditures and economic growth in 1989. His main conclusion from a regression with 76 countries was that "government consumption is inversely related to growth, whereas public investment has little relation with growth."[29] His paper was followed by a large number of academic articles, representing a convergence of views. A conventional wisdom became that "productive government expenditure enhances growth, whilst nonproductive expenditure does not."[30] Hansson and Henrekson concluded that government transfers, consumption, and total outlays had negative effects, while education expenditures had a positive effect.[31] Barro found a significant negative impact of all government consumption, apart from defense and education.[32] Recent research makes the argument that government consumption, subsidies and government investment had a "sizeable, negative and statistically significant effect on growth."[33]

The critical findings refer to excessive government consumption, subsidies and social transfers, whereas basic public activities are not criticized. Bernhard Heitger has offered a nice summary: "The central hypothesis is that government expenditures on core public goods . . . have a positive impact on economic growth, [but]. . . this positive impact of government tends to decline or even reverse if government further increases expenditures in such a way that it ultimately also provides private goods."[34] Nobody questions the benefits of a substantial and well-functioning state, but the question is at what level it becomes more costly than beneficial. For that purpose, comparisons among developed economies or OECD countries are most relevant.

Given the large size of the Swedish public expenditures, Swedish economists have been particularly concerned with the state becoming too large. In 2010, Andreas Bergh and Magnus Henrekson published a useful book, *Government Size and Implications for Economic Growth*. Their conclusion was that in studies of growth of real GDP per capita over longer periods, "the research is actually close to a consensus: In rich countries, there is a negative correlation between total size of government and growth."[35] They noted: "No OECD country has collected taxes of more than 40 percent of GDP *and* during the same decade achieved an average annual growth rate exceeding 3 percent."[36] They conclude: "The most recent studies find a significant negative correlation: an increase in government size by 10 percentage points is associated with a 0.5 percent to 1 percent lower annual growth rate."[37] A vital condition for these results is controlling for initial GDP and demography and the causality is important. Many rich countries have large states, but notably the Scandinavian countries had well-functioning states before they become rich and they did not become rich because they had large state sectors.

Vito Tanzi's overall conclusion is that until the 1960s the rise in public spending was correlated with a considerable increase in welfare, but the extra spending mandated in the 1960s and 1970s did not bring about any apparent further benefits. The level of public expenditures diverged greatly above the level of 35-40 percent of GDP, but the big spenders achieved no better results than the low spenders.[38]

Naturally, the specifics depend on many factors such as the quality of the public service and the tax system. Yet the needs that a well-functioning state can satisfy seem to be in this range. This suggests a scaling back of the social welfare society, to what is proven justified and efficient. Then the question is what should be financed and done by the private sector and the state, respectively. Most of the variation of public expenditures originates in social transfers. At present, Europe's highest public expenditure ratios have fallen from a peak of 71 percent of GDP in the early 1990s (in Sweden) to 59 percent of GDP (in Finland), while the lowest ratios linger around 35 percent of GDP (Lithuania and Romania) and the average was 46 percent of GDP in 2014.

The most obvious reason for limiting public expenditures is that governments cannot finance them. "There appears to be an enormous divergence between what the Portuguese believe the state should deliver and the amount of taxes they are prepared to pay," Portuguese Finance Minister Vitor Gaspar told parliament in November 2012.[39] But redefining the state's responsibilities is highly contentious for many Portuguese, who see universal health care and education as fundamental achievements of the 1974 revolution that overthrew 48 years of dictatorship. This sentiment is shared by other South Europeans, for example in Greece and Spain, who equate the advance in democracy in their countries with the expansion of the welfare state.

In the long term, the limit of feasible tax revenues appears to be about half of GDP to judge from the development in the Scandinavian countries. Higher public expenditures tend to lead to large budget deficits and rising public debts. At a time of an average EU public debt of about 90 percent of GDP, far above the Maastricht ceiling of 60 percent of GDP, public expenditures must be checked. Private co-payments may become necessary in some public sectors like healthcare and education, but they will only be accepted if services are viewed as of high quality. "Paying more for better services would make sense, but not just to keep things as they are," says Cidália Juste, an unemployed clerk in Lisbon.[40]

Demands for pensions, social transfers and health care expenditures may be un-limited if the state takes full responsibility for them, but since fiscal resources are limited, European governments need to set a ceiling. The question is how and where to set the limits. For pensions, this is relatively easy, as discussed in Chapter 4 on pensions, while the financial boundaries for public health care are much more difficult to establish. The comprehensive access to services like education and health care are rightly accepted as basic human rights in developed societies.[41] The state can look elsewhere for savings.

WHAT THE STATE DOES AND HOW MUCH IT COSTS

Tanzi and Schuknecht have analyzed the major items of public expenditures in 17 Western countries.[42] Some categories of expenditures are similar in most counties, while others vary greatly regardless of income level. Items with great variation are particularly worthy of scrutiny. We base our examination upon the excellent Eurostat statistics on public expenditures.

The first task of a state is to defend the national borders. Average defense expenditures in EU countries have fallen from 3.4 percent of GDP in 1960 to 2 percent of GDP in 1995 and 1.3 percent of GDP in 2015. NATO demands a rise to 2 percent of GDP, but the only European countries that meet this target are Greece, at 2.1 percent of GDP, and the United Kingdom, at 2.3 percent.[43]

The second most important function of a state is law and order, courts, prosecutors, police, and prisons. This is a true public good where the private sector is far less efficient, that is, if everybody has to take care of his or her own security. Yet, law enforcement is not very expensive costing 1.8 percent of GDP on average in 2015 with minimal variations across Europe.[44] The largest expenditures are incurred in Slovakia (3.3 percent of GDP in 2015) and Bulgaria (2.7 percent). The lowest expenditures are incurred in Denmark and Lithuania, both at 1 percent of GDP.

A third basic state function is public administration, which cost on average 2.1 percent of GDP. Public service is needed where no measurement of performance is easily available, but that sphere is rather limited. The state administration should be kept small but be well paid, fostering an elitist sense of esprit de corps. The United Kingdom, generally considered to have an excellent public service, spends only 1.5 percent of GDP on its maintenance, to compare with 4.2 percent of GDP in Croatia and Hungary.[45]

In public discussion about fiscal stimulus, public investment, primarily in infrastructure plays a prominent role. In reality, however, public investment in Europe is remarkably stable at around 3 percent of GDP, although the Anglo-Saxon countries invest much less.[46] Moreover, European infrastructure is well developed, and Eastern European countries are fast catching up through the use of cohesion funds from the European Union.

Some attempts have been made to increase private sector investment in infrastructure, including at the European level. In November 2014, European Commission President Jean-Claude Juncker proposed a European Investment Plan that aims to stimulate private investment in infrastructure. "We need an investment plan like the one we are now presenting because there is a real breakdown of investment in the European Union, in all the member states. For example, private investment in Germany fell by 52 percent between 1991 and 2013."[47]

The Juncker Plan, as it has become known, leverages public investment on the European and national level and aims to attract €315 billion to address infrastructure needs. The European Investment Bank (EIB) and the EU budget have contributed €21 billion in guarantees that allows the EIB to raise new funds in the private capital markets that can then be invested in previously unfunded projects. Countries with fiscal space are reluctant to spend more, while those willing and in need of it the most are restricted by the rules. This is even though investment in the EU has plummeted by €430bn during the Eurozone crisis, with Greece, Ireland, Spain, Portugal and Italy suffering the most. 2015 is the first year after the crisis that infrastructure investment started rising again.

Education is one of the oldest public services delivered to all inhabitants. Many European countries have a tradition of private schools, but financing is predominantly public for primary and secondary education. Surprisingly, the public cost of education is rather limited at an average of 5 percent of GDP and the variations between countries are small (figure 2.3).[48] Denmark spends the most, at 7 percent of GDP; followed by Sweden, at 6.6 percent. Romania and Bulgaria spend the least, below 4 percent of GDP. They are followed by Italy, Greece, and Spain, who spend below 4.5 percent of GDP. The PISA measurements of school attainment indicate no clear correlation between spending on education and outcome.

Health care is of great importance to people's wellbeing. In total, Europe spends half as much of its GDP on health care as the US, whereas most health outcomes are substantially better in Europe. Public expenditures on health care have risen with life expectancy. In 2013, they amounted to a European average of 7.2 percent of GDP, ranging from 3.1 percent of GDP in Cyprus to 8.7 percent of GDP in Denmark (figure 2.4).[49] Countries that spend a small share of GDP on healthcare include Romania (4 percent), Bulgaria (4.6 percent) and Poland (4.6 percent). Finland, France and the Netherlands spend more than 8 percent of GDP on health care.

The cost of public pensions surged until the 1990s and then stabilized at about 9 percent of GDP (9.2 percent in 2013).[50] Public pension costs vary greatly from 4 percent of GDP (Ireland) to 14.4 percent of GDP (Greece) depending on retirement age, level of benefits and public responsibility. The highest public pension costs were recorded in Greece, Italy, France and Austria.[51] There is a well-tried pension reform, which the World Bank has promoted since 1994. It consists of three elements: a public minimum pension, a mandatory private saving pension, and optional private pension saving.[52] Chapter 4 discusses the merits of pension reforms. As pension costs have become too high, countries have tended to adopt such a reform. The Netherlands has done so most successfully having cut public pension costs to 6.9 percent of GDP in 2013, while offering very generous pensions thanks to sound private pension savings.

Unemployment benefits attract much public attention, but they are actually quite cheap, costing merely 1.6 percent of GDP in 2014. Here, the differences are great ranging from 0.1 percent of GDP in Bulgaria to 3.8 percent of GDP in Spain. In addition, some countries, notably the Netherlands, Sweden and Denmark, have expensive labor market programs.[53] It is doubtful whether they offer value for the money.

Other social benefits consist of a complex array of disability pensions, sickness, maternity and family allowances, early retirement, social welfare, and housing subsidies. By the early 1990s, they had reached 5 percent of GDP, and in 2013 they averaged at 6 percent of GDP. Though they varied greatly, being three times higher in Scandinavia and the Netherlands.[54] This area deserves critical scrutiny. Housing subsidies and early retirement schemes are not very desirable. Social support should be given in the form of financing and not for the consumption of any particular goods, such as housing. Early retirement means a permanent disconnection with the labor market. Social welfare needs to be carefully analyzed to identify programs

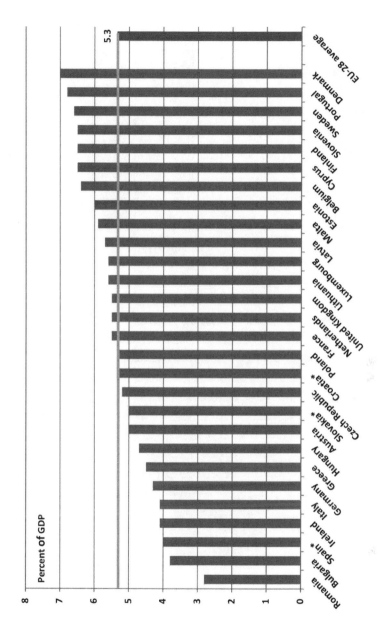

Figure 2.3 Public Spending on Education, 2013

*Provisional value

Source: Eurostat, available at: http://appsso.eurostat.ec.europa.eu/nui/show.do

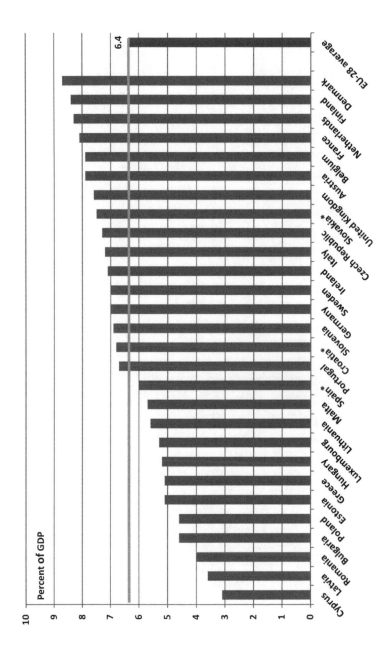

Figure 2.4 Public Spending on Health Care, 2013

*Provisional value

Source: Eurostat, available at: http://appsso.eurostat.ec.europa.eu/nui/show.do

that keep people in the labor market. The same is true of disability programs, which may be abused when unemployment or pension programs do not provide sufficient coverage.

It is difficult to generalize about social benefits because they come in many shapes. They can be direct public expenditures, tax deductions, tax credits or tax expenditures. Often, only direct public expenditures are recorded. Especially the United States has ample tax deductions and tax credits.[55] In addition, there are many hybrids of joint state and private financing. Taken together, total public expenditures on social protection are huge. On average, EU countries spent 19.6 percent of GDP on social protection in 2013, ranging from 11 percent in Latvia to 25 percent in Denmark (Figure 2.5).[56] There is a clear pattern where Eastern Europe spends less on social benefits—11.4 percent in Lithuania, 12 percent in Estonia, and 13 percent in the Czech Republic.

Research and development (R&D) are vital for technical progress. The countries with the highest R&D costs in Europe—Finland and Sweden—spend 3.5 percent of GDP, slightly more than the United States. Of this spending, two-thirds come from private sources, and only one-third from the state. Thus, R&D should cost the state approximately 1 percent of GDP if innovations are to be best stimulated. Chapter 9 goes further into this topic. Similarly, environmental protection costs on average 0.8 percent of GDP, with the Netherlands spending 1.5 percent of GDP, while Portugal spending just 0.4 percent of GDP. Recreation and culture 1 percent of GDP, and a few wealthy Northern European countries spend up to 1 percent of GDP on development aid.[57]

A sometimes large but undesired public expenditure is interest payments on public debt. After the global financial crisis, public debts in relation to GDP have risen sharply, but interest payments have been untypically small because of very low interest rates. In the mid-1990s, countries with traditionally large public debts, such as Italy and Belgium, had annual public interest payments of as much as 10-11 percent of GDP.[58] Public interest payments should be minimized through governments paying down the public debt, which can be best done by privatizing superfluous state-owned assets. The public interest cost should not exceed 1 percent of GDP.

If we add up the relevant public expenditures with actual current averages or our normative targets we get as shares of GDP: True public goods 8.3 percent (defense 2 percent, law and order 1.8 percent, state administration 1.5 percent and basic infrastructure 3 percent), essential services paid for by the state 11.8 percent (education 5.3 percent and basic health care 6.5 percent), essential social transfers 15.6 percent (basic public pensions 8 percent, unemployment benefits 1.6 percent and some other social benefits 6 percent), research and development 1 percent and public debt interest 1 percent. This total amounts to 38 percent of GDP. This is not a minimal but a advantageous level of public expenditures, which could be generalized as 35-42 percent of GDP. The best policy would be to keep public expenditures to within these boundaries. This is true both of highly-developed and les developed EU countries.

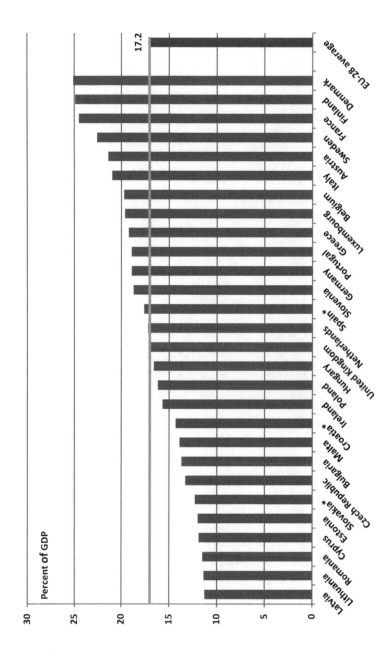

Figure 2.5 Total Social Protection, 2013

* Provisional value

Source: Eurostat, available at: http://appsso.eurostat.ec.europa.eu/nui/show.do

HOW PUBLIC FINANCES CAN BE BALANCED

Wasteful public expenditures in Europe can be trimmed. The most obvious starting point are enterprise subsidies, which have proven largely inefficient and prone to corruption. In 2013, the average EU country spent 4.3 percent on GDP on such "economic activities," with Greece and Slovenia spending nearly 15 percent of their GDP on such subsidies.[59] One example is the construction of an international-standard racetrack that can be used for staging Formula One car racing in Xalandritsa near the western port city of Patras in Greece, at a cost of €100 million.

A similar group of public expenditures are price subsidies that used to be common in energy and agriculture sectors across Europe. Remaining price subsidies are mainly rent controls in big cities. Fortunately, they are not large, averaging only 0.5 percent of GDP. [60]

Privatization offers one-off opportunities to improve public finances, and to keep them stable in the long run. Various state-owned enterprises can be sold off, such as manufacturing, steelworks, mines, communication, energy, banking, and superfluous real estate. Such sales can be spread out over time to maximize revenues. Privatization proceeds can be used to reduce public debt service, another public expenditure that does not improve social welfare.

The next step should be to render the public sector more efficient. One means of doing so is to open up as much as possible of public procurement to open and transparent competition. Given that public procurement typically amounts to about 8 percent of GDP and the cost is likely to be smaller with open competition, thus reducing public costs substantially. Similarly, the efficiency of the public sector can be raised when it is being exposed to competition with private suppliers of services. Chapter 5 on services discusses ways to achieve this efficiency.

Two complex reforms are usually needed in most countries, namely in pensions and social sectors. Pension reform is so essential and beneficial that we discuss it as a separate Chapter 4. Its aims are multiple—to reduce public cost, to increase pensions, to improve incentives by tying pensions closer to earnings, to stimulate private savings, and to strengthen financial markets. The public sector should guarantee a minimum pension for all, while additional pensions should be earned. The Dutch pension system stands out as the most successful in Europe.

Social welfare reform is not complicated technically, but it is politically difficult since it concerns many voters. The Scandinavian countries adopted manifold social benefits during their years of excessive public expenditure through the 1970s. To a considerable extent, they have trimmed benefits that were subject to wide abuse and corruption, rendering full compensation for unemployment or sickness rare. These efforts can be used as examples in other countries.

With such steps, public finances can be balanced. In the period 1993-2007, seven current EU members cut their public expenditures as a share of GDP by more than 10 percent of GDP. Sweden cut its public expenditures by 20 percent of GDP in the course of 15 years (figure 2.6). Governments enjoy far greater freedom of policy choice once inefficient expenditures are curtailed.

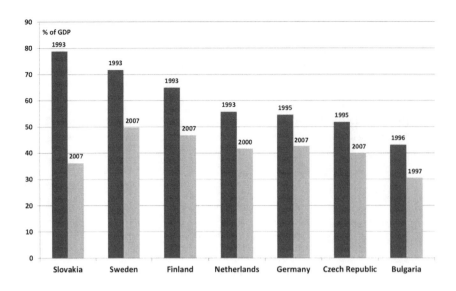

Figure 2.6 Large Drops of Public Expenditures, **1993-2007**
Source: Eurostat Statistical Database (accessed on March 8, 2013)Available at: http://epp.eurostat.
ec.europa.eu/portal/page/portal/statistics/search_database

Similarly, many EU countries have cut their public debt sharply. At least six nations have slashed their debt by 30 percent of GDP or more from 1995-2011. Most impressive was Bulgaria's reduction of its public debt from 97 percent of GDP in 1997 to 14 percent in 2008, partially through official debt relief, but mainly though privatizations that some years reaped public incomes of as much as 25 percent of GDP (figure 2.7). Such improvements in public finances can be fragile, however: since 2013 Bulgaria has doubled its debt to GDP ratio, due to increasing budget deficits and unwise handling of the bank failures.

THE MAASTRICHT CRITERIA: A WELCOME STEP

Until 1992, the EU played no role in fiscal policy, which was entirely the concern of national governments. This changed when the EU adopted the Treaty of the European Union in Maastricht in 1992, in preparation for the introduction of the euro. The Maastricht Treaty introduced two fiscal rules. The general government deficit must not exceed 3 percent of GDP and the ratio of gross government debt to GDP must not exceed 60 percent of GDP if a country were to join the Economic and Monetary Union. These standards were imposed upon all EU members from 1998 as the Stability and Growth Pact. This principle was sound, and the EU countries greatly improved their fiscal balances in the 1990s.

Since the early 1990s, many countries have introduced strict national budget rules, which have helped to improve budget discipline. In general, governments have reduced the possibilities of parliaments to introduce new public expenditures. A common practice is that a parliament cannot authorize new public expenditures

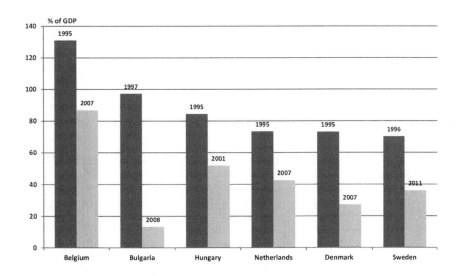

Figure 2.7 Big Public Debt Declines, **1995 – 2007**
Source: Eurostat database 2015. Available at: http://ec.europa.eu/eurostat/tgm/table.do?tab=table&init=1&language=en&pcode=teina225&plugin=1

without securing corresponding revenues. Another useful devise is medium-term budgets that bring more stability to public finances. The European Commission now mandates 3-year medium-term budgets, and these documents are reviewed in Brussels before being voted on by parliaments.[61]

In 2003, however, three big EU countries, France, Germany and Italy, all had too large budget deficits. They compelled the European Council to decide that the criteria did not apply to them and in 2005 the Council "reformed" the SGP rendering it toothless.[62]

Because many EU countries ended up in public debt crisis after the Eurozone crisis of 2008, the EU has attempted to reinforce these fiscal criteria more rigorously. The European Commission pursues this control, but the ultimate decision about sanctions remains with the Council and the governments of the EU countries, which means that the standards cannot be imposed on the big and powerful EU countries. To deal with that problem, the EU encourages countries to adopt legislation against large budget deficits and public debts. Countries such as Poland and Germany have even adopted constitutional amendments as checks.

Only a few EU countries have adopted balanced budgets as their standard, notably the three Baltic countries and Bulgaria, which based this policy on their currency board regimes. From 2006-14, the conservative Swedish government declared its policy to be an average budget surplus of 1 percent of GDP over the business cycle, but the ensuing red-green government abolished this restriction. Only Estonia and Luxembourg, the two smallest EU countries, pursue a policy of minimal public debt. In general, small countries tend to have less public debts, partly because they feel more vulnerable, partly because their government bond markets are comparatively shallow.

Neither the EU nor any member country has adopted any norm with regard to the size of public expenditures. One of us tried to impose a 40 percent limit on public expenditures through constitutional amendments in Bulgaria, but the parliamentary vote came short. Various analyses acknowledge that accumulated public debt "represents a deadweight burden on the economy, dimming both its investment and growth prospects." The idea that large public expenditures in themselves are undesirable has only recently come to light during the painful restructuring of public finances in Southern Europe.

Interestingly, a recent ECB study of fiscal consolidation finds that when consolidation is implemented via a cut in government primary spending, the debt ratio, after the initial increase, falls below its pre-shock level. When instead the consolidation is implemented via an increase in government revenues, the initial increase in the debt ratio is stronger and, eventually, the debt ratio revers to its pre-shock level, resulting in self-defeating austerity.[63] This result seems robust and appeals to common sense, suggesting that public expenditure cuts are preferable to an increase in tax revenues when public expenditures exceed 40 percent of GDP.

CONCLUSIONS: TOWARDS BALANCED PUBLIC BUDGETS

Larger public expenditures than 55 percent of GDP appear indefensible in peacetime, and smaller and poorer European countries need to be careful not to expand public expenditures too fast because it can lead to fiscal crisis and high levels of unemployment over a long period.[64] Lower public expenditures than 35 percent of GDP appears politically impossible in developed democracies and are hardy desirable. How can European countries choose within this range?

Our recommendation to EU countries is to reduce their public expenditures from the current average of 48 percent of GDP to the range 35-42 percent of GDP. We suggest a European-wide ceiling of public expenditures in peacetime of 42 percent of GDP, much like the Maastricht criteria of maximum 3 percent of annual budget deficits to GDP and the 60 percent of public debt to GDP (figure 2.9). This level is likely to be optimal for economic growth in a developed economy, and most European countries fell within it before the Eurozone crisis struck.

At present, nine EU members are in that range: Bulgaria, Estonia, Ireland, Latvia, Lithuania, Romania, Slovakia, Poland and the Czech Republic. Eight of them are former communist nations that have lived through the disadvantages of a large and inefficient state and downsized it. Ireland, which carried out far-reaching structural reforms in the 1980s, has once again reduced its public outlays after the Eurozone crisis. For most other countries, such an adjustment would take years, but the goal should be clear and explicit.

Most EU countries, however, have allowed their public expenses to swell simply because they could collect the taxes or sell bonds without much consideration of whether it would be beneficial for their economic growth or employment.[65] In this chapter, we have suggested where the great discrepancies lie and what needs to be revised. The goal of the analysis is to improve the balance between state and private sector in order to promote economic growth.

3

Taxes That Support Entrepreneurship
and Growth

Europe's large public expenditures require high taxes for their financing. High taxes on labor have not helped income equality in European countries rising in the past quarter century, since that means that low-income earners pay higher taxes than those who live on capital income. The bottom half of income earners in France paid a rate of 40-45 percent in 2010; the top 1 percent paid only 35 percent, an example of regressive taxation.[1]

Europe's high tax rates are a post-World War II phenomenon. Until the war, even Sweden had lower taxes than the United States.[2] The vast costs of World War II prompted most Western European countries to adopt high taxes, with marginal personal rates usually over 90 percent. Corporate profit taxes also surged to pay the rebuilding of Europe. The high taxes could be collected because of the strict regulation of financial flows characteristic of the postwar period until the mid-1970s.

From 1945 to about 1975, European governments exploited closed financial markets and control over monetary policy to force companies and individuals to invest in government bonds, while offering these captive investors low or negative real interest rates.[3] In the 1970s, the old Keynesian model collapsed as unemployment and inflation in Europe rose in parallel. Margaret Thatcher led a move to lower public expenditures and reduced taxes in the United Kingdom. A decade later, the Nordic social welfare states entered a financial crisis, also leading to reduced public expenditures and eventually lower taxes. After the collapse of communism in Eastern Europe in 1989, the state's role in European economies diminished further.

This chapter focuses on the four major European taxes—the corporate profit tax, the personal income tax, the value-added tax (with other indirect consumption taxes), and the payroll tax. In the last few decades, these four taxes have evolved differently. The corporate profit tax has converged due to tax competition. Value-added taxes (VAT) have also converged but because of harmonization within the European Union (EU). Both the VAT rates and their share of tax revenues are similar in most European countries. In contrast, taxes on labor, the personal income taxes and the payroll tax have not converged but their level has declined somewhat. As a consequence, taxation has been concentrated to labor, while capital enjoys increasingly lighter taxation. This is the main problem with Europe's tax systems.

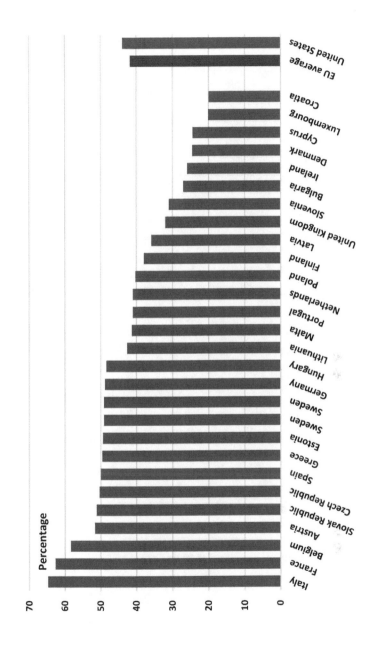

Percentage

Source: Doing Business Database

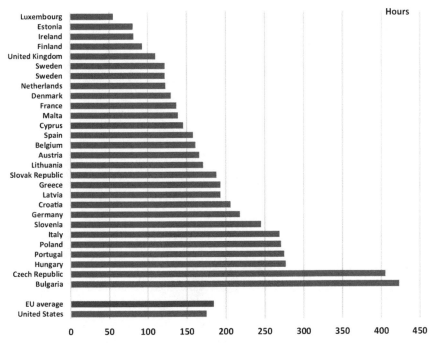

Source: Doing Business Database

Figure 3.1 Figure 3.1a - c Data from Doing Business Database
Source: Doing Business Database

EUROPE'S EVOLVING TAX SYSTEMS

In the late 1970s, following a period of extended economic growth a rethinking of taxation started in Europe. The question arose what level and form of taxation is most amenable to entrepreneurship. An extensive literature on the theory of optimal taxation evolved.[4] It showed that high taxes can have a negative effect on output by introducing a tax wedge between supply and demand. A high marginal tax can persuade a person not to work as much as she would otherwise. High taxes on the formal economy drive people to work less or informally, to exchange services, or to carry out their own domestic services rather than deliver professional services. Then they see less return in investing more in their own human capital, which limits their productivity and the quality of their work. This is likely to lead to less innovation. High formal tax rates also encourage taxpayers to lobby for loopholes for themselves.[5]

Since most taxes involve some distortion, economists have favored few and low taxes while broadening the tax base. Tax administration should be simple, leading many economists in the 1980s to favor lump-sum taxes. Yet, lump-sum taxes are widely refuted by politicians as being regressive. Memorably, the policy issue that ended Margaret Thatcher's political career in 1990 was her insistence for a "poll tax," a lump-sum tax equal for all individuals.[6]

The advent of the internet has made tax administration easier both on the taxpayers and the public officials. Over half of the EU countries now collect taxes electronically, without any paperwork, greatly facilitating tax collection. Europe has accomplished quite a lot in simplifying its tax laws. Relative to other regions, Europe has light administrative burden of taxation on business, with the Baltic and Nordic countries leading the way. The average Swedish business pays only 6 times a year, while in Latvia and Poland businesses only make 7 payments a year to the tax authorities.[7] In Estonia, Finland and Ireland, businesses spend on average less than 100 hours a year filing with the tax administration (figure 3.1). Firms in Bulgaria, Croatia, Ireland and Denmark pay about 25 percent of their profits in taxes, among the lowest in countries around the world.

Italy and Greece suffer from severe problems of "glass ceilings" in their tax and regulatory systems, making it difficult and expensive to scale up from a small firm with a maximum of 15 employees to a larger one. As a consequence, these two countries have an unusually large share of their employment in small family firms.

Remarkably, fixing tax systems in Europe has taken place without external help. The International Monetary Fund (IMF), the main global institution dealing with public finances, has opposed many changes in the tax legislation in a conservative vein, fearing that new tax models may reduce public revenues. Since countries in crisis tend to be dependent on IMF emergency financing, tax reforms rarely occur in severe crises. Tax models change when state revenues suffice.

Europe has not undertaken coordinated tax reforms, as tax law is not part of the European Commission's responsibilities. However, several features of the evolving tax system are common. Changes have been driven by tax competition, attempts at European tax harmonization, and concerns over the deleterious effects of tax regimes on labor participation and the size of the formal economy. These considerations have moved politicians towards simpler and flatter tax structures. In particular, the flat-tax model was introduced across Eastern European countries by conservative as well as socialist governments. Likewise, reducing of the top marginal income tax rate was introduced in Western Europe by social democrats as well as liberals.

The inherent interest of the public sector is for a larger state, that is, higher taxes and more rigorous tax collection. European social democracy has represented this tendency so well in the past 50 years that it was widely perceived as the natural development. EU tax harmonization has coalesced with these forces, facilitating higher tax rates. It has been most effective in standardizing and boosting value-added taxes (VAT), particularly after the Eurozone crisis.[8]

Against this tendency stand two forces. One is globalization that has made it possible for taxpayers to move abroad. This was made possible when European currencies became convertible and financial regulation eased. In 1958, the European Payment Union ended and in 1973 the Bretton Woods fixed exchange rate system broke down. With international financial flows freed, high tax rates were no longer

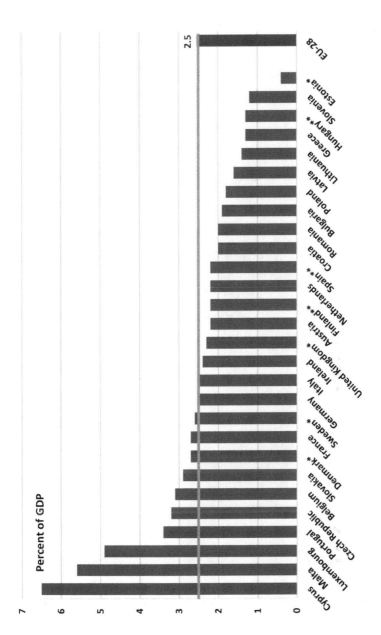

Figure 3.2 Corporate Tax Revenue, 2013

* Figure from 2014; ** Figure from 2012

Source: Eurostat, available at: http://appsso.eurostat.ec.europa.eu/nui/show.do?dataset=gov_10a_taxag&lang=en, retrieved 2015-08-05

feasible. The resulting tax competition has forced countries to reduce tax rates, especially corporate income taxes.

The second force for lower taxes was the fight against the informal economy. Politicians in Eastern Europe have generally opposed high public expenditures and taxes due to their effects on increasing the share of the informal economy and corruption, and discouraging workers from participation in the formal labor force. Estonia's Prime Minister Mart Laar was the first to propose this view in 1992. His ideas can be summarized as few taxes, broad tax bases with minimal loopholes, and low flat tax rates. Consumption should be taxed rather than labor and entrepreneurship.[9]

More recently, concerns over inequality haves driven some European politicians towards taxing capital and moving away from payroll taxes. Thomas Piketty's *Capital in the Twenty-First Century* (2014) has illustrated the regressive nature of labor taxes, and its punitive effect on social mobility. However, his plea for a Europe-wide capital tax is hardly implementable, and the prescription of an 80 percent marginal top personal income tax rate is even less so.

FALLING CORPORATE PROFIT TAX RATES

Since 1990, European corporate profit tax rates have fallen sharply, but revenues have on the contrary risen from about 2 percent of GDP in the early 1980s to 3.4 percent of GDP in 2006-7. They declined with the global financial crisis and have since recovered to 2.5 percent of GDP in 2013 (figure 3.2).[10] The reason for politicians

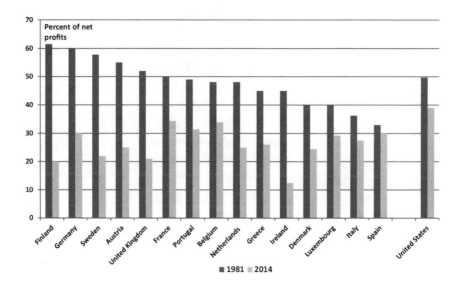

Figure 3.3 Corporate Tax Rates: EU-15 Vs. US, 1981 and 2014
Source: Organization for Economic Cooperation and Development (OECD) Tax Database. Acessed on March 12, 2013. Available at: http://www.oecd.org/ctp/tax-policy/Table%20II.1-May-2014.xlsx

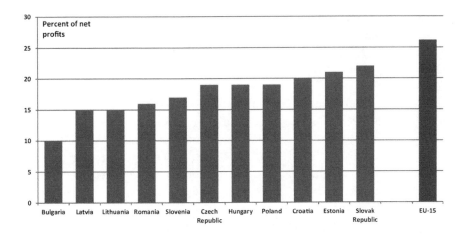

Figure 3.4 Corporate Tax Rates in Eastern Europe, 2014.
Source: EU-15: Organization for Economic Cooperation and Development (OECD) Tax Database. Acessed on March 12, 2013. Available at: www.oecd.org/dataoecd/26/56/33717459.xls. All others: KPMG Corporate Tax Rates Table, 2013. Available at: http://www.kpmg.com/global/en/ services/tax/tax-tools-and-resources/pages/corporate-tax-rates-table.aspx

favoring lower corporate tax rates is simple: "that effective corporate tax rates have a large and significant adverse effect on corporate investment and entrepreneurship," even when controlling for other related variables.[11] In addition, revenues have risen with lower tax rates.

A comparison between the pre-2004 members of the European Union (EU-15) and the United States is illuminating.[12] In the EU-15, the average corporate profit tax rate plunged by 22 percentage points from an average of 48 percent in 1981 to 26 percent in 2014, and rates converged across countries. In 1981, the highest EU profit tax rate was 61.5 percent (Finland) and the lowest 33 percent (Spain). In 2014, France topped with 34.4 percent, while Ireland had merely 12.5 percent. The United States and Japan are outliers. In 1981, the United States had a corporate profit tax of 50 percent, close to the EU-15 average, but it has only fallen to 39 percent, leaving the United States with a higher rate than any EU country. Japan has a corporate tax rate of 33 percent, down from 41 percent before 2011, but still higher than any European country but France (figure 3.3).

Corporate profit taxes have never generated large revenues because big companies can reduce their profit taxes in several ways. For example, they lobby for loopholes for their sector or type of investments. Also, businesses shop around the world for the lowest tax. As a consequence of such behavior, corporate profit tax revenues have *increased* with falling tax rates in 12 of the pre-2004 EU member countries.[13] The countries with lowest tax rates are Cyprus, Malta and Luxembourg. Luxemburg, Ireland and the Netherlands have also negotiated special deals for big foreign companies, which have attracted complaints in the rest of the EU and the United States.[14]

After 1995 Eastern Europe has induced tax competition, which has spread to Western Europe. Eastern European "governments have repeatedly lowered corporate tax rates ... to attract and motivate investment," and their public statements "indicate that they are paying attention to the tax rates set by their counterparts abroad."[15] Eastern European corporate tax rates fall in the range of 10-22 percent (figure 3.4). In 2000, Estonia decided that corporate profit taxes are harmful to the economy and abolished taxation of reinvested profits completely. In 2007, Bulgaria adopted a corporate income tax of 10 percent, lowest in Europe, and in 2012 lowered the dividend tax to 5 percent. Initially, some of the old EU members (notably France and Germany) attacked these countries for "tax dumping," but such accusations have petered out. Instead, they have reduced their corporate profit taxes themselves, and German companies have thrived in their expansion eastward through outsourcing, integrating these countries into the German supply cycle, which has increased employment and investment in Germany.

While cutting corporate tax rates, governments have usually succeeded in abolishing most loopholes for industries or individual firms, further leveling the playing field. This change also lowers tax administration costs and thus reduces the incentive for tax evasion.

PERSONAL INCOME TAXES: DRIVEN DOWN

Governments have realized that they cannot tax corporations heavily as these emigrate or lobby for loopholes. But individuals are not so resourceful, partly because they do not have large legal teams to advise them on optimal tax locations. Therefore, they tend to be taxed far more than businesses.

After World War II, personal income taxes tax rates skyrocketed in the west, while they were reduced in the east. Many Western European countries had marginal income taxes of 90 percent or more. In the two decades after World War II, personal income taxes were the dominant source of public revenue. In the United Kingdom, the top marginal income tax rate was 96 percent in the mid-1960s.[16] In Sweden, Astrid Lindgren, the country's most famous author of children's books, and a social democrat, had to pay 102 percent income tax in 1976.[17] Her public complaint was seen as a major cause of the electoral loss of the social democrats after 44 years in government.

The negative effects of high marginal income taxes were hardly discussed until the 1980s. The highly progressive income tax was seen as "an ideal instrument for social engineering."[18] The objective was to check the wealth of the rich and "it was considered an efficient tax because at that time most economists dismissed its potential negative effects on work efforts or incentives."[19] This was not a subject of empirical study until the 1980s, and studies on income taxation of the period did not even mention tax evasion as a consideration.[20]

Eventually, the stifling effect of high marginal taxes on economic activity became a concern. The change came from America and the influential work of economists Milton Friedman, Friedrich Hayek, and James Buchanan. They all emphasized

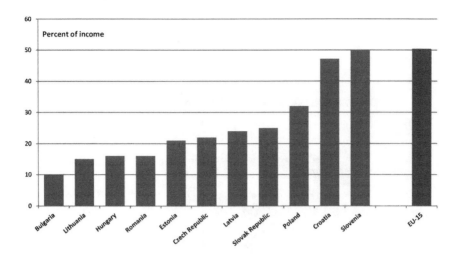

Figure 3.5 Top Personal Income Tax Rates, Eastern Europe 2014
Source: Eurostat, "Taxation Trends in the European Union", 2014 Available at: http://ec.europa.eu/
taxation_customs/resources/documents/taxation/gen_info/economic_analysis/tax_structures/
2014/report.pdf

that high marginal taxes perverted incentives. National economies were no longer
closed and strictly regulated and globalization offered ever more opportunities for
tax avoidance and tax evasion. President Ronald Reagan transformed US taxation.
To begin with, he cut the highest federal personal income tax to 50 percent. In 1986,
he succeeded in reducing the top federal income tax to 28 percent, while abolishing
many loopholes. Admittedly, this low level of taxation lasted for only a few years,
and soon the highest federal tax rate went up to 40 percent.[21]

Reagan's tax reform had an impact in Europe, and Margaret Thatcher pursued
the same ideas in Britain. The end of communism in Eastern Europe brought about
a new challenge for the West European tax system. In the East state banks had carried out tax collection, and these countries did not have any system to collect taxes
from workers and entrepreneurs. Tax evasion thrived and the issue was how taxes
could be collected. The Soviet standard had been low flat income taxes at around
13 percent, though some countries, notably Hungary, pursued social democratic ex-
periments at the end of communism with marginal income taxes as high as 60 percent.[22] But personal income taxes were rather insignificant for state revenues, and
hence received little attention.

Initially, Eastern Europe adopted progressive income taxes, but they malfunc-
tioned, due to widespread evasion. In 1994, Estonian Prime Minister Mart Laar
pioneered a new tax model. "Its basic principles were clear and simple: few taxes,
broad tax bases, no loopholes, simplicity and low rates."[23] The main novelty was
a flat income tax. Initially, the Estonian flat tax was at 26 percent but it has gradually declined to 21 percent. The IMF opposed it, claiming that it would reduce
tax revenues, but they did not suffer. Estonia subsequently equalized the personal

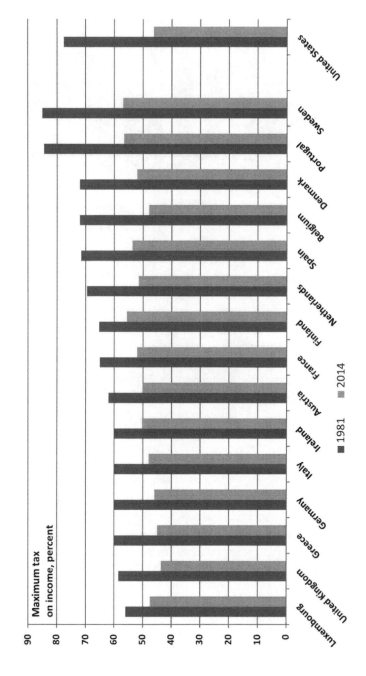

Figure 3.6 Top Marginal Personal Income Tax Rates, EU-15, 1981 and 2014

Source: OECD Special Feature: Trends in Personal Income Tax and Employee Social Security Contribution Schedules. (Accessed March 13, 2013). Available at: http://www.oecd.org/ctp/tax-policy/S0131824.pdf Data for 2012 available at: http://www.oecd.org/tax-policy/Table%201.7_Mar_2013.xlsx

income tax with the corporate profit tax, because these taxes tended to be fungible for wealthy people, and the wealthy should not be taxed less than other people.[24]

Latvia and Lithuania soon followed Estonia's example. The big breakthrough came in 2000 when Russia cut its progressive personal income tax of maximum 30 percent to a flat income tax of 13 percent, while revenues increased from 2.4 to 2.8 percent of GDP the same year. Tax evasion declined persistently and the gap between consumption and income, a measure of tax evasion, declined very significantly by 9-12 percent in one year.[25]

Since then, further 16 post-communist countries have enacted flat taxes ranging from 10-25 percent, usually setting the flat personal income tax rate at the same level as corporate profit tax rate.[26] Bulgaria made the most significant cuts in tax rates, setting its personal income tax and corporate profit tax at 10 percent in 2008, with a socialist government ushering in the change. Its argument runs that as the poorest EU country with problematic governance, Bulgaria needs low taxes to be competitive and avoid corruption in tax administration.[27] In Eastern Europe only Croatia, Poland and Slovenia stuck to progressive income taxes, but the Czech Republic and Slovakia abandoned their flat income taxes after center-left parties gained power (figure 3.5).

The difference in the top marginal income taxes is remarkably great, being 75 percent in France but only 10 percent in Bulgaria, or 65 percentage points. The highest marginal income taxes declined during a long period, and in 2008 several West European countries had maximum tax rates of 40 percent (Luxembourg, the United Kingdom, Greece, Ireland and Portugal), and the average had fallen to 47 percent. But after the global financial crisis the average top marginal tax rate has surged to 50 percent (figure 3.6). This policy change was driven by a new political aspiration to tax the rich as inequality had increased.[28]

Personal income taxation varies greatly between Eastern Europe and the rest of the European Union. The significance of personal income taxes for total state revenues in Europe varies more than for any other tax from 3-30 percent of GDP.[29]

In the EU-15, personal income taxes compose a large share of tax revenues and high marginal income taxes are standard (figure 3.7).

High taxes on personal income dissuade people from formal work and reduce the division of labor as people prefer to stay home to pursue domestic chores amateurishly rather than working more professionally and hire able service professionals. Thus, high marginal income taxes reduce overall national productivity. A reasonable approach would be to set personal income taxes in Western Europe to account for about 8 percent of GDP as in Spain and Portugal, and in Eastern Europe for about 4 percent of GDP as in Lithuania or the Czech Republic. This corresponds to a flat personal income tax of about 25-30 percent in a West European country and of 15 percent in an Eastern European country. Such a tax system would be transparent and easy to administer.

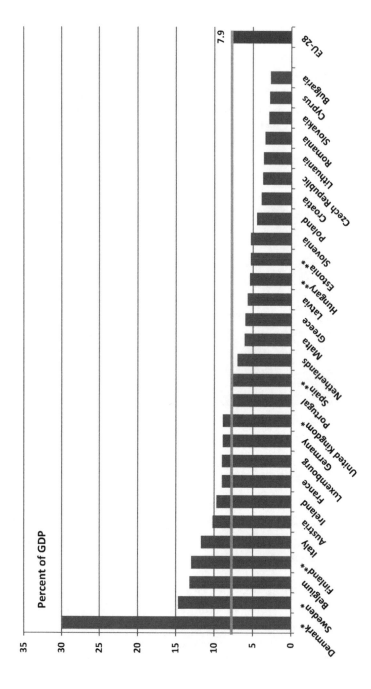

Figure 3.7 Personal Income Tax Revenues, 2013

* Figure from 2014

Source: Eurostat, available at: http://appsso.eurostat.ec.europa.eu/nui/show.do?dataset=gov_10a_taxag&lang=en, retrieved 2015-08-05

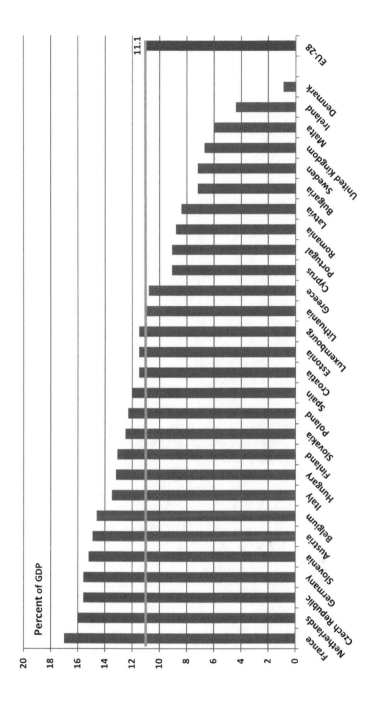

Figure 3.8 Payroll Tax Revenues, 2012

Source: "Taxation trends in the European Union", 2014 Available at http://ec.europa.eu/taxation_customs/resources/documents/taxation/gen_info/economic_analysis/tax_structures/2014/report.pdf

PAYROLL TAXES: LIMITING OFFICIAL WORK

Originally, payroll taxes arose in Europe as social insurance contributions to finance pensions, medical care and unemployment benefits. Where actual insurance systems persist, this remains true, but in many countries "social insurance contributions" are taxes that are paid into the central state budget and only partially relate to social benefits. These taxes are often concealed from the taxpayer, as employers usually pay social security taxes as a ratio to the payroll, leaving their workers in the illusion that the employers pay these taxes, while employers rightly consider payroll taxes costs of their employees. Salary costs include both salaries and payroll taxes, so that payroll taxes and income taxes together amount to the real tax on labor. Moreover, payroll taxes are paid proportionally from even minimum incomes, rendering payroll taxes the most regressive of all taxes.

Payroll taxes have decreased in a number of European countries during the Eurozone crisis. The Netherlands and several Eastern European countries have done so to boost employment and stimulate the economy. France cut the payroll tax from 50 to 38 percent in 2012. As a share of GDP, payroll taxes accounted for an average of 11 percent in 2012, but the variation is enormous. Denmark alone has refuted the idea of payroll tax altogether, minimizing it to 1 percent of GDP in 2012, while France's payroll tax generated 19 percent of GDP in revenue in 2014. Other countries with payroll taxes bringing in more than 15 percent of GDP include the Czech Republic, Germany and Slovenia (figure 3.8).[30]

The bulk of the payroll tax revenues goes to pensions, but as discussed in Chapter 4 employees can be encouraged to pursue their own pension savings. The countries that have cut their payroll taxes sharply—Denmark, Ireland, the United Kingdom, the Netherlands and Poland—have all done so by carrying out major pension reforms. Public minimum pensions come from the general budget, financed with other taxes. Unemployment insurance should be a real insurance. Some countries have health care insurance, connected to the payroll, but it should be a real insurance and not a tax. A study on taxation in 14 European Union countries finds strong negative effect of the payroll tax on employment, especially among the youth.[31]

VALUE-ADDED TAXES: RISING AND STANDARDIZED

In sharp contrast to the personal income and payroll taxes, Europe's indirect taxes are fairly standardized, through the value-added tax (VAT) that all EU members have been compelled to introduce. This trend concurs with a rising view among economists that consumption should be taxed rather than production or labor.

After World War II, many European countries introduced sales taxes to tax consumption. They applied only to some goods in retail, but not to services and were easily evaded. Therefore sales taxes were so distortive that they could hardly be higher than 10 percent and they did not generate large revenues. Instead, the VAT was introduced, first in France in 1954.

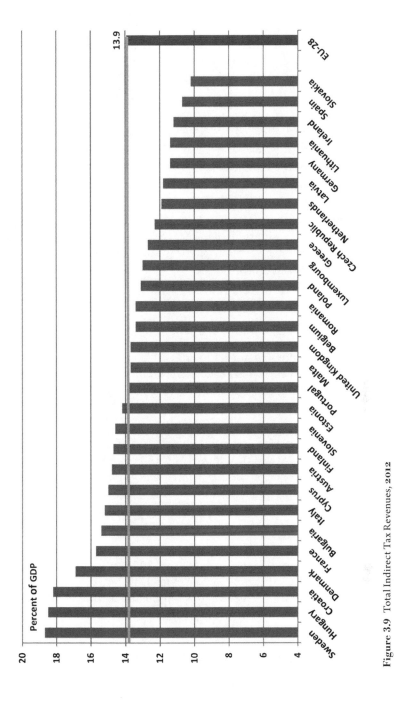

Figure 3.9 Total Indirect Tax Revenues, 2012

Source: "Taxation trends in the European Union", 2014 Available at: http://ec.europa.eu/taxation_customs/resources/documents/taxation/gen_info/economic_analysis/tax_structures/2014/report.pdf

The EU VAT harmonization has taken place in several stages. In 1967, the two first EU VAT directives were adopted. They laid down the general structure of the new tax system but left it to the member states to determine coverage and rates. In 1977, the sixth VAT Directive established a common VAT system for all member states. In 2007, the rates VAT were harmonized, requiring a minimum rate of 15 percent, and allowing a reduced rate of at least 5 percent to only two sets of goods in any country.[32]

The VAT applies to the value added in each step of production. Each enterprise is allowed to deduct VAT incorporated in services and goods that it has purchased from the VAT paid for the goods and services it sells. Thereby most distortions specific to the sales tax can be avoided. Any payer of VAT wants to show receipts of incoming VAT, thus assisting the tax authorities in taxing others. VAT applies to all goods and services that are bought and sold for use or consumption. When an enterprise exports, it is allowed to have its VAT refunded, which stimulates exports. Thus, goods, which are sold for export or services to customers abroad, are not subject to VAT. Conversely imports are taxed to keep the system fair for EU producers so that they can compete on equal terms on the European market with suppliers situated outside the European Union.

The VAT together with other indirect taxes, mainly excise duties on alcohol, fuel and tobacco and energy taxes, have become important for state revenues in Europe yielding nearly 14 percent of GDP on average (figure 3.9). VAT rates range from 17-25 percent with an average of 21.6 percent. Hungary is an outlier with a VAT rate of 27 percent, which was introduced in 2011 to bring additional government revenue and close the large budget deficit. The revenues from these consumption taxes vary less than for other taxes, from 10.2 percent of GDP (Slovakia) to 18.7 percent of GDP (Sweden).[33]

The introduction of the VAT has greatly facilitated the large increase in public expenditures in Western Europe. It is the main explanation for the United States having lower public expenditures than Europe.[34] This tax involves some difficulties: first, VAT bookkeeping involves a certain cost, which may be cumbersome for small and poor firms wanting to stay outside the system. Second, VAT fraud, especially for exports, is a problem in some European countries, particularly for energy products. Third, an argument often raised against VAT is that it is regressive, as the poor spend a larger share of their income on consumption than the rich, but high excise taxes on luxury goods and expensive cars have countered that impact.

In sum, a VAT rate of 20-23 percent being as comprehensive as possible appears a sound policy, and together with other taxes on products and services it should reap about 13-15 percent of GDP in annual state revenues.

THE QUESTION OF TAX HARMONIZATION

One of the important policy discussions in Europe is to what extent tax harmonization is desired. Some countries, for example France, have complained about "tax dumping" and called for a unified tax policy in Europe.[35] This sentiment has been met with stiff resistance from Eastern European countries who favor low taxes. Northern European countries like Finland and the Netherlands favor standardization of corporate accounting for the sake of transparency and European integration.

The first question about the need for tax harmonization is whether the problem to address is insufficient tax revenues. The average EU public expenditure was 46 percent of GDP in 2014, 10 percentage points above that in developed Asian countries and the United States. Clearly, there is no reason Europe should be collecting more taxes. The second alleged issue is inequality. Taxes are imposed on capital, labor or consumption. Tax competition across the world has driven capital taxes down because capital is most footloose. Optimists, going back to the seminal works of Simon Kuznets in 1955, have argued that economic growth will bring more equality in Europe on its own.[36] Pessimists like Thomas Piketty have argued that a unified tax rate is needed to fight inequality. But the higher the total harmonized taxation, the greater the discrimination against labor may be. The third issue is efficiency. The high labor taxes in Europe have contributed to hold back the development of the service sector, which is one of Europe's main economic drawbacks, as detailed in Chapter 5.

Two taxes have been harmonized across Europe: foreign trade taxes and the VAT. Given that the EU is a customs union, the foreign trade taxes are uniform, and the design of the VAT implies a far-reaching harmonization. Further harmonization seems out of reach in the next decade, except possibly in one area: a "financial transaction tax." This idea arose in the wake of the Eurozone crisis combining three different motivations: to tax the financial sector more, to hike taxes, and to give the European Union a tax of its own. In September 2011, the European Commission proposed that the "tax would be levied on all transactions on financial instruments between financial institutions when at least one party to the transaction is located in the EU. The exchange of shares and bonds would be taxed at a rate of 0.1 percent and derivative contracts, at a rate of 0.01 percent. This could approximately raise €57 billion every year."[37]

Since then, the European Council has discussed this proposed tax repeatedly. The number of countries that were interested soon shrunk to 11 out of 28 member countries. The main proponents of the financial transaction tax are France and Germany. They were supported by Austria, Belgium, Greece, Italy, Portugal, Slovakia, Slovenia and Spain. In February 2013, the European Commission noted that when "applied by the 11 Member States, this Financial Transaction Tax is expected to deliver revenues of 30-35 billion euros a year."[38] Eleven countries have subscribed to a unified financial transactions tax since 2013. Efforts are underway to convince others to follow, but none has done so, and there are serious doubts that this tax will be adopted.

The countries that supported the financial taxation tax were largely those with relatively small financial markets, while the United Kingdom, Ireland, Scandinavia, and most of the East European members opposed the tax. Sweden was particularly strongly opposed, because it had tried a financial transaction tax from 1983, and abolished it in 1991 since the results had been negative. Most Swedish trade in securities went abroad, stocks mainly to Oslo and bonds primarily to London, and much of it never returned. Consequently, the revenues ended up being just a few percent of the expected amount.[39]

Another tax that is being discussed for introduction across Europe is some form of an environmental tax. Its precise shape has yet to emerge.

EUROPE HAS EXAMPLES TO FOLLOW

The main goal of taxation is to generate sufficient revenues for necessary public expenditures. The average European country collects 40 percent of GDP in taxes out of total state revenues of more than 45 percent of GDP. The need for these large state revenues arises from Europe's large social expenditures. While Europe generates about 20 percent of global GDP, it spends about 50 percent in social welfare, thus burdening the tax system.

The tax system should combine the aims of minimizing tax evasion and the administrative burden on citizens and enterprises. It should be as simple as possible, with few taxes, few but clear rules, and minimum loopholes. In many European countries most taxpayer already file their returns electronically, and the standard tax return in Sweden is only four pages long. People accept paying taxes as long as taxation appears just and limited and the deliverance of public services credible and efficient.

Transparency is the best reinforcement. Scandinavian countries benefit from a far-reaching public information policy, according to which all tax returns are available to the public. In 1766, Sweden adopted the first Freedom of Information Act in the world. Since then, all declarations of income and wealth in Sweden have been available to any member of the public. Five years later, Denmark adopted a similar law, also in order to expose the ill deeds of the aristocracy. These laws stuck, and they were shared by the then dependent nations of Norway, Iceland and Finland. Many other countries have freedom of information acts, but none that is as far-reaching as the five Nordic ones.[40] Every year, Swedish newspapers publish the names and incomes of the richest in each town. Under such circumstances, it is very difficult to hide illicit revenues or fortunes. Therefore the Nordic countries have less corruption than other countries.[41]

The tax system must not discriminate against labor and should not generate inequality. If capital flees to tax havens to avoid taxation altogether, taxation of the wealthy is ineffective. Much wealth in the Western world is shielded in trusts, foundations, insurances and corporations. The high taxes then apply to people of more modest means. For this reason taxation of labor should be reduced and equalized with the taxation of capital gains.

Several more concrete conclusions can be drawn from this analysis. First, to encourage entrepreneurship and growth taxes should be few in number, low, and relatively flat. Loopholes favoring one industry or another should be minimized. The example of Estonia, Bulgaria and Slovakia can be followed as has been the case in a number of other European countries. Overall, Europe is ahead of the United States in simplifying tax laws and reducing the cost of tax administration.

Second, labor in Europe is subject to excessive taxation through income taxes, high payroll taxes and VAT. These taxes hamper innovation and discourage official work, preventing job-seekers from finding their first employment. Personal income tax and payroll tax are the two taxes that need to be trimmed the most to encourage participation in the labor force, especially among European women.

Third, marginal income taxes are too high in many European countries. Europe suffers from high tax wedges on labor. Studies have documented the high tax wedge for labor in Sweden, which has resulted in falling labor supply and shorter working hours in sharp contrast to the US development.[42] The initiative of the UK government to reduce the marginal rates is an example to follow.[43]

Finally, Europe may consider introducing a luxury tax to encourage the efficient use of financial wealth and to temper the increase in inequality. So far, the European Commission has been skeptical to luxury tax proposals, a particular form of consumption taxes. Hungary's Prime Minister Viktor Orban proposed the introduction of a 35 percent VAT on luxury goods in 2011, but the European Commission turned it down.[44] Such a tax, albeit on a limited number of good, was launched the same year in Greece. It involves an annual levy of 13 percent on recreational boats over five meters (16ft). Other countries that have discussed the introduction of luxury taxes include Bulgaria and the Czech Republic. Taxable items include expensive residences, cars, yachts, and art.

West European countries can take the new thinking on taxation from Eastern Europe. The Baltic countries, Slovakia, Romania and Bulgaria have only the taxes we have advocated here. Bulgaria, for example, collects most of its taxes through VAT and excise taxes with a VAT rate of 20 percent, thus getting 15.4 percent of GDP out of its total tax revenues of 28 percent of GDP in 2013. It has a flat personal income tax at 10 percent, which coincides with its corporate profit tax of 10 percent. The personal income tax yield 3 percent of GDP and the corporate profit tax 1.9 percent of GDP. Other taxes of significance are environmental taxes (2.8 percent of GDP), capital gain taxes (1 percent of GDP) and property taxes (0.6 percent of GDP). Thanks to other revenues, Bulgaria can maintain a balanced budget at 36-38 percent of GDP.

4

Reforming Pensions

Europe is ageing rapidly, and the old need pensions and care. As a share of the active population aged 15-64, the European population aged 65 or more is projected to increase from 28 percent in 2016 to 53 percent in 2060.[1] Consequently, an increasing share of national income will cover pension expenditures. In 2013 old-age pensions accounted for an average of 9.2 percent of GDP in the EU-28 to compare with 6.1 percent of GDP in the United States.

Some European countries have inordinately high public pension expenditures. In 2013, Greece spent 14.4 percent of GDP on public pensions, more than any other developed economy. Italy followed at 14 percent of GDP. Other countries with high public pension spending are also European: Austria and France at about 13 percent of GDP, and Finland, Poland, Portugal and Sweden at about 12 percent of GDP. Pensions account for one-quarter to one-third of total public expenditure in these countries. Yet the public pension costs vary greatly with the share of public versus private pensions. In Ireland, it was only 4 percent of GDP (figure 4.1), while actual pension benefits vary much less.

Projections of the economic impact of ageing on EU countries' public finances include private mandatory pensions and span the period to the year 2060.[2] The European Commission assesses the average statutory pension expenditure of the EU countries at 11.4 percent of GDP, and expects these expenditures to increase to 12.9 percent by 2060. Pension expenditures in Finland are projected to reach a peak in 2032, at 15.6 percent of GDP. According to the Commission, pension expenditure in Europe will increase the most in Luxemburg (9.4 percentage points), Cyprus (8.7) and Slovenia (7.1). Pension expenditure in Luxemburg and Slovenia would be the highest in the world in 2060 at 18 percent of GDP. Yet the ratio will fall in some countries, which are experiencing a large outflow of citizens to other European countries. Thus pension expenditures are projected to decrease in Latvia (-3.8 percentage points), Poland (-2.2), and Estonia (-1.1).

Pensions are just one part of the overall cost of caring for the elderly. Public health care expenditures, excluding what patients pay out of pocket as co-payments or the cost of medicine, in the European Union are expected to increase from 7.3 percent of GDP in 2015 to 8.3 percent in 2060, while public spending on long-term care is projected to double, increasing from 1.9 percent of GDP in 2015 to 3.4 percent of

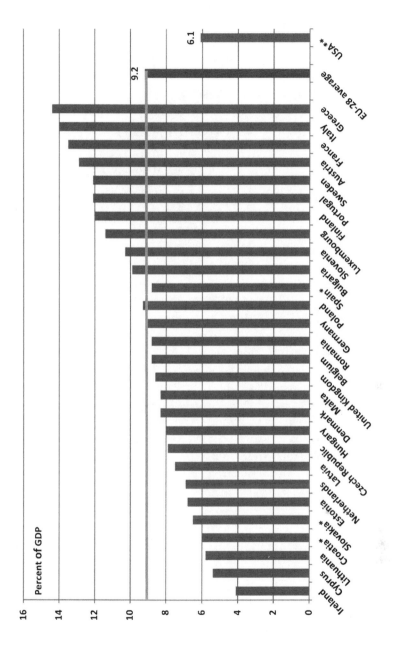

Figure 4.1 Share of Pensions in Public Expenditure, 2013

* Provisional; ** Data from OECD, 2012

Source: EU: Eurostat, available at http://appsso.eurostat.ec.europa.eu/nui/show.do; USA: OECD, available at https://stats.oecd.org/Index. aspx?DataSetCode=SOCX_AGG, both retrieved July 30, 2015.

GDP in 2060.[3] Hence the burden of paying for pensions, health and social care is a serious challenge to Europe's stability.

The first section of this chapter discusses how European pension systems have evolved. Section 2 analyzes the need for change. The three following sections discusses changes, namely tightening of early retirement schemes, rising retirement age, and more fundamental pension reform. Section 6 examines private pension funds across Europe. Section 6 reviews the impact of the global financial crisis on pension systems, and section 8 concludes with a recommendation for European governments to pursue more changes to their pension model.

HOW PENSION SYSTEMS HAVE EVOLVED

Pension systems have evolved over a long time. Since their aim is to provide for old age, they are characterized by a great deal of inertia. Goals and means chosen decades ago have persisted in today's economic and demographic environment. Pension systems have evolved in in different fashion across Europe, with several countries providing watershed developments.

The initial step was Bismarck's Old Age and Infirmity Bill of 1889, which marked the beginning of public pensions. It offered a subsistence pension to those who became permanently disabled or reached the age of 70, when the average German life expectancy at birth was 36 for men and 38 for women.[4] Similar systems spread to other developed countries. Until World War II, all publicly managed pensions were modest, providing for no more than 15-20 percent of the average wage.[5]

Everything changed after World War II. The Beveridge Report in England advocated a significant increase in retirement benefits and the right of all old-age pensioners to receive a minimum income at public expense. The consequence was the proliferation of expensive public pension plans across wealthy European countries. They were financed with payroll taxes on current employees to the benefit of those already retired. The combination of the Bismarck and Beveridge pension schemes established several principles in Northern Europe: Pensions were predominantly public; they were financed with payroll taxes; the current taxpayers financed older generations (pay-as-you-go); and pensions were usually set as a share of the last salary before retirement.

In parallel, alternative pension arrangements existed, such as the so-called occupational pension plans. They went back to the American war of independence in 1776 when such plans provided half-pay for life to soldiers disabled during the revolutionary war. Occupational pension schemes became popular in Europe too. They were based on savings pension funds, and they cover a large part of the population in Western European countries. Unlike the public pensions, the occupational pensions were based on private insurance savings, and pensions were thus related to the accumulated value of the contributions.[6]

A third form of pension systems has been personal saving plans, which evolved after World War II in Europe. These private schemes initially developed in former British colonies that combined a strong market-economic tradition with distrust in the state. The first national mandated private pension was established in Malaysia in 1951. In addition, voluntary private pension plans have existed for a half century, and they often benefit from tax preferences.

As the old public pension schemes grew too expensive, the question arose whether countries should turn to alternative collective or private schemes based on savings. Exceptionally, Chile replaced its old public pension scheme with a mandatory pension scheme in 1981.

Since 1990, pensions systems in Eastern European countries have evolved rapidly, with many countries adopting a three-pillar pension system recommended by the World Bank in its seminal report *Averting the Old Age Crisis,* published in 1994.[7] Yet Europe retains two distinct pension models. One has emerged from Beveridge anti-poverty considerations after World War II, while the other has evolved into performance-rewarding schemes in the 1970s and 1980s.

As a result, two basic pension models prevail in Europe. In social insurance systems the state provides the greatest share of individual pension income according to the principles of defined benefits. A single public pillar pursues a goal of maintaining income with generous benefits and general coverage, reducing or eliminating the need for supplementary pensions. Financing is usually pay-as-you-go: current contributions and tax revenues are immediately disbursed to finance pensions. The United Kingdom, Germany, France, Italy and Spain developed such pension systems after World War II. Sweden and Finland followed the same path somewhat later. These pension systems aimed not only at security but also at redistribution of income.

The second system is based on defined contributions to private pension funds, which have evolved since 1990. The leader in this group is the Netherlands, followed by the United Kingdom, Ireland and Denmark. Most Eastern European countries have adopted such systems as well. The government maintains a responsibility to offer security for all at old age and in the case of disability, whereas additional incomes come from individual private savings, whether voluntary or mandatory.

THE NEED FOR CHANGE

A need for change of pension system has grown over time and it became more widely felt in the late 1970s. The fundamental problem was that the costs of the public pension systems became too large. Rising life expectancy meant more retired people. When the old were few and real incomes were rising fast, as in the "glorious 30" years between 1945 and 1975, it made sense that the young were paying out of their incomes for the older generations. After 1975, however, incomes stagnated, and fewer young people were available to pay for the pensions, as the ratio of working people to pensioners declined with lower birth rates.

The high payroll taxes prompted tax evasion and offered a disincentive to work. Furthermore, in many countries an employee had to work for many years to secure any public pension, so it discriminated against migrating workers. Another source of irritation was that the poor financing led to frequent political meddling in the pension system, which meant that citizens harbored little security or trust in the pension system and felt compelled to participate in private pension funds. Nor was the public pension system transparent. Few knew what pension they would receive upon retirement. For these reasons the public pension systems were subject to periodic crises, when overall economic conditions sour. In one country after the other, the public pension system became financially unsustainable. This problem was aggravated by the tradition to finance pensions with a payroll tax.

Sweden offers an illuminating example. In the 1990s, it was clear that the old Swedish pension system had run its course. Three features led to its demise: the lack of the financial sustainability, perceived unfairness and the negative economic stimuli it created. In the 1980s the Swedish pension system fell into a significant deficit in spite of the high payroll tax of 20 percent. According to the Swedish Ministry of Health and Social Affairs, it would needed to be raised to 36 percent of the average wage, to keep the system financed, which was deemed politically unsustainable.[8] The system was also increasingly perceived as being unfair, since calculations of pensions were based on the 15 highest-earning years, favoring white-collar workers with peak-earnings years, while high-income earners were dissatisfied with the highly redistributive character of the pension system.

Finally, taxes paid by an individual into the system did not correspond to his or her benefits, giving workers an incentive to quit the labor force prematurely.[9] Swedes did not trust the public pensions, with most working Swedes paying for complementary private pensions. These deficiencies forced the center-right government of Prime Minister Carl Bildt to enter negotiations with the opposition Social Democratic party as well as with labor unions. In 1998, after a decade long process of consultation and research, Sweden enacted a radical change, introducing defined-contribution rules for public pensions as well as new supplementary pillars.

TIGHTENING OF EARLY RETIREMENT SCHEMES

In Europe, early retirement schemes vary substantially across countries. Labor statistics suggest that around 22 percent of workers aged 55 to 59 take early retirement, with another 18 percent taking out early retirement in the age group of 60 to 64. With regard to early retirement, European countries fall into three categories: less than 10 percent of workers opt for early retirement in Spain, the Czech Republic, Cyprus, Germany, Portugal, Ireland and Latvia; average of 10-20 percent in France, Bulgaria, Denmark, Estonia, Slovenia, Slovakia and the United Kingdom; and more than 20 percent in Belgium, Luxembourg, Poland, Hungary, the Netherlands, Lithuania, Romania, Finland and Sweden.[10] Most early retirement is justified with hazardous or physically demanding work.

In recent years, early retirement has been scaled back in many countries because excessive costs, longer life expectancy, improving health, and suspicions of abuse. In 2011, the early retirement age in Greece was raised from 53 to 60 years, including for workers with 40 years of contributions and those in heavy and arduous professions. At the same time, the list of jobs deemed heavy or unhealthy, and which thereby qualify for early retirement, was reduced in half, as safety standards have improved. In Portugal, access to early retirement was suspended for five years, starting in 2011, while Poland has withdrawn some of its early retirement schemes, and Slovakia has decreased pensions for early retirement by up to 25 percent.[11]

In 2012, President of the European Council Herman van Rompuy attended the meetings of finance ministers (Ecofin) on two occasions and requested a discussion on reforms of early retirement schemes.[12] The main focus was on how to link career planning for workers in the army, police, and mining so that they could continue gainful employment after finishing their primary round of duty. The result of this discussion was the inclusion of recommendations on reducing early retirement schemes in the annual European Council report on national economic programs.[13]

Recent changes also include a tightening of eligibility conditions for early retirement and disability schemes and a reduction of generous indexation. In Bulgaria, members of the military and police could retire after 18 years of service, sometimes as early as at the age of 40, but in 2011 and 2015 the mandatory minimum retirement age was raised to 52 years for army officers and the police. Other reforms have improved the conditions for credits for child rearing and care responsibilities to encourage families to have more children.

The longer people work, the more socially engaged they are. The reduction of early retirement schemes allows workers to stay socially active for longer, and thus avoid depression and diseases related to lack of active life. Recent studies have found that workers who have taken early retirement are 40 percent more likely to fall into bouts of depression relative to working people of similar age and physical health.[14] Another study, using data of Belgian early retirees, has observed that the risk of obesity and cardiovascular diseases nearly doubles, due to insufficient adaptation (in terms of food consumption and physical activities) of the retired to the new lifestyle.[15] Early retirement is, in other words, not only a fiscal problem but also a healthcare issue. Politically, the tightening of early retirement schemes has proven quite easily accepted.

RETIREMENT AGE RISING

As life expectancy rises and the cost of public pensions spike, the increase of retirement age has become necessary. All European countries, with the exception of France, have done so in the last two decades. These decisions are politically controversial, because they involve a large share of the population, and many perceive it as a deterioration in their future standard of living.

The general retirement age in Europe is 65 years (table 4.1). Following the recent financial crisis, many countries have decided to raise the retirement age from 65 to 67 years, which is about to become the European standard, while the goal is 68 years in the United Kingdom and Ireland. Especially in the years following the Eurozone crisis many European countries have raised retirement ages. Fourteen countries—including all on the front lines of the Eurozone crisis, such as Italy, Spain, Portugal, Greece and Ireland—passed legislation to increase retirement ages to between

67 and 69, by 2050.[16] The retirement age is set to rise further. As Germany's EU Commissioner Günther Oettinger suggested in 2015. "We have to talk about 70 as the new retirement age in Europe. We have to prepare people for a longer working life."[17]

Denmark, Greece, Hungary, Italy and the Netherlands have linked future increases in pension ages to changes in life expectancy, meaning that retirement ages in both Denmark and Italy, for example, will go well beyond age 67 in the future. However, automatic adjustment is scheduled to run only from 2020. This is likely to become the next European standard. In Italy the automatic adjustment of age requirements was brought forward and the revisions of pension ages and annuity divisors were scheduled to take place together, every other year from 2021. The pensionable age is expected to rise to 70 years by 2050.

Previously, it was common to have a lower retirement age for women, down to 60 years of age, especially in the former communist countries. This makes little sense, considering that European women presently have a life expectancy that is 4 years longer than for men. Most countries that had a gender differentiation are abolishing it and raising the retirement age for women faster than for men to equalizing them.

To raise the retirement age is hardly ever popular, and people of upper middle age are politically very active. Many a government has lost elections for such a deed. One early victim was the Estonian reform government of Mart Laar in 1994. More recently, the socialist Spanish Prime Minister José Luis Rodríguez Zapatero was voted out of office in 2011, after he raised the country's retirement age from 65 to 67. In France, President Nicolas Sarkozy provoked a nationwide strike when he backed a proposal to lift the minimum retirement age from 60 to 62. He was ousted in elections in May 2012 by socialist challenger François Hollande, who vowed during his campaign to roll back the measure and did so shortly after taking office.

The most significant policy proposal that Italian Prime Minister Mario Monti managed during his short tenure was to hike the retirement age in 2012—to 68 for men and 63 for women in the private sector or 65 in the public sector. Soon after, he lost popularity and early elections ousted him.

In Bulgaria, the Ivan Kostov government carried out the initial pension reform in 2001. Since then, population ageing and emigration to the richer EU countries have resulted in a large pension system deficit. Yet the mandatory retirement age remained 60 for women and 63 for men, among the lowest in Europe. In early 2010, the center-right government proposed an increase in the retirement age to 65 years for both men and women, to be phased in gradually by adding four months each year. The new retirement age would be reached in 6 years for men and 15 for women. The proposed changes encompassed eliminating the provisions that allowed members of the police and the military to retire after just 15 years of service. After months of hard work, enough members of Parliament were lined up to make this change happen. But the prime minister wavered under pressure from the labor unions, and the legislation was stopped before reaching a formal vote in the Parliament. In early 2011, an identical proposal for changes in pension legislation passed Parliament.

Rising unemployment in Europe and pension changes in neighboring Romania had convinced the prime minister of the necessity to change.

The reform was short-lived, however. The next government repealed these changes as of January 2014, increasing the size of the deficit in the Social Security Fund. Most recently, in July 2015 a partial re-institution of the new pension legislation took place, with a more gradual increase in the mandatory retirement age to 65 by the year 2037, and the introduction of a minimum retirement age for police officers at the age of 52. Other parts of the earlier proposal were left untouched.[18]

Understandably, politicians have been reticent to implement changes to their pension model, unless forced by large fiscal deficits. In fact, France and Germany, have gone in the opposite direction as the rest of the European Union. France has gone back to a lower retirement age of 60. After the elections in 2014, the newly-formed German Christian Democratic and Social Democratic coalition government adopted a pension package, allowing eligible workers to retire at 63. Workers who have worked for 45 years can retire two years before the standard retirement age of 65 without any loss of pension.[19]

To reduce the burden on pensions without implementing unpopular legislative changes, some countries encourage workers to continue their employment beyond mandatory retirement. The Swedish government increased its Earned Income Tax Credit, which is designed to stimulate incentive to work for workers above the age of 65. The employer's social security contribution is also lower for workers over 66. The United Kingdom abolished the default retirement age in order to afford workers greater opportunities for longer working lives.[20]

COMPREHENSIVE PENSION REFORM

Around 1990, many European countries realized that their pension systems needed greater changes than the restriction of early retirement and an increase in the retirement age. The privatization of the Chilean pension system in 1981 was an important source of inspiration, but European politicians perceived it as being too radical. Instead, they wanted to scale down the public pension system and standardize it as a minimum social security for all retirees.

A new concept arose of a three-pillar pension system. The first pillar was a public pay-as-you-go pension providing a basic minimum rate for all for the sake of poverty prevention. The second pillar was the novelty inspired by Chile, a mandatory private savings scheme. Typically a certain percentage of the payroll was allocated to such pension funds, and the individual in question owned that fund. The owner could decide how to invest his or her share and was the beneficiary of the returns. The third pillar consisted of voluntary private pension savings, which were encouraged through favorable taxation. Sometimes employers financed these schemes, sometimes employees themselves. This reform concept was popularized by an influential 1994 book by the World Bank, *Averting the Old Age Crisis.*

Three different groups of countries opted for a multi-pillar system. Ireland and the United Kingdom embraced its personal choice backbone. The same was true of the formerly communist countries in Eastern Europe that inherited a poorly functioning public pension system. A third group was the North Europeans--the Netherlands, Denmark, Sweden and Finland, whose public pension systems had become financially unsustainable.

The method of financing tends to be mixed in three-pillar pensions: the first pillar of pay-as-you-go for public programs as well as the second pillar are usually funded through a payroll tax. Legislation mandates what share of the collected contributions goes to the second pillar. Though exceptionally Denmark has minimized its payroll tax and let employees finance their pension out of their earnings. However, if payroll tax revenues are insufficient for ordinary pensions, the ordinary state budget tends to top them up. Either employers or employees can provide private funding for supplementary funds, and they usually enjoy tax exemption, while disbursed pensions are taxed in some countries but not in others.

The transition to a multi-pillar pension system made pensions defined by contributions, and no longer based on previous earnings. Sweden took the lead in making public pensions above the minimum pension actuarially correct, giving people an annual statement of their public pension savings and their expected pensions. Employees could control their pension funds with considerable but not complete freedom and decide how to invest their mandatory pension savings. Private pension funds vie for the resources of this second pillar and the voluntary third pillar.

The driving motivation for reforms was to reduce the gap in public finances. In the early post-communist period, Hungary was considered the country that had the earliest transformation of the pension system in Eastern Europe. The program, designed by finance minister Lajos Bokros, included several important changes, notably mandatory private pension funds for people entering the labor market for the first time. It came into force in 1998.[21] Poland followed suit in 1999, where Minister of Finance Leszek Balcerowicz drove the transformation. A major reason for these two countries reforming first was that they had the highest pension costs, which peaked at 16 percent of GDP in the mid-1990s.[22]

In 1998, the main Swedish political parties agreed on a major pension overhaul, introducing an account-based system, where the money paid into the pension system would be associated with an individual pension account. Here an additional motive was to render pensions more stable and secure, since the pension system was subject to frequent political tampering. Payments were divided into two different accounts: one notional, based on a "pay-as-you-go" system, where 16 percent of the payroll was credited. The money went directly to current pensioners, but was assigned to an individual's account, to be accessed at retirement. Additionally, a fully funded component of 2.5 percent of the payroll was invested in pension funds according to the individual's choice.[23] Furthermore, a balancing mechanism was introduced, to ensure financial sustainability of the pension system. In a downturn, pension disbursement decreases with economic growth. This happens automatically, and without political control, ensuring that the system is sustainable as well as kept free from political meddling.

In the 2000s, Bulgaria, Estonia, Latvia, Romania and Slovakia introduced mandatory private pensions. The most significant transformation took place in Slovakia. The center-right government elected in 2002 introduced a strong second pillar that allowed employees to set aside resources for retirement in funds managed by pension management firms. This reform, implemented by Finance Minister Ivan Miklos, was important not only to increase the size of future pensions but also to promote the-long-term sustainability of public finances.[24] Had a second pillar not been added, public finances would likely have suffered a complete collapse in the future. The Slovak government also reformed the pay-as-you-go pillar, moving from an annual politically negotiated valorization to an automatic mechanism based on the rate of inflation and the growth rate of nominal incomes. It also raised the retirement age and provided tax incentives for saving through the third, voluntary pillar of the pension system. Moreover the Miklos reform added a life expectancy component to future retirement ages. The pace of retirement age increases leads to a slight fall in the highest earners' pension wealth, as there is a ceiling on contributions.

The macroeconomic effects of a successful pension reform are widely recognized. An IMF Working paper suggests that they "can have a positive effect on growth in both the short run, propelled by rising consumption, and in the long run, due to lower government debt crowding in higher investment." Greater savings lead to more capital accumulation. Needless to say, an increase in the retirement age yields the strongest impact in the short run because higher labor income leads to more demand and in the long run positive supply effects come to the fore.[25]

THE ROLE OF PENSION FUNDS

Several European Union countries have created compulsory individual pension accounts. These accounts are funded with earnings-related pension contributions. Figure 4.2 presents the sizes of pension funds in different countries in relation to the country's GDP. These statistics cover statutory (1st pillar) and individual mandated pensions (2nd pillar), but not individual pension insurance (third pillar). The most striking observation is how small most of these funds are. Only five EU countries have pension funds exceeding 20 percent of GDP, namely the Netherlands, the United Kingdom, Ireland, Denmark and Finland.

The extensive pension assets in the Netherlands are a result of compulsory and fully funded individual accounts, constituting the second pillar. In Finland, the mandated earnings-related pension scheme is partly funded by the government since the scheme came into force in 1962. In most other European countries, the second pillar was created as late as in the 1990s. Therefore, the accrued statutory pension assets are relatively small compared to those in the Netherlands and Finland. Eastern European countries, in particular, implemented second pillar private pensions after 1998. In some cases, younger workers adopted these new schemes. Many of them have yet to begin paying benefits, and often the share of the payroll devoted to the second pillar is small.

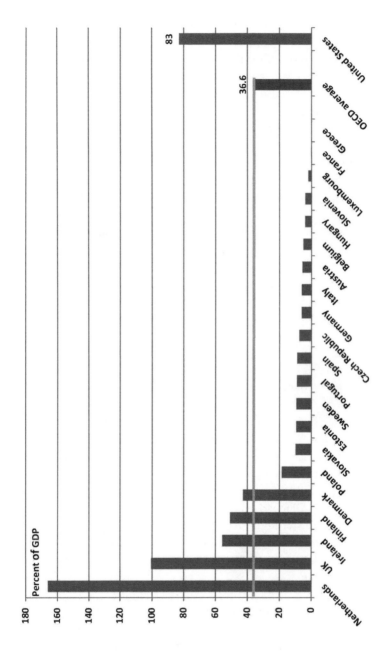

Figure 4.2 Size of Pension Funds, 2013

Note: Savings in pension funds from all types of pension plans are included (occupational and personal, mandatory and voluntary), covering both public and private sector workers. All elements of pay-as-you-go systems, such as pension insurance contracts, are not included.

Source: OECD, Pension Markets in Focus, available at: http://www.oecd.org/daf/fin/private-pensions/Pension-Markets-in-Focus-2014.pdf

Pension funds are subject to many restrictions on what investments they are allowed, often compelling them to invest to a large extent in domestic government bonds. In Belgium, 46 percent of total pension funds' assets are invested in bonds as of early 2015, and only 35 percent in equities. At the extreme end of the spectrum is Spain, where law compels pension funds to be fully invested in domestic government bonds.

Figure 4.3 shows an overview of the national maximum limits on different types of assets in select European countries. Generally, the legislation prefers government bonds, and gets strict for equity and real estate. About half of countries have no limitations on publicly-traded equity, while most of the other countries have limits on the range of 50–75 percent of equity. Investment in real estate is heavily regulated, only allowing shares below a quarter of the total pension fund's holding.

Eastern European countries like Hungary, Poland and Slovakia have no limits on investment in domestic government bonds, but they have imposed a 20-40 percent maximum limit on foreign government and domestic corporate bonds. Regulations of real estate holdings by private pension funds limit the total amount invested in a single real estate position. This is motivated by a fear of real estate price bubbles as well as of corruption.

The greater the opportunities are to invest in diverse assets, the lower is the risk and the greater the likelihood of good returns. The latter aspect has become the focus of intense debates in some European countries, where policy makers have questioned the efficiency of private pension funds. Indeed, the available statistics

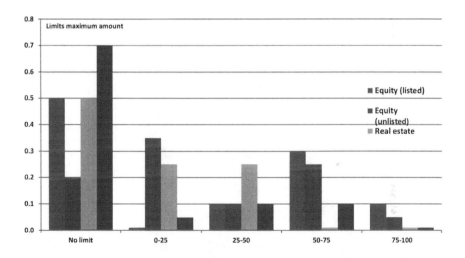

Figure 4.3 Where Can Pension Funds Invest
Note: This represents all OECD-countries in the European Union, in total 21 countries.
Country notes: The data for Czech Republic is based on the "balanced scheme" requirements for savings; Finland is based on the "statutory pension plan", Germany is based on the rules for 'Pensionskassen' and Slovakia refers to the rules for the second pillar.
Source: OECD; Table 1, Portfolio Limits, available at http://www.oecd.org/daf/fin/private-pensions/ 2014%20Survey%20of%20Investment%20Regulations%20of%20Pension%20Funds%20FINAL.pdf

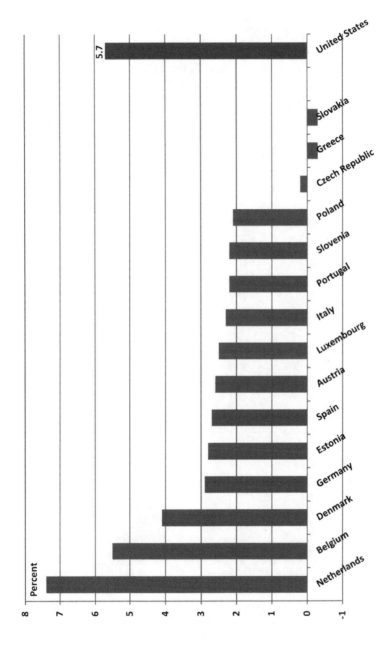

Figure 4.4 Real Return of Pension Funds

Note: this is a selection of EU countries, based on OECD's Pension Markets in Focus report.

Source: OECD, Pension Markets in Focus, available at: http://www.oecd.org/daf/fin/private-pensions/Pension-Markets-in-Focus-2014.pdf

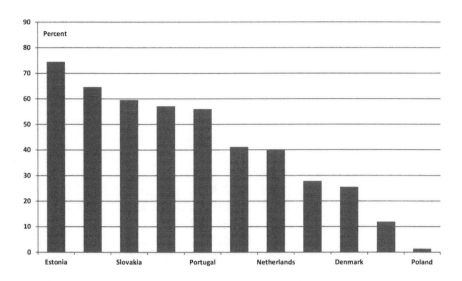

Figure 4.5 Foreign Assets of Pensions Funds in Select EU Countries, **2013**
Note: this is a selection of EU countries, based on OECD's Pension Markets in Focus report.
Source: OECD, Pension Markets in Focus, available at: http://www.oecd.org/daf/fin/private-pensions/
Pension-Markets-in-Focus-2014.pdf

show that in many countries, the return on investment of private pension funds is below the respective market index (figure 4.4).[26]

Slovakia, Greece and the Czech Republic even show negative returns on their pension funds. All three countries had their pension assets almost exclusively invested in bonds as of 2013 (Czech Republic 85 percent of total pension assets, Slovakia 75 percent and Greece 70 percent), while they held the rest as cash and deposits. By contrast, the Netherlands and Belgium, which had the highest returns, had around 40 percent of their pension fund assets invested in shares of publicly-listed companies. [27]

If a viable pension fund industry is to develop, regulators need to allow a diversification of investment opportunities, both at home and abroad. This is particularly important for small countries with tiny stock markets. In Estonia, 75 percent of pension funds' money is invested in foreign assets, in Luxembourg—about 65 percent (figure 4.5). This is particularly important in smaller countries when the country's economy is experiencing a downturn. When the Greek stock market suspended operations during the summer of 2015 and later re-opened with significant losses, Greek pension funds were hit hard, as a quarter of their portfolio was in publicly-listed stocks on the Athens Stock Exchange, and Greek regulation bars pension funds to invest in foreign stocks.

IMPACT OF THE GLOBAL FINANCIAL CRISIS

Pension reforms were quite popular in Europe during the boom years 2000-2007, but the global financial crisis had an even bigger impact and reverse impact on pension reforms. Concerns were raised both by pension holders and governments. Government wanted to safeguard the public pension system, which led to a tightening of benefits and a hiking of retirement ages, especially in crisis countries like Ireland and in Southern Europe. Several Eastern European countries transferred some of the pension contributions from mandatory private savings to the public pension system.

Given that stock markets plummeted, private pension savings appeared much less attractive to the pension savers.[28] They lost a large share of their accumulated capital at least temporarily. Many were not ready for such a shock and called for greater security. Also in the good times, savers in some countries had complained because their government had compelled them to keep a large share of their savings in low-yielding government bonds. In effect, this was a means of indirect taxation through financing the government's fiscal deficits.[29]

The greater threat to the mandatory private pension funds came from the governments. In 2008/9, most of the East European countries reduced the share of the payroll going to private pension savings and redirected the funds to the state treasury instead in order to finance the ordinary pay-as-you go system. In two cases, the government's appetite grew extreme. The Hungarian government of Viktor Orban simply nationalized the second pillar in 2010-11, claiming that it was really state property. The Polish government of Donald Tusk nationalized half the mandatory pension funds in 2013. The government's argument was that the funds were invested in government bonds in any case, so why not swap bonds for pension obligations?

Slovakia allowed workers to move back to the state-run scheme from private defined-contribution plans in June 2009 and made occupational pensions voluntary for new labor market entrants. However, the move was short-lived: in 2012, private pensions were again made compulsory. Its example was, however, contagious. Bulgaria took a similar turn in 2015.

Of the Eurozone crisis countries, only Ireland had substantial private pension savings. The crisis magnified the shortcomings of its pension system, too little anti-poverty protection and inadequate regulation of private pensions. The government responded by increasing its contribution to the national pension fund and it centralized the management of national pension fund investments with the Ministry of Finance. It also reduced tax incentives for voluntary retirement savings and made employer pension contributions taxable income for the employee.[30]

Portugal, Spain and Greece all tightened pension benefits and raised retirement ages. Through various legislative measures, they have brought their pay-as-you-go system closer to defined contribution models. Portugal reduced the starting pensions and related pensions more closely to the length of work. In effect, the retirement age was hiked from 65 to 66 years as of 2014, and it is supposed to reach 67 years by 2029.

Prior to the Eurozone crisis the Spanish state pension system was the third most generous in Europe, behind Greece and Italy. According to the OECD, a Spanish pensioner typically received 74 percent of his salary before retirement—compared to an OECD average of 54 percent. Spain's pension regime is being squeezed by a falling birth rate and rising life expectancy. For every Spaniard above the age of 65 in 2010 there were 3.6 potential contributors to the system aged 16 to 64."If current demographic trends continue, that ratio will be 2.5 in 2030 and 1.6 in 2050," the study said, adding: "To continue to fund its pensions, Spain will need 26.5 million immigrants over the next 40 years, or roughly 665,000 per year. But only 70,000 immigrants arrived in 2010."[31] In 2011 and again in 2013, Spain reformed its pensions, by extending the number of years of contributions used to compute the pensions, delaying the retirement age, and effectively transforming the Spanish pay-as-you-go system into a defined-contribution system by tying pensions to the evolution of life expectancy. By 2037, these reforms will reduce the real value of the average pension by approximately 20 percent. This legislation uses the experience of Portugal.[32]

Greece had the most generous pension system, especially for public employees, and it has carried out drastic changes too. Before 2010, the pay-as-you-go pension system was fragmented and inequitable with unfunded liabilities of 170 percent of GDP. The average dependency ratio of 1.7 workers per pensioner in Greece was below the viability ratio of 2:1. Total state pension commitments amounted to 16 percent of GDP. Without change, this ratio would have risen to 26 percent by 2060. Pensions paying over €2,000 per month were cut by 40 percent, while pensions of less than €1,000 per month were cut by 14 percent. The government reduced the number of annual pension payments from 14 to 12, eliminating bonus payments for Easter and Christmas. In July 2015, as part of the negotiations over the release of the third rescue package by the European Union, Greece committed to reducing another 1 percent of GDP in pension expenditures, while protecting the poorest pensioners. The measure is, however, difficult to fulfill, after five years of prior reductions in pensions.

CONCLUSIONS: CONVERGENCE AROUND PENSIONS BASED ON DEFINED CONTRIBUTIONS

Europe's pension models have varied greatly, but current trends show considerable convergence. The most significant transformation of European pension systems is the extension of the number of years of active labor force involvement. This is occurring through a reduction of early retirement schemes, an increase in the number of years required for mandatory retirement, and greater participation of women in the labor force (as discussed in Chapter 6). These changes have made the pension system more financially sustainable.

Another major change that is taking place both in public and private pension schemes is to move from defined benefits to defined contributions. The benefit of this transformation is that the pension benefits adjust automatically to the financially feasible, avoiding the need for frequent political meddling in pensions. It also greatly improves the transparency of the pension system. Pension contributions become real savings and are no longer perceived as a tax. Everybody can receive a statement of their pension capital and expected pension each year. A person can take the pension capital to another country, which is not true of the old European public pensions, which can make it prohibitively costly to move from one country to another in the middle of a career. The disadvantages of the move to defined contributions for a pensioner is that the economic risk is transferred to the pensioner from the state or employer and the pension might be lower.

A serious challenge to sustainability of pension systems has been the reduction of private mandatory savings during the global financial crisis and the nationalization of the second pillar in Hungary and Poland. The crisis response suggests that it is difficult to safeguard small pension funds. They must grow and be successful to seem attractive. An obvious way of doing so is to enact regulations that allow individuals greater choice over the way their retirement savings are invested, which is currently taking place.

Estonia and Bulgaria have adopted a flexible pension policy, moving people automatically into less risky investments as they get closer to retirement. Several countries have relaxed restrictions on investment options to foster greater diversification of pension funds' portfolios. Sweden, Finland and Estonia have followed this path, with Slovakia allowing pension funds to take larger shares in foreign investments in order to hedge the risk of national default or fall in the value of corporate stocks listed on the Bratislava Stock Exchange. Finally, voluntary pension plans can expand investment options for workers and thus increase competition for customers among funds. The Czech Republic, Poland, Slovakia and the United Kingdom have introduced such schemes since 2012.

Considering the starting point, EU governments should have the ambition to cut public pension costs to no more than 8 percent of GDP to limit the fiscal burden;[33] to render most of the public pensions actuarially correct and transparent; to promote solid private pension savings, whether mandatory or voluntary with sound regulation. The Dutch pension system appears the example to follow. It is seen as "having reached an enviable position, coming closer than any other country's system to the ideal combination of complete coverage, inflation-indexed benefits at a reasonable level and predictable contribution rates."[34]

The Dutch system combines all the best features of a pension system. Its first pillar is a public old-age pension under a statuary insurance scheme financed with a payroll tax in a pay-as-you-go system. It provides all with a flat minimum pension amounting to 70 percent of the minimum income, rendering it very stable. The outstanding feature of the Dutch system is its second pillar, a very large private occupational pension that is quasi-mandatory. It is financed with 18 percent of employees' earnings, giving the Netherlands the largest private pension funds in Europe far exceeding its GDP.

Together with the state pension, the Dutch occupational pension is supposed to offer pensioners 70 percent of their salary. The occupational pensions cover both private and public employees. They are agreed through collective bargaining

Table 4.1: Retirement Age in Europe

	Current general retirement age (2014)	Future retirement age
	Men/ Women	General retirement age or men/ women
Netherlands	65y.1month	67+ (2024, GP 2021)
Belgium	65	
UK	65 / 61	67+ (2028), 68 (2046)
Spain	65.1	67 (2027)
Ireland	65	68 (2028)
Italy	66 / 62.3month	67+ (2022)
Austria	65 / 60	65 (2033)
Greece	65	67(-), 67+ (2021)
Luxemburg	65	-
Portugal	65	-
France	65	67 (2018)
Sweden	61-67, 65	-
Germany	65y.2month	67 (2029)
Finland	63-68, 65	-
Denmark	65; 67	67+ (2022, 2030)
Bulgaria	63.8/60.8	65 (2017) / 63 (2020)
Cyprus	65	-
Latvia	62	65 (2024)
Lithuania	62.10/60.8	65 (2026)
Malta	62	65 (2027)
Poland	65.3/60.3	67 (2020) / 67 (2040)
Romania	64.3/ 59.3	65 /60 (2015), 65 (2030)
Slovakia	62 / 57-61	62 (2024)
Slovenia	63 / 61	-
Czech	62.8/57.4-61.8	66.8 (2041)
Hungary	62.6	65 (2022)
Estonia	63 /62	65 (2026) / 63 (2016), 65 (2026)
Croatia	65	67 (2038)

between employers and trade unions. In 2011, there were 459 pension funds that are non-profit firms with strictly regulated management fees. The Netherlands maintains actuarially correct defined benefits, but it has switched from basing it on final pay to average wages with conditional indexation, which means that benefits can be reduced if returns on investment falls.[35] The system considers all conceivable risks and it is strictly regulated by the Dutch central bank. An added benefit of the Dutch system is that any resident of the Netherlands earns 2 percent of his or her public and private pensions each year he or she lives in the country, and this pension capital is treated as individual property regardless of country of residence.

Not surprisingly, it is copied in other countries, for example in the United Kingdom.[36] Its main attract is the collective pension funds that are shown to be less vulnerable to shocks in capital markets. The UK Treasury calculates that retirement incomes can increase as much as 30 percent if the Dutch model were implemented.

5

Opening Up Services and Digital Trade

Services have come to dominate the European economy, as in all developed econo-mies. They account for over 70 percent of economic activity in the European Union, ranging from 87 percent in Luxembourg to 52 percent in Romania, but European trade in services remains very limited. That is a great and costly anomaly.

In 2014, intra-EU trade in services amounted to €835 billion, which is only 28 percent of total intra-EU trade,[1] which corresponds to only 5.8 percent of the European Union's GDP (Figure 5.1). The service sectors that contribute the most towards trade within the European Union are business services (for example, ac-counting and audit)—amounting to 31 percent of total service trade, travel—15 percent, financial services—8 percent, communications—5 percent and construction—3 percent.

The contrast with the single market for goods is great. After the single European market was introduced in 1992, trade between EU countries has grown more than between other high-income countries. Among the twelve original members of the single market, the proportion of GDP accounted for by trade grew by an average of 1.7 percent per year between 1992 and 2014 (from 34 percent to 58 percent of GDP). The Nordic members like Finland and Sweden that joined in 1995 have done even better, averaging 2.1 percent, and Eastern European countries' trade has grown by an average of 3.7 percent per year since 2004, when eight countries joined. In comparison, other OECD countries' trade grew by 0.7 percent a year between 1992 and 2014.[2]

The stark disparity between the success of the single market for goods and the failure of trade in services indicates a potential major source of growth in the European economy. When the European Parliamentary Research Service tried to assess the cost of lacking EU cooperation in 2014-19 it found the two biggest losses in the missing digital single market (€340 billion) and single market for consumers and citizens (mainly for services €330 billion).[3] These are the two biggest costs of partial EU integration. The question is what to do to alleviate these shortcomings.

In this chapter section one presents the 2006 EU Services Directive. Section two shows that Europe's service market remains fragmented. Section three details recent changes to legislation on regulated professions and what more could be done to alleviate trade in services that rely on regulated professions. Section four dis-cusses the possible impact of the Transatlantic Trade and Investment partnership.

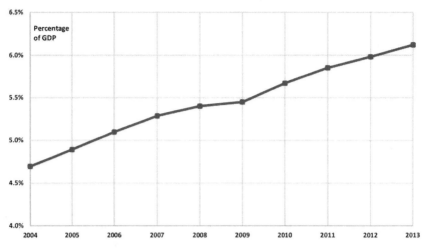

Source: average of import and export reported by Eurostat

Figure 5.1 Intra-EU Trade on Services, 2004-14
Source: Eurostat, average of import and export

Section five moves beyond the services direction, discussing the integration of capital markets, and section six concludes.

THE EU'S 2006 SERVICES DIRECTIVE: AN ATTEMPT TO OPENING SERVICE TRADE

The EU has been tardy in promoting service trade. Its first attempt to reduce barriers to intra-EU service trade was its adoption of the Services Directive in 2006.[4] This directive aims at removing obstacles in service markets in two ways. First, it eases the establishment of service companies in other European Union countries, by preventing host countries from demanding a more onerous registration process or more stringent regulation for foreign companies. Second, it requires all European countries to set up one-stop shops, so that companies entering the market do not have to register with multiple agencies.

The Services Directive covers most services accounting for almost half (47 percent) of Europe's GDP: business-related services, real estate, wholesaling and retailing, construction, tourism and the entertainment industry. The exceptions are quite important, financial, transport and postal services, telecommunications, health care, as well as electricity and water supply. A combination of intentional disregard of some member countries and gaps in the Directive's coverage means that many barriers to service trade remain in place, and European firms have to comply with onerous regulations. The services directive is often likened with a Swiss cheese because of its many loopholes. "The internal market program," warned Wim Kok, former Dutch prime minister, "is felt to be yesterday's business and does not receive the priority it should. This is a fatal policy error."[5]

This flaw in the European single market has attracted increasing attention. Mario Monti has been among the most-active supporters of further opening up of service trade. In 2010, while still president of Bocconi University, he submitted a report to the European Commission president, José Manuel Barroso, identifying a list of restrictions that hampered cross-border trade in services.[6] As a result, in 2011 the European Commission and national regulators conducted an evaluation exercise, through which member-states reviewed each other's implementation of the Services Directive. The Commission published the results, which showed the extent to which member-states had failed to reduce barriers to entry.

The findings suggested that Ireland and the United Kingdom had the most open service sectors in Europe. Some member-states, such as Slovakia and Slovenia, cut the numbers of barriers most aggressively—by more than half. However, France, Germany, Italy and Austria retain highly protected service industries. Across the European Union, the average number of restrictions on establishment or cross-border provision fell by one-third, though the majority of barriers remain, as member-states label them "proportionate." Fears of losing the dominance of national suppliers and having to rely on foreign companies drive much of this reticence.

The benefits from opening up service trade can be large. Implementation of the Services Directive could boost GDP by 0.8 percent a year, with a low of 0.3 percent for Bulgaria and a high of 1.8 percent for Cyprus across the European Union.[7] For Germany an increase of 0.45 percent is forecast, while the figure for the UK is 1 percent. Additional growth of 0.4 percent is possible, if all countries implemented the Services Directive to the same extent as the EU average. If all barriers to service trade were removed, the European Union would benefit from additional growth as much as 1.6 percent a year for five successive years.[8] Another study finds that fully opening up the EU services markets would add to Europe's GDP almost €300 billion a year.[9]

This additional economic growth can be achieved in three ways. A significant productivity boost can be gained by reducing the number of regulated professions. In total, 800 different occupations in the European service sector are subject to state regulation. Of these, 25 percent are regulated in just one country, which suggests that a substantial number of regulations might be unnecessary. Construction is one example where big gains from reducing the burden on regulated professions can be made. The sector constitutes 6 percent of Europe's GDP. There are over 4 million small construction companies confined to national European markets. Productivity growth in construction has been slower than in other services and significantly slower than in the United States.[10]

Apart from the Service Directive, some international agreements also serve to promote intra-EU trade in services to increase productivity and potentially reduce consumer prices. One example is the Open Skies Agreement in air transport between the European Union and the United States, which allows any EU airline and any US airline to fly between any points in these territories. Research indicates that this arrangement resulted in a 15 percent drop in travel costs to passengers on these routes.[11]

But the biggest potential gain from opening up service trade in Europe is in areas not regulated by the Services Directive. In February 2012, UK Prime Minister David Cameron and 11 other EU leaders sent a letter to the European Commission calling for a single energy market by 2014 and a digital single market by 2015.[12] In digital services, the focus is on trade on-line, by simplifying licensing, building an efficient framework for copyright, providing a secure and affordable system for cross-border on-line payments, establishing on-line dispute resolution mechanisms for cross-border on-line transactions and amending the EU framework for digital signatures. Each of these allows European companies to conduct business across borders more efficiently.

EUROPE'S SERVICE MARKET REMAINS FRAGMENTED

The implementation of the Services Directive has been hampered by differing national rules remaining in place that benefit incumbent suppliers. Some EU states still have restrictions based on the nationality or the residence of the service provider, which is prohibited by EU directives.[13]

The statistics on the service sectors show a worrying lack of openness. Between 2006 and 2010 just 3.4 percent of all public-sector contracts in the EU were awarded to foreign bidders.[14] The European Commission estimates that trade integration—measured by the average of imports and exports divided by GDP—in the single market for goods amounts to approximately 22 percent, but only 5 percent for services. While some services are local in nature—for example haircuts or taxi rides—the majority of services could be traded across Europe.

The barriers to service trade in Europe remain many and severe. Often, entry barriers to foreign competition take the form of domestic regulation. In order to establish themselves in another member state many service providers face lengthy authorization procedures even if they have already obtained similar licenses or permits in their home country. For instance, professional qualifications of another country are not recognized or service providers are obliged to have a certain legal form or capital requirements when trading across borders. National rules relating to labor, taxation, health and safety, consumer protection, and company insurance contribute to a fragmentation of the single market.

If a construction firm based in Sweden wants to build in Germany, it must first hire architects from a pre-approved list. Yet the 2005 recognition of professional qualifications directive lists only three architecture schools in Sweden whose qualifications are recognized by all member-states. Architects who received their education at other universities are automatically disqualified. Next, Germany requires proof that foreign architects have good standing with their national regulator, but Sweden does not regulate architects and thus has no national regulator for them. Third, electricians and plumbers must submit a certificate showing they have taken a vocational qualification, whereas Sweden allows electricians and plumbers to train on the job and does not issue such certificates. These German regulations make it difficult for Swedish construction companies to operate in Germany, even though Sweden's quality of house construction is ranked highest in the European Union by the European Construction Association.[15]

The lack of integration in the service sectors is reflected in member states' price levels, which vary much more than those for goods across the euro area. Mobile phone users across the European Union face huge price differences. The monthly subscription fee for local phone calls is three times higher in Finland than in Lithuania (Figure 5.2). The biggest price difference is in domestic mobile calls, which cost 774 percent more in the Netherlands, the most expensive, than in Lithuania, the cheapest country. These price disparities cannot be explained by differences in quality, cost of provision of the service, or by consumer purchasing power.[16]

Europeans use online trade extensively, but cumbersome regulations retard international online trade and the provision on online services. Seventy-five percent of the EU population reports that they used the internet at least weekly in 2014. Close to two-thirds (63 percent) of those shop online (Figure 5.3), and more than half (57 percent) of EU Internet users use online banking. Yet only 15 percent of citizens in 2014 were buying from another EU country, and only 3 percent use banking services from other EU countries.[17]

An additional obstacle to online trade in services is the imposition of roaming charges when calling or using data from another European Union country. Due to pressure from member states, such charges are now regulated at €0.05 per minute over the cost of a local call, €0.02 per text message sent, and €0.05 per MB of data, and will be phased out completely by June 2017.

Also in trade in music entertainment digital barriers across Europe make citizens miss out on goods and services: only 7 percent of small businesses sell cross-border. At present Netflix and Spotify, which operates a subscription streaming service for music, offer different catalogues with different prices for each European country. Licenses are currently carefully segmented for different geographic markets to maximize sales, and it is impossible to buy music and other entertainment online from one European state to another. Harmonizing such services across the EU would require copyright holders to change the way they license their materials. For this reason Jean-Claude Juncker, the president of the European Commission, has made the creation of a single market for digital services one of his top five policy priorities. A fully functional Digital Single Market could contribute €415 billion per year to European economic growth.[18]

The same is true of postal services. According to the European Commission, a standard 2 kg parcel delivery in Austria with the national postal operator costs €4.44, but to send the same parcel to neighboring Italy would cost €14. If the same parcel were sent from Italy to Austria, it would cost €25.[19] Similar examples are found throughout Europe. To send the 2 kg parcel from the Netherlands to Spain would cost €13, but to ship it back from Spain to the Netherlands costs €32.74.[20] The main reason for such disparities is the lack of competition in some markets.

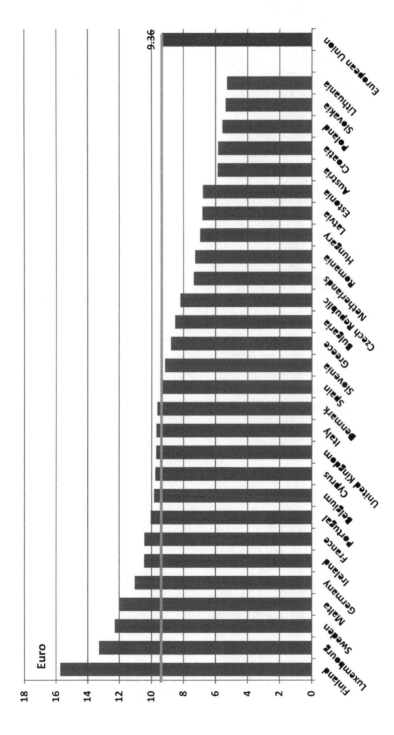

Figure 5.2 Average Cost per Minute in Mobile Communications

Source: Electronic communications market indicators, available at http://digital-agenda-data.eu/datasets/digital_agenda_scoreboard_key_indicators/indicators

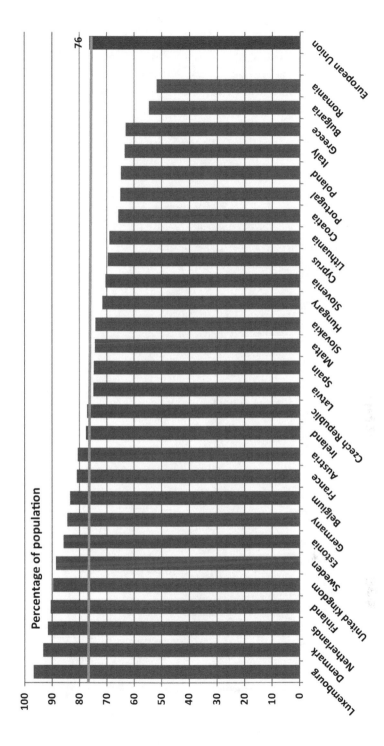

Figure 5.3 Regular Users of the Internet, 2014.

Source: European Commission, Digital Agenda Scoreboard, accessible at http://digital-agenda-data.eu/charts/

Prices diverge 400 percent: with Romania offering the lowest price and Denmark the highest (Figure 5.4).[21]

In December 2015, France's competition authority fined 20 parcel delivery companies €672 million for colluding over transport costs.[22] Executives from courier service companies, including Federal Express, Germany's DHL, U.K.'s Royal Mail and TNT, routinely met on the sidelines of an industry group to agree on annual price increases imposed on French customers between September 2004 and September 2010. The largest courier firm in France, Geodis SA, a unit of French state-owned railway operator SNCF, was penalized with the highest fine of €196 million. Such collusive behavior is facilitated by the acceptance of price discrimination across European markets.

More generally, studies comparing service prices across the European Union, find differences of over 300 percent in housing, local transport, audit and other financial services, controlling for purchasing power parity.[23] These differences mean that markets are still segmented and a further push towards opening is required.

To combat these differences, the Juncker Commission has announced that it will provide annual statistics on developments in the letter and parcel markets in the EU, including on prices. These statistics can be used to benchmark progress towards the full market opening of postal services, whose deadline has already passed in 2012.

The entry of Eastern European countries into the European Union in 2004 demonstrated how closed the service sectors are. The work of Polish plumbers in the France, first coined by the satirical magazine *Charlie Hebdo*, was seen as a symbol of taking away jobs from local workers, while allegedly providing inferior quality. In fact, limited supply, high prices of plumbing services and

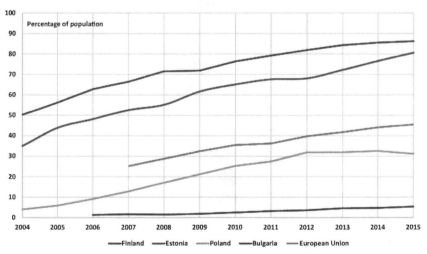

Source: European Commission, Digital Agenda Scoreboard; available at: http://digital-agenda-data.eu/charts/

Figure 5.4 Online Banking Usage, 2004-14
Source: European Commission, Digital Agenda Scoreboard; available at: http://digital-agenda-data.eu/charts/

unsatisfactory workmanship in France were the reason that many families did not use such services even when required. The entry of new firms offering such services dramatically reduced prices—by over 40 percent—while increasing quality as well.[24]

WHY REGULATE PROFESSIONS?

Some professions have their diplomas recognized immediately in other European countries—architects, doctors, nurses, midwives, pharmacists, veterinaries and lawyers, but others face administrative difficulties when applying for a job in another member state as they have to obtain recognition from the host country. Further, they can be asked to exercise their profession under the supervision of a locally qualified professional for a period of up to three years in order to be certified.

Regulating professions amounts to keeping local monopolies, preventing new entry and boosting costs for consumers. Some professions are so well-organized nationally and so apt at maintaining their sinecure that various EU initiatives have so far failed to reduce substantially the number of regulated professions. One example of such a profession is notaries. They form a special class of lawyers, who oversee most commercial transactions and maintain official registers of property. They object to reducing regulation, which would diminish their work load. In Italy, the government provoked strikes in 2006, 2012, and again in 2015 by attempting to trim the rules of that profession. The number of notaries is restricted, as is the region in which they can work; their fees are fixed, too. The average self-employed French notary earned very well at €190,812. In Italy, in 2013, the figure was €210,400.[25] These costs are borne by those buying and selling assets, particularly housing. Legal fees add 1 percent to the bill for buying a home in France and 2 percent in Italy.

The Italian government of Matteo Renzi wants to open up the profession, by allowing notaries to practice anywhere in Italy rather than in a designated region. It also aims to abolish the arrangement whereby notaries pool their income to ensure a minimum for everyone—a system that dampens the incentive to compete. More dramatically, it would permit all lawyers to sign off on certain transactions that are currently the exclusive preserve of notaries, such as the sale of non-residential properties worth less than €100,000 and the registration of particular types of companies. This will pave the way for lawyers from other EU countries to perform such transactions too. It would be even better to abolish the need for notarization as has been done long ago in Scandinavia.

Real estate professions offer another example of harmful regulation hindering Europe to achieve its economic potential. These professions are regulated in a number of European countries. These include Belgium, where a federal agency is charged with the regulation of real estate professionals and France, which has a national supervisory structure for the real estate sector. In some countries new regulations are being introduced, as was done in Ireland in 2012 with the establishment of its Property Services Regulatory Authority. In 2015 a new regulation of real estate professionals was introduced in the Czech Republic.

The stated rationale for regulating real-estate agents as a profession differs across countries: from national requirements with which real estate professionals must be familiar such as energy performance certificates; to mandatory training on mortgage credit rules; to being skilled in precautionary procedures about anti-money laundering during the purchase of real estate. All these concerns can easily be dealt with if aspiring real estate agents from other European members pass aptitude tests—which can be made available online and taken from their home country. The fact that professional regulation in real estate remains in place in a half-dozen European countries suggests that it is not safety that drives the regulator, but rather an aspiration to keep competition at bay. The regulation of professions should be minimized, preferably through an EU directive.

THE TRANSATLANTIC TRADE AND INVESTMENT PARTNERSHIP: A MEANS TO LIBERATE SERVICE TRADE AND E-COMMERCE

The problems both to formulate a relevant EU Services Directive and even more to implement it can arouse despair. A major source of hope for deregulation of the service trade is the Transatlantic Trade and Investment Partnership (TTIP), currently being negotiated between the European Union and the United States. It aims at creating the world's biggest free trade area. It is a work-in-progress.

TTIP's scope is still expanding, for example adding a chapter on services and public procurement markets, and perhaps on financial services' regulation. A comprehensive TTIP deal has been assessed to increase the size of the EU economy around €120 billion (or 0.5 percent of GDP) and the US by €95 billion (or 0.4 percent of GDP).[26] However, this could be much more if TTIP would be seen as the tipping point for the EU carrying out major reforms that it has aspired to but so far failed to carry out.

While negotiations on the goods trade have been progressing since 2013, texts on the service sectors have been a recent welcome addition. A study on international service trade showed that firms typically associated with the production of goods are also the largest importers and exporters of services. Manufacturing firms might export intellectual property that they hold in exchange for royalties and licensing fees and import or export design support, research and development, or product testing.[27] It will be much easier for such companies if service markets are open too.

Government procurement could benefit greatly from inclusion into TTIP. Procurement activities include buying software, healthcare insurance and transport services for government employees; providing water treatment services; and building roads or buildings for the public. The current proposal agreement is to open up public procurement, so that European and American companies have equal access to each other's market. In doing so, TTIP will also force a harmonization of procurement rules across the 28 member states. These are currently disparate and create opportunities for both inefficiency and corruption. In the process of negotiating opening up government procurement across the Atlantic, European member states are likely to uncover ways to integrate their own public procurement into a single European system.

The economic significance of public procurement in Europe is considerable: in 2010 a total of €2,406 billion—or around 20 percent of EU GDP—was spent by governments, the public sector and utility service providers on public works, goods and services. Not all areas of public expenditure are covered by public procurement rules, however. Only public procurement worth €447 billion (19 percent of this total expenditure) was published in the Official Journal and the European Commission's TED-database in 2010.

The lack of transparency facilitates corruption. Corruption in European public procurement is estimated at €1.4 to €2.2 billion annually (Table 5.1). Four main types of corrupt practices are frequently encountered. First, bid rigging: the contract is "promised" to one contractor, with or without the consent of the public official issuing the tender. Bid rigging takes the form of bid suppression, complementary offers, bid rotation and subcontracting. Second, the public official demands, or is open to, a bribe, which will be accounted for in the tendering process. Third, the public official has personal interests in the winning company. Finally, the public official has not properly carried out checks or followed procedures where this is required and ignores overt deliberate mismanagement by a contractor.

Table 5.1: Direct costs of corruption in public procurement

Another proposal in TTIP is to remove burdensome regulation in telecommunications and water transport, including in the ownership and management of port infrastructure. This step will allow more efficient investment and over time reduce the fragmentation in these service markets. TTIP also stipulates common licensing rules for individuals and firms in business services: audit, management consultancy and legal advice. Finally, the agreement seeks to open up trade in financial services and e-commerce.[28]

TTIP can greatly increase productivity is in the telecommunications sector. Currently, over 650 telecommunication providers offer mobile services, entertainment and high-speed data in the European Union.[29] This fragmentation increases costs and is a barrier to the sector becoming a basis for the advance of informational technologies. In contrast, four companies—ATT, Verizon, Comcast and Time Warner Cable—provide the bulk of telecommunications services in the United States. As a result, Deutsche Telekom is the only European company in the top-5 telecommunication providers globally. Telefonica (Spain) and Vodafone (UK) join it among the top-10. The opening up of the European telecommunication sector would increase investment by 30 percent and create a wave of mergers and acquisitions to reduce providers in half.[30] This, in turn, may increase the adoption of new technologies, boosting productivity.

A major point of contention in TTIP is whether to include financial services and their regulation. So far the United States demurs. Some American politicians want to address regulatory discrepancies between the U.S. and EU financial systems, stating "confusion caused by inconsistent and conflicting regulations have already spilled over into the broader economy, reducing investment, creating higher compliance costs, lowering employment, and hindering economic growth."[31] Others worry about lowering financial regulatory standards, such as reducing consumer protections. The same arguments have been used in previous attempts to open up the financial markets in Europe.

Another contentious issue is the inclusion of audiovisual services. Many European countries provide budget support to domestic industries they consider culturally sensitive through broadcasting quotas, subsidies, and local content requirements. In particular, France maintains cultural exceptions for its film and television industries. These measures limit market access to such industries for both other European and US companies.

The final area for service trade considered in TTIP is e-commerce. EU negotiators have expressed concerns that any potential measures as part of the agreement must not undermine EU privacy standards. Trade negotiators are facing strong push from companies like Google, Facebook, IBM and Hewlett-Packard to include the free streaming of data in the agreement. But the US does not have as far-reaching privacy legislation as does Europe, which makes this area of negotiations an easy target for opponents.

While some of the current areas of TTIP negotiation may in the end fall out of the potential agreement, the main benefit of these negotiations for the opening of the European service markets is that in the negotiation process many national peculiarities and inefficiencies in regulations are documented and analyzed. This procedure will undoubtedly help when Europe's own initiatives on a single digital market, a single capital market and a unified public procurement come to fruition.

INTEGRATING CAPITAL MARKETS

The Eurozone crisis has taken a heavy toll on the European financial sector. The public costs of bailout programs for banks surpassed 5 percent of GDP or more in Belgium, Greece, Ireland, Luxembourg, the Netherlands, Austria and the United Kingdom. As a result of deleveraging, between 2009 and 2015 the level of investment (even when taking into account public investment) in the EU dropped by about 12 percent. During the Eurozone crisis, cross-border lending in Europe declined by about 18 percent. At the same time, banking activities concentrated on home markets.[32] The capital markets that could have alleviated this effect were not present, due to the limited size of capital markets in the EU.

It is very difficult to enter banking in another country because European countries have widely differing regulations. They may be harmonized within the Eurozone group of 19 countries with the advent of the single banking supervisor. Currently all European countries have the same deposit insurance threshold—of 100,000 euro—but regulations differ for how this insurance is paid out. Regulations on access to online banking also diverge, resulting in great variations in online usage, being nearly 90 percent in Finland, but less than 5 percent in Bulgaria (Figure 5.5).

Integrated capital markets have three main benefits for European companies seeking finance: they improve access to funds; reduce capital costs by creating

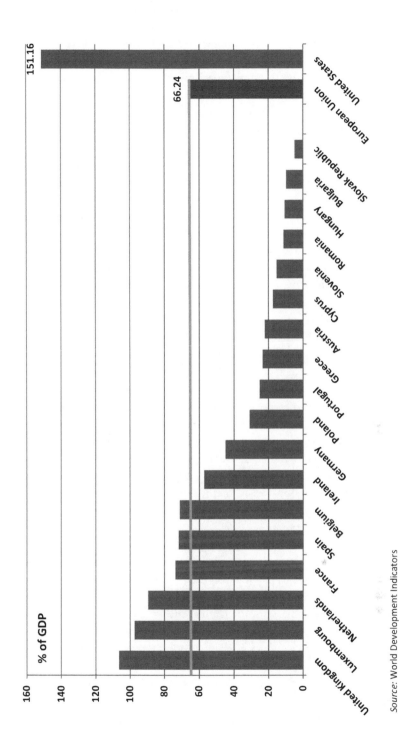

Source: World Development Indicators

Figure 5.5 Size of Capital Markets, Excluding Banking

Source: World Development Indicators

competition among investors; and decrease the risk of disruption in financing through diversification of sources of funding. European Commission President Juncker commented in July 2014 that "[t]o improve the financing of our economy, we should further develop and integrate capital markets. This would cut the cost of raising capital, notably for [small and medium-sized enterprises], and help reduce our very high dependence on bank funding."[33] Juncker's belief in the benefits from consolidating capital markets comes from the understanding that EU capital markets are underdeveloped, and that less dominance of banks in the system would improve economic growth.[34]

Several EU states—Luxembourg, Ireland, Denmark and the Netherlands—have larger capital markets than the USA in relation to their GDP, suggesting that conditions in the EU can be supportive to the development of large capital markets if the European Union adopts legislation and institutions already present in some of its members (Figure 5.6). These are particularly useful for the growth of companies which are young and small and cannot provide collateral, when their investments are particularly risky or large compared to firm size, or when their corporate or financing structure needs to be restructured. In such situations, European companies may use corporate bonds, leveraged loans, securitization, or private equity markets, which are now underdeveloped in many EU countries.

The most significant EU initiative in response to Juncker's call for creating a single capital market has been the preparation of new legislation to harmonize insolvency law. The outcome of insolvency varies greatly across Europe, returning 90 percent of creditors' money in Belgium and Finland, but only 30 percent in Croatia and Romania and 34 percent in Greece. The time it takes to resolve bankruptcy differs as well, from half a year on average in Ireland to 4 years in Slovakia. The legal and administrative costs of insolvency are lowest in Finland, at 3.5 percent of the value of the estate, and highest, at 22 percent, in Italy.[35]

Research on the efficiency of insolvency regimes finds that foreclosure procedures—the prevalent insolvency method in common-law countries like Ireland and the United Kingdom—work well when the whole business is pledged as collateral, but poorly when only specific assets have been pledged. This result is consistent with the observation that the senior creditor has the socially optimal incentives to dispose of the business as long as he can gain control of it in default. The efficiency of foreclosure rises when the senior creditor is allowed to take collateral in an out-of-court procedure.[36]

Turning to bankruptcy proceedings, legal rules that require the company to suspend operations, or that allow suppliers and customers to rescind contracts while the company is in bankruptcy, reduce efficiency. Moreover, extensive appeal of judicial decisions during insolvency proceedings and the failure to continue the proceedings during appeal are both detrimental to efficiency. The most likely result of such efficiency is that the business continues operation as a whole, as in Sweden, and does not get sold piecemeal, as in Greece or Hungary.

Even if the harmonizing of insolvency laws across Europe proves to be successful, other obstacles to capital market integration remain untouched, including divergent accounting enforcement regimes, fragmented market infrastructure, and varying taxation of financial investments.[37]

A more thorough reform would require new institutions. Some of these institutions are already in place because of the establishment of a Europe-wide banking union. The Five Presidents' Report, which outlines the most-needed reforms of European institutions, argues that the capital markets union should lead ultimately to a single European capital markets supervisor.[38] In 2014, the Banking Union's supervisory two arms were set up under the auspices of the European Central Bank. One is the Single Supervisory Mechanism and the other is the Single Resolution Board, which establishes a recovery regime for banks in the Eurozone.[39]

The application of uniform standards by a single European banking supervisor enhances integration of banking services across Europe, and is a step towards capital markets integration. To complete the institutional set-up for a banking union, Europe needs is a common scheme to protect savers. The creation of such a scheme was first approved in December 2012, but progress towards its completion has been uneven because of objections from Germany and Finland.

A fiscal union could also be a building block towards the creation of a capital markets union, but here progress has stalled altogether. A fiscal union can open opportunities for new financial instruments to be used in Europe, thus enhancing the value of a single capital market. Currently, negotiations among European governments center on two projects. The first aims at mutualizing part of the sovereign debt of Eurozone countries. In the eyes of its supporters, issuing common sovereign debt would create an effective, common risk-free yield curve that is the necessary precondition for a single capital market. Opponents, including these authors, argue that such issuance will create opportunities and incentives for laxer fiscal policy.

The second project is to create a centralized fiscal buffer for the euro area, funded proportionately by member-states. Its anticyclical nature can serve as a cushion to alleviate banks' losses, and support countries through their fiscal adjustment. In 2011, at the height of the Eurozone crisis, ECB President Jean-Claude Trichet and several other senior European officials proposed the establishment of an EU-wide ministry of finance, to rule on major fiscal spending items and to veto budgets in states in breach of the Eurozone deficit criteria.[40] However, this idea was quickly scrapped because of objections by European politicians defending their countries' sovereignty.

Since the Eurozone crisis has abated, progress towards opening and consolidating the capital markets across Europe has proceeded in small steps. A recent initiative involves changes to the Prospectus Directive, with a view to making it easier and less expensive for small and medium-sized companies to raise capital.[41] This proposal focuses on four groups of issuers: issuers already listed on a regulated market, which want to raise additional capital by means of a secondary issuance, small companies, frequent issuers of securities and issuers of non-equity securities. It encourages the use of the cross-border "passport" for approved prospectuses, to reduce legal and administrative costs.[42] The new disclosure regimes for secondary issuances and small companies would result in lower compliance costs for issuers and also reduce the work load of competent authorities as less information is disclosed and examined. Transforming the prospectus summary in a document similar to the key investor information document would also mean a considerable reduction in compliance costs as the summary would be shorter.

The Prospectus Directive proposes a high threshold to determine when European companies must issue a prospectus. No prospectus will be required for capital raisings below €500,000. Member States will also be able to set higher thresholds for their domestic markets, up to €10m. Companies that frequently tap into capital markets will also be able to use an annual "Universal Registration Document", a registration containing all the necessary information on the company that wants to list shares. Issuers who regularly maintain this registration with their supervisors benefit from a 5 day fast-track approval when they are ready to tap into capital markets by issuing shares, bonds or derivatives.

It helps that a number of commissioners in the current European Commission, including President Juncker, have previously been finance ministers during the Eurozone crisis and understand the value of integrated capital markets. This gives life to the initiative and in doing so extends the reach of opening up the financial sector across Europe.

CONCLUSIONS: SERVICE TRADE NEEDS TO BE DEREGULATED

Service trade across Europe has been surprisingly neglected, which has led to very limited intra-European trade in services in stark contrast with the successful liberalization of the single market for goods. Only in 2006, the EU adopted its Services Directives, and it contained too many loopholes to be effective. In addition, it encountered great resistance from vested interests, such as regulated professions. The variety of cultures and customs in European countries has ensured that services have been treated as local in nature.

This situation needs change. New technologies and business practices, notably in digital trade, render the old protectionism untenable, and the evidence mounts that opening up the service sectors in Europe can bring about significant economic growth. The larger migration flows within Europe also assists this opening: as people move from one country to another, they bring with them knowledge of using services at home. It is common for such migrants to continue to use services at home, from online banking, to postal services, to transport.

The question is how to accomplish this. We would suggest three parallel paths. To being with, the EU as such should reinforce its Services Directive so that it becomes an effective support for the evolution of intra-European service markets. Its coverage should be expanded to most if not all services, and it should set much firmer rule for opening of EU service markets. The European Commission should also pursue its implementation more forcefully. The establishment of service companies in other EU countries should be facilitated and one-stop shops for registration should

Table 5.1: Direct costs of corruption in public procurement

Sector	Sector Direct costs of corruption (in million €)	% of the overall procurement value in the sector in the 8 Member States
Road & rail	488 - 755	1.9% to 2.9%
Water & waste	27 - 38	1.8% to 2.5%
Urban/utility construction	830 - 1 141	4.8% to 6.6%
Training	26 - 86	4.7% to 15.9%
Research& Development	99 - 228	1.7% to 3.9%

Source: PWC (2010)

be instituted throughout Europe. Unnecessary regulation of professions should be reined in through an improved Services Directive.

Much can be enforced through integrated public procurement: once Europe starts using a single procurement system for municipal, national and cross-national projects, the many services involved in making this procurement successful will also be integrated.

A second line of action would be national policymaking. For example, each country has an interest in reducing its list of regulated profession at the national level and to improve the efficiency of communications services. This is simply a rational national competition policy.

A third line of action lies in the current negotiations with the US about a new TTIP agreement. It would naturally incorporate most of the issues of liberalization of service trade and digital trade. It should lead to increased competition on the telecommunications market and presumably to its consolidation. It should certainly lead to an integration of the now completely fragmented digital market. Hopefully, it would also open up most of public procurement for competition. An added advantage is that TTIP would presumably also be accompanied with a stricter legal enforcement than the current Services Directive. Thus, TTIP can be a means for the European Commission to implement what it wanted to accomplish in any case in the service market.

6

Creating Jobs

The decline in Europe's economic growth and productivity has been accompanied by the stagnation of Europe's labor force. It remained constant in the period 1990-2014, with the prospect of a rapid decline in the next 25 years. In 2014, Europe's labor force comprised 243 million people, an increase of 0.8 million on 2013.[1] This increase was fully due to immigration into the European Union. The fundamental insight is that the size of Europe's labor force depends on migration, which can go into or out of the continent.

Therefore Europe's demographic trends are not given but can change quickly should the immigrants' waves that currently flood Europe continue. In 2015 alone, Europe received about 1.5 million refugees from Syria, Iraq and other countries in the Middle East. This may alter the labor force significantly, either by further exacerbating the already high youth unemployment or contributing to more productivity thanks to vocational training and reduced tax wedges on labor. Both the size and impact of immigration depend on policies chosen.

The easiest way to create new jobs is to increase the overall number of employed workers among those in working age. In 2015, the employment rate of the population of the age 15-64 was only 64.3 percent in the European Union. The discrepancies within Europe are great. In general, northern countries have high employment rates, while they are very low in Greece, Croatia, Italy and Spain. The employment rate for the population aged 15-64 exceeds 70 percent in only six European countries (Figure 6.1). The highest rates are recorded by Sweden (74.9 percent), the Netherlands (73.9 percent) and Germany (73.8 percent). Would every European country exceed 70 percent in terms of working-age employment, the gain would be about 20 million workers.

Not only do few Europeans work, those who do work too little. The average hours worked during 2014 averaged 4.9 percent more than in the US than in Europe. Yet in eight EU countries the average employee worked longer hours than in the US, but none of these countries had a high employment rate. The leader is Greece, followed by Latvia and Poland. Germany has the shortest working hours, followed by the Netherlands and Denmark (figure 6.2).

To make sense of these statistics, we examine how average working hours have changed over time. Figure 6.3 contrasts the development in France and the US from 1960-2014, because they provide the most dramatic contrast. In 1960, French

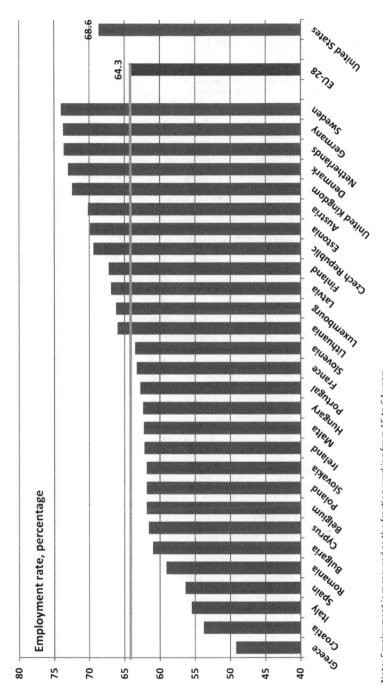

Figure 6.1 Employment rate, 2015

Note: Employment is measured as the fraction working from 15 to 64 years.

Source: For EU-28: http://appsso.eurostat.ec.europa.eu/nui/show.do?dataset=lfsq_ ergan&lang=en; For USA: http://stats.oecd.org/

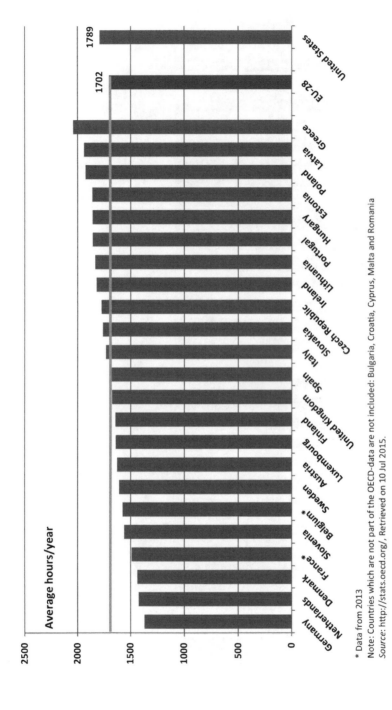

Figure 6.2 Average Working Hours, 2014

* Data from 2013

Note: Countries which are not part of the OECD-data are not included: Bulgaria, Croatia, Cyprus, Malta and Romania

Source: http://stats.oecd.org/, Retrieved on 10 Jul 2015.

employees worked 12 percent longer hours than Americans, but 17 percent less than Americans in 2014. "In the early 1970s, Europeans and Americans worked about the same number of hours; today Europeans work much less."[2] Americans have reduced their working hours but only by 8.2 percent, whereas the French have cut their official working hours by 32 percent in this period. Thus, the short working hours are no old European tradition but a relatively recent development conditioned on labor market regulations, taxation and welfare.

The negative demographic trend affecting Europe's labor force can be reversed through five sets of policies. One opportunity is to increase labor participation among the youth. In 2014, the youth unemployment rate in the European Union was on average 22 percent, but it varied greatly. It was above 50 percent in Spain (53 percent) and Greece (52 percent), and around 10 percent in Germany (7.7 percent), Austria (10 percent), and the Netherlands (10.5 percent). These great differences largely depend on how youth are being prepared for the labor market and labor market regulation.

A second direction is to increase labor participation by European women. In 2014, almost half or 48 percent of all employees were women. To increase this share, policy makers can invest in child care, legislate flexible work hours, and create incentives for returning to the labor force after children have left home. One promising venue is to allow more flexible hours, for example through part-time employment. The share of employees working part-time is highest in the Netherlands (52 percent of employees), followed by Germany and Austria (28 percent), Denmark, the United Kingdom and Sweden (26 percent). Yet this practice is virtually unused in Eastern Europe: the lowest shares in the European Union are recorded in Romania (0.7 percent), Bulgaria (2 percent), Croatia (3 percent), Slovakia and Latvia (6 percent).

The third direction is to increase labor mobility, including from outside the European Union. In 2013 and 2014 each, more than one million persons took up

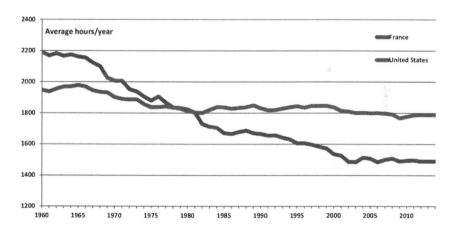

Figure 6.3 Working Hours in France and the US, 1960-2014.
Source: http://stats.oecd.org/, Retrieved on 10 Jul 2015.

residence and worked in a European state other than their country of citizenship. Of these, 41 percent took up residence and worked in the United Kingdom, 22 percent in Germany, 8 percent in Belgium and 4.5 percent in Austria. Other European countries are less inviting or attractive to job seekers. But to compensate for demographic decline, European countries have to consider ways to absorb immigrants.

A fourth direction is increasing the productivity of incoming workers through better education. An example in this regard is the vocational training system, which nearly 60 percent of German youth go through. Even for Germany, higher capital intensity is unable to compensate the expected productivity decline due to the decline in the labor force.[3] On average, European productivity growth was half of that in the United States in the past decade.[4] This difference is mostly driven by certain sectors like IT, education and energy, where US workers are over twice as efficient as their European peers.[5] Improving higher education is discussed in Chapter 9.

Beyond these employment-augmenting measures, governments can limit the adverse demographic trends by reducing the labor tax wedge and by giving tax incentives for people to work longer. Recent studies identify tax incentives among the reasons that American workers stay longer in the labor force relative to their European peers.[6] Both reforms have shown results in some European countries and are discussed in Chapter 3.

The chapter is organized in seven sections. The first section discusses ways to reduce youth unemployment through vocational training. The second section suggests ideas of increasing labor participation of women. The third section discusses policies to absorb immigrant workers. Section 4 reviews Germany's experience with attracting and training immigrants. Section 5 focuses on reducing the labor tax wedge as a way of increasing employment. Section 6 documents recent reforms of labor regulation aimed at increasing jobs in Southern Europe. The final section summarizes the main policy recommendations.

EXPANDING EDUCATION AND VOCATIONAL TRAINING

Comprehensive public education has also been a great pride of Europe. In general, Europe has good education, though as the level of education rises the worse Europe manages in relation to the US. The US used to be the outstanding global leader in the share of the population that has graduated from high school, but that is no longer true. Eighty-eight percent of the US adult population has completed high school, but six East European countries supersede that level. Yet, the South Europeans are lagging seriously behind. Only 42 percent of the Portuguese have completed high school, and Spain, Italy and Greece are also suffering from limited secondary education (figure 6.4). For these four countries, expansion of high school education appears a major cure of poor employment rates and growth.

After World War II, the US stood tall as the undisputed leader in higher education, but it has leveled off. The picture varies greatly with choice of measurement, but the completion of higher education for the age cohort of 25-34 appears most

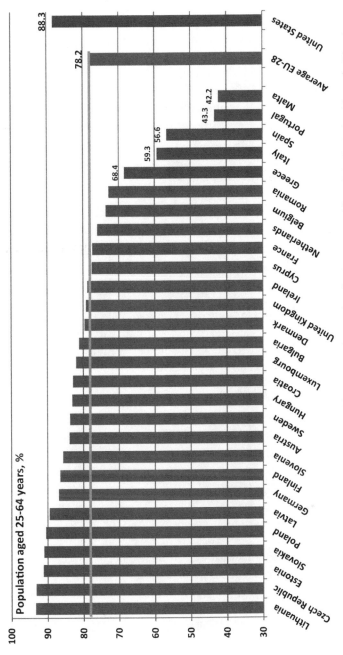

Figure 6.4 High-School Completion Rate, 2014

Source: EU: Eurostat Statistical Database, available at http://ec.europa.eu/eurostat/web/products-datasets/-/tps00065; USA: National Center for Education Statistics, available at http://nces.ed.gov/programs/digest/d14/tables/dt14_104.10.asp, both accessed July 30, 2015.

relevant. In 2011, Europe fell into two large categories divided between north and south with Ireland leading the successful north, and the south headed by Italy. In 16 EU countries 35-50 percent of the young have completed higher education, and nine surpass the US. In the remaining 12 only 20-30 percent of the youth had completed higher education (figure 6.5).

Germany and Austria have low rates of high-school completion, but these two countries have extensive apprenticeships delivering vocational achievement, which are not considered higher education. In their apprenticeship systems, students do several years of training for a specific occupation, gaining practical experience in a company, while also attending theoretical classes at a training center. Such systems that combine education at school and on-the-job training provide an easier transition into the labor market and therefore also generally lead to lower youth unemployment rates.

Spain, Portugal and Greece, by contrast, have few people with vocational training. These Southern European countries have focused in the past on subsidizing companies to temporarily hire and train young people to reduce youth unemployment. The Eurozone crisis has contributed to shift the emphasis towards strengthening vocational training. For example, in 2011 the Spanish government facilitated for companies to integrate apprentices into their business, and the Spanish car company SEAT announced the introduction of the dual vocational training in its factories.[7]

In December 2012, the European Commission announced that Germany would assist six other EU countries—Spain, Greece, Portugal, Italy, Latvia and Slovakia—in strengthening their vocational training systems. The German apprenticeship program, which dates back to the medieval guild system in Northern Europe, went through an overhaul in 1969. It is widely considered to explain Germany's high youth employment. Vocational training, similar to that in Germany, is also present in Austria and the Netherlands, and is resurrected after several decades of communism in the Baltic countries.

In German vocational training students apply directly to employers for apprenticeships. High-school students spend a few days of the week at work, earning a small stipend, and a few days at school, learning the theoretical side of their prospective jobs. The process usually lasts three years and ends with a certification exam. About 360 professions are recognized as training occupations in Germany, and more than 60 percent of high school graduates participate in vocational training. In recent years this percentage has fallen somewhat—to 56 percent in 2015—due to the increase in popularity of bachelors programs. The high quality of Germany's vocational training secures jobs for a large proportion of the country's school graduates. Vocational training is also responsible for the high-growth of German industry, as companies train their future workers at small cost and an early age. Turnover tends to be small once the apprentices have joined their employers after graduating.[8]

The choice of vocational over academic education is encouraged by some incentives. First, throughout their training, companies in Germany pay the equivalent of $1,200 a month, about one-third of the starting wage a qualified employee, which

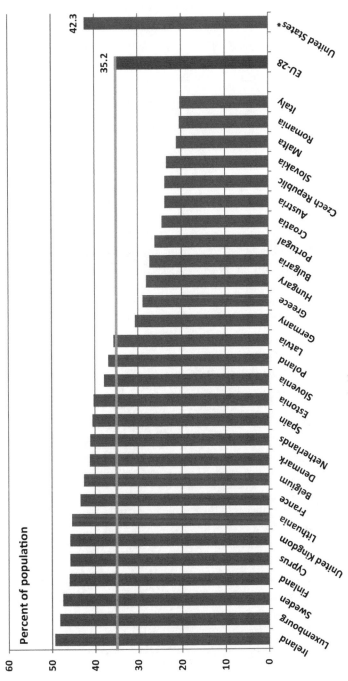

Figure 6.5 Completion of Higher Education, 2014

Note: completion of higher education or higher (bachelor equivalent, ISCED 5-6), 30-34 years of age

Source: EU-28: http://ec.europa.eu/eurostat/statistics-explained/index.php/Educational_attainment_statistics, USA: http://stats.oecd.org/

means that the apprentices can support themselves rather than paying tuition fees while taking lines. Second, mid-way through the training apprentices can sign contracts to work with the company. Third, apprentices who show interest in further education may complete bachelors and masters programs at the employer's expense. All these features comply with a long-term working relationship that is unusual for emerging economies—in Eastern Europe but also increasingly in Southern Europe.

Such vocational training is remarkably robust. From bakers and car mechanics to carpenters and violin-makers, about 90 percent of German apprentices successfully complete their training. British Prime Minister David Cameron has called for his country to emulate parts of the German system. "I think what we are going to see with the expansion of the higher level apprenticeships is many people going into them as they leave school, spending time doing that and then going on and doing a university degree linked to their apprenticeship skill," Cameron said. "That is what has happened for years in Germany and it is going to be happening much more in Britain."[9] German companies are successful proliferating their apprenticeship system in the US.

European vocational training adjusts quickly to shifting needs. "Because it is so decentralized, vocational training has proved very flexible, allowing it to meet the demand of industry very quickly," says Ekkehard Ernst, director at the International Labor Organization.[10] Such flexibility implies that if a new factory opens doors in a community, vocational training with the local schools can be swiftly re-designed to fit the needs of the new employer.

Vocational training is well suited to also address the adoption of work skills by recent immigrants, who may need to receive new qualifications. With the upsurge of asylum seekers across Europe, traditional education would be hard-pressed to create the necessary skills in time for immigrants to join the work force without substantial spouts of unemployment. In contrast, the vocational training system can be tailored to fill such gaps.

INCREASING PARTICIPATION BY WOMEN

Much of the expansion of the labor force in Europe in the last few decades can be explained by rising female labor force participation: among prime-age women (aged 25-54), participation rates climbed steadily from an average of 54 percent in 1980 to 71 percent in 2010. Cross-national differences are wide, however, with female employment rates being persistently high in Denmark around 80 percent and persistently low in Greece at around 30 percent, showing the impact of differences in culture and policy (figure 6.6).

The increase of employment in the service sector has considerably increased women's job opportunities. In 2008, an OECD average of one-third of the female working population was employed in the service sector. In addition, the expansion of service activities (health and education, sales, hotels and catering, and domestic workers) has relied particularly on part-time workers, which has contributed to women increasing their labor force participation.

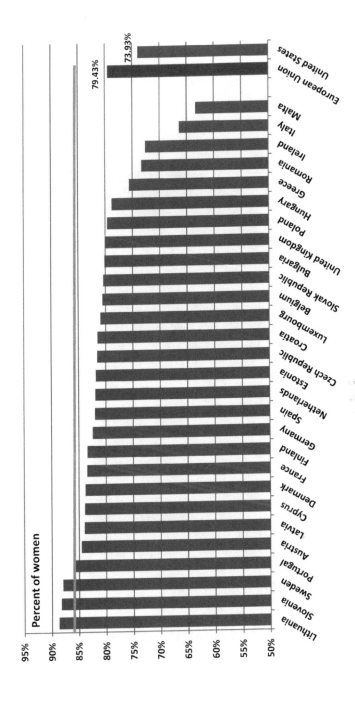

Figure 6.6 Labor Participation by Women
Source: OECD, Labor Force Statistics

In the 1970s, Nordic countries faced a demographic challenge of a shrinking population and low female labor participation. They responded by implementing policies boosting female labor participation, ranging from comprehensive parental provision and public childcare facilities, to statutory right to paternal paid leave. As a result, the gender gaps in both wage and labor force participation in those countries are among the smallest today of any developed country.

Paternal involvement in childrearing and flexible work arrangements are also notable features of Nordic countries. This helps women to continue their careers after childbirth and indirectly promotes higher fertility rates. Finland was the first Nordic country to introduce child home care allowance in the mid-1980s. The allowance is paid if the child is sick and not in public childcare. The amount of the fixed allowance varied with a means-tested supplement and a possible municipality supplement.[11] Finland also stands out in the concentration of female labor in the public sector: women make up for 70 percent of public-sector employment.

Women's employment rates react to changes in tax rates and leave policies, but the rising provision of childcare to working parents with children under three is the main driver of increased female labor force participation. Its absence in southern European countries explains why so few women—less than a third—stay consistently in the work force there.[12]

Women may face less discrimination in the public than in the private sector and, in some countries, may earn higher wages if they belong to certain categories of employees. They may also prefer the greater employment protection and/or opportunities to combine work and family formation.[13]

ABSORBING IMMIGRANTS

Europe has had and will have substantial migration. The question is not whether migration will take place, but how it will be managed, how much it will cost society, and how great benefits it will generate.

In 2014, 15.2 million people were living and working in a European state of which they were not citizens, accounting for 7.0 percent of total EU employment. Of those 7.3 million were citizens of another EU country and 7.9 million were non-European citizens. The highest proportions of foreign workers among all employed persons are seen in Luxembourg (45.9 percent) and Cyprus (11.9 percent). The share of foreign-born residents is about twice as high, since many countries offer citizenship after five years or so (table 6.1 and table 6.2).

Compared to the United States, intra-EU labor mobility is tiny. In the United States, mobility across states, measured as the share of persons who lived a year ago in a different state, accounted for 2.7 percent of the population in 2011-12, while mobility within the European Union relative to the population was 0.2 percent in the same span, or fourteen times less than in the United States.

Labor mobility is beneficial for the European Union in several ways. In the host country, incoming workers benefit the destination economy—for example, Germany or Spain, by reducing skills shortages. They help widen the range of

Table 6.1: Foreign Workers in the Labor Force, 2013

Member State of residence	Number of EU workers in thousands	In % of total employment in the residence country
Austria	283	7
Belgium	316	7
Cyprus	45	12
Czech	43	1
Germany	1883	5
Denmark	87	3
Estonia	2	0
Greece	54	2
Spain	765	5
Finland	33	1
France	598	2
Hungary	19	1
Ireland	204	11
Italy	793	4
Luxembourg	110	46
Latvia	2	0
Malta	2	1
Netherlands	173	2
Poland	10	0
Portugal	26	1
Sweden	132	3
Slovenia	4	0
Slovakia	4	0
United Kingdom	1482	5
EU-28	**7072**	**3**

Note: No data available for Belgium, Croatia, Lithuania and Romania and the values for Estonia, Latvia, Malta, Poland and Slovenia are of limited reliability due to small sample size.

Source: Eurostat, EU-LFS

Table 6.2: Share of Workers with Jobs in Other European Countries, 2013

Member State of residence	Number of EU workers in thousands	In % of total employment in the residence country
Austria	140	3.4
Belgium	110.7	2.4
Bulgaria	232.4	7.9
Cyprus	21.4	5.7
Czech	68	1.4
Germany	388.3	1
Denmark	60.5	2.3
Estonia	27.3	4.4
Greece	236	6.5
Spain	232.4	1.4
Finland	45	1.8
France	334.7	1.3
Croatia	214.9	15.5
Hungary	154.3	0.9
Ireland	188	10
Italy	677.3	3
Lithuania	158.1	12.2
Luxembourg	15.7	6.6
Latvia	78	8.7
Netherlands	240.3	2.9
Poland	1059.2	6.8
Portugal	571.1	12.7
Romania	1290.7	14
Sweden	60.9	1.3
Slovenia	18.6	2
Slovakia	121.1	5.2
United Kingdom	318.6	1.1
EU-28	**7071**	**3.3**

Note: No data available for Malta

Source: Eurostat, EU-LFS

services available and boost competitiveness. In the countries of origin, mobile workers alleviate the burden on public finances, if previously unemployed, and increase the standard of living of their families by sending remittances. In the longer-run, workers who have gained experience and contacts abroad can bring useful know-how and capital in developing new businesses and sectors in their home country.

Labor mobility also absorbs temporary economic shocks: a rise in unemployment in one country during an economic downturn can be contained if workers look for jobs abroad. This helps to improve employment prospects for those not moving, as the labor market in their country experiences reduced labor supply.[14] During the financial crisis of 2009, large numbers of Latvian and Lithuanians emigrated and thus escaped unemployment.

Numerous studies have gauged the importance of labor mobility for increasing productivity of the American economy.[15] Recent studies have shown this effect in Europe. Researchers estimate that post-enlargement mobility flows over the period 2004 to 2009 have increased the GDP of the EU-15 countries by around 1 percent, with higher figures in the major countries of destination, such as Ireland, the UK, Spain and Italy.[16] Another study found that higher labor mobility across Europe boosted the employment rate, increased entrepreneurship, spread knowledge and consequently fostered innovation.[17] This can also be seen in aggregate labor data: 80 percent of the working-age EU citizens residing in another European country are economically active, 6 percentage points higher than the average among those residing in their own country of citizenship. A broad consensus among economists sees increased labor migration as the best means of enhancing economic growth both in the countries of immigration and emigration, but the positive impact depends on government policy.

Migration has evolved in waves. In the 1990s, few European workers considered looking for jobs in another European country. Labor mobility increased greatly after the 2004 and 2007 expansions of the European Union towards the east. In 2004 about a million citizens from Central Europe and the Baltics and another million from Bulgaria and Romania resided in the European Union. By 2009, the total number of nationals from the new accession countries residing in the EU-15 states increased to 4.8 million.[18] During the migration peak in 2007, one percent of the citizens of new accession countries moved to Western and Southern Europe.

Due to the Eurozone crisis and its effect on European economies, the annual number of westbound immigrants within the European Union fell to roughly 600,000 since 2008. Still, the latest statistics suggest that 6 million East Europeans work in other EU states. This group has more than doubled the previous labor mobility in Europe, and constitutes the biggest factor in improving productivity across the European Union.[19]

East-to-west migration will probably pick up once economic growth has returned to Western Europe.[20] With convergence in economic standards in some Eastern European countries, however, it is unlikely to be high as in the early accession period. Recent flows show that labor mobility is highly dependent on economic conditions: during the Eurozone crisis in 2009-2012 the number of Polish job seekers fell down by 44 percent—in part thanks to the relative strength of the Polish economy, while the number of job seekers from Hungary and Latvia increased by 58 percent and 39 percent, respectively.[21] Both countries experienced sharp declines in economic growth during this period. These statistics are grounds for optimism, as they show that labor mobility in Europe follows economic logic and that the free movement of labor works well.

In the meantime, a new trend in labor mobility in Europe has emerged. Tens of thousands of Greeks and Spaniards have gone north, due to the lack of job prospects in their own countries. By 2014, GDP per capita in Greece had dropped by 27 percent relative to 2007 and in Spain by almost 11 percent. The unemployment rate in both countries crossed the threshold of 25 percent with over half of its active young (15-24 years) population being unemployed In 2014 alone, there was a 38 percent increase year-to-year of the job seekers coming from Southern Europe to Germany and Great Britain. Their share of overall labor mobility in Europe has jumped from 11 percent in 2010 to 19 percent in 2014.[22]

To assist in this process, the European Commission has initiated a job-search platform to make it easier for European citizens in finding jobs in other countries. The pan-European job search network EURES has about one thousand EURES advisers in daily contact with jobseekers and employers across Europe. The EURES portal gives information on living and working conditions in all participating countries in 26 languages, and as of September 2015 allows access to 1.6 million job vacancies and 1.3 million CVs.[23] The platform is a useful initial step to bridge the information gap in finding jobs and learning about labor conditions in other European countries. It does not address, however, some of the major other deterrents to labor mobility.

One obstacle to greater labor mobility across Europe is the lack of certainty of whether on social benefits. In principle European regulation states that anyone is entitled to benefits, where he or she pays taxes and social contributions. For example child allowances are granted in the country of work and reflect the costs of raising children there. In some member states public debate has concentrated on this issue, fueled by the suspicion that people move not in the search for employment but rather to obtain higher allowances than those granted in the country of origin where family and children still reside.

In reality, the exported benefits are limited. Less than 10 percent of the child benefits paid to Romanian citizens working in Germany is exported to Romania and some 30 percent of Polish citizens to Poland.[24] After Greece experienced severe cuts in its public expenditure, immigrants from Eastern Europe have complained that their pensions and other social benefits have been significantly delayed, unlike those of their Greek peers. Clearly, much more can be done to ease exportability of benefits.

A related issue is the accumulation of social benefits during the life of a migrant worker. A mobile worker's rights to social security benefits should be based on the sum of all social contributions made, both in her home country and the country of present work. However, pension systems are national and they are not coordinated within the EU. The contradiction between national rules has sparked controversy in both source and destination countries. Many countries require that a person has worked for decades in that country to be entitled to pension. In other cases, the resulting social payments can be significantly higher than if actual earnings during the relevant period had been taken into account, making nationals complain that mobile workers are favored. Needless to say, migrants have to adjust their moves to the inconsistencies in the national social benefit systems. The EU countries need to harmonize their regulations for migrant workers, and the European institutions can help making the actual rules clear and transparent, both to improve these rules and to inform EU citizens.

A third deterrent is the so-called regulated professions, which require certain qualifications by law. These professions differ across member states but they usually include medical professions (40 percent of all regulated professions) along with architects, educators and the transport sector. Malpractice in these professions can cause direct harm to the customer that is not able to evaluate the service provided herself. The European Commission has issued a list of all regulated professions so that mobile workers can be aware of such requirements.[25] A Eurobarometer survey in 2014 found that 23 percent of European citizens expect recognition problems abroad. However, only 4 percent of people who actually moved experienced problems. This suggests that public information needs to improve, but it might also reflect that many people in regulated professions are deterred to migrate.

Not all countries are welcoming job seekers from other European countries. At times, job seekers may add to the pressure on public services, schools and housing. In 2014, for example, prior to the lifting of barriers to the free movement of labor to the United Kingdom for Bulgarians and Romanians, a fierce media campaign raged against "welfare tourism" in Britain, and it has become a major argument for the United Kingdom leaving the EU. Previously, other campaigns had emerged spontaneously in some countries, perhaps best illustrated by the "Polish plumber" debate in France. Fears were exacerbated by the Eurozone crisis, causing a surge of anti-immigration sentiment in several EU member states. In most cases, however, such campaigns have been short-lived. The economic benefits far outweigh the costs: Most studies find a positive effect for destination countries, both in terms of added economic growth and higher public income. Immigrants typically take on jobs no longer sought by nationals and increase competition in certain services sectors, thus reducing consumer prices.[26]

GERMANY'S LABOR IMMIGRATION POLICIES

The shrinking original population because of lasting low birth rates has caused major shortages of labor in economically successful countries. Often the real choice is between illegal or spontaneous immigration and orderly, regulated immigration. Germany offers a stark example of hanging immigration policies. Its aging population is shrinking, with the 2011 census showing a loss of about 1.5 million people since the 1986. Analysts estimate that worker shortages already cost Germany as much as $40 billion a year. Despite various measures that have been introduced to attract job seekers, demographers estimate that Germany's working population will drop by 6.5 million by 2040—a decrease equivalent to losing every worker in Bavaria, Germany's rich southern state.

Germany has experienced two waves of immigration, coinciding with its need for skilled workers. It is instructive to study the experience of the first wave and apply what worked to increase the attractiveness of Europe in general.

In the late 1950s, the West German economy was booming and the demand for labor seemed endless. There were labor shortages in several industries—starting for industrial assembly. German companies were mainly interested in semi-skilled employees on assembly lines and in shift work. The solution was found in October 1961, with the signing of a labor recruitment agreement between West Germany and Turkey. Hundreds of thousands of Turks boarded special trains in Ankara and Istanbul and were taken to Germany as "guest workers" (*Gastarbeiter*). The workers arrived in Munich and were then distributed among the country's industrial zones. The immigrant workers were expected to live together without their families in newly built dormitories near the factories where they worked, and return to their native countries after working for a few years.

All this changed when the oil crisis threatened to stall the German economy in 1973. Immigrants were suddenly seen as an economic burden. The official policy focused on "promoting the desire to return home," at times by offering the guest workers monetary rewards to return. This policy is reflected even today in natu-ralization laws. Foreigners born in Germany must decide by the age of 23 between their parents' nationality and German citizenship.

Faced with these challenges, the German government has acknowledged the country's dependence on immigrants to sustain economic growth. In recent years, German policy has pragmatically becoming friendlier toward immigrants, as the shortage of labor has grown worse. In 2012, Germany simplified the process for immigrants from outside the EU. In 2013, Chancellor Angela Merkel said Germany needs to become an immigration country and that "increasing diversity also means enrichment."[27] Germany introduced a "Blue Card" system, inspired by the US green car, effectively granting entry to anyone with a university degree and a job offer with a minimum salary of $50,000 to $64,000 a year, depending on the field. As a result, the average immigrant moving to Germany in 2015 is better educated and more skilled than the average German.

Multilingual immigrants have started to fill the gap in the labor market, leverag-ing the relatively high level of English spoken in international companies in Germany to find work. David Fernandez, an unemployed social worker from Madrid, decided in 2014 while marching in a street protest that "nothing in Spain was ever going to change." He had never been to Germany, but "everyone was talking about how you could get work, how you could build something real. So I decided, I will go."[28]

In 2015, the German government demonstrated this immigration-friendly at-titude, by welcoming hundreds of thousands of Syrian and Iraqi refugees. Such an influx can solve the long-term problem of declining labor force, but it poses an enormous challenge: how to absorb a wave of immigrants seeking accommodation with their families, unlike temporary workers from Turkey in the 1960s, who initially came alone. The current immigrants also require schooling for their children, healthcare for their spouses and parents. If they are successfully integrated into society, they would become permanent citizens. Their integration requires not only active labor market policies, but also policies to accommodate and socialize the newcomers. In a recent interview in *Sueddeutsche Zeitung*, the President of the Bundesbank, Jens Weidmann noted that "in the long term, Germany in any case faces considerable challenges, if one thinks for example of the ageing society, increasing competition from emerging markets or the energy (policy) change, [. . .], Given the demographic change, Germany needs additional manpower to be able to keep up its prosperity."[29]

REDUCING THE LABOR TAX WEDGE

Most European countries impose high taxes on labor. The European Commission's 2014 Annual Growth Survey demonstrated the need to shift taxation away from labor to other sources of taxation as a way to support job creation.[30] The tax wedge is defined as the difference between gross income and after-**tax** income. It encompasses employers' social security contributions, the personal income tax and employees' social security contributions. In 2015, the tax wedge was lowest at 20 percent in Malta and highest at 56 percent in Belgium (figure 6.7). The tax wedge was around 50 percent in Austria (49.4 percent), Germany (49.3 percent), Hungary (49.0 percent), France (48.4 percent) and Italy (48.2 percent).

A high tax wedge increases the cost of labor and thus limits employment, which is particularly true of low-skilled individuals in countries with high labor taxes as well as for part-time workers, who are primarily women. A study of the EU countries found that an increase in tax wedge of one percentage point decreases the employment growth in the EU-27 by 0.04 percentage points.[31] A comprehensive study of 20 OECD countries between 1983–1994 showed that a decrease in the average tax wedge by 5 percentage points would reduce the unemployment rate by 13 percent.[32] A companion study reported that a 10 percentage point rise in the tax wedge reduces labor input of the working age population by 1-3 percent.[33] By comparing the big three countries of continental Europe (France, Germany and Italy) with the United States, the study found that the difference in the tax wedge (around 16 percentage points) explains around one quarter of the overall difference in the employment rate.

Given the large potential gains in employment creation from a reduction of the tax wedge, many European countries have attempted to do so. The direction of change is to replace the high tax burden on labor with a combination of consumption taxes, property taxes and environmental taxes. However, social security taxes have not been reduced. They are easily collected by the national tax authorities. Therefore they are often increased during economic downturns when the government lacks

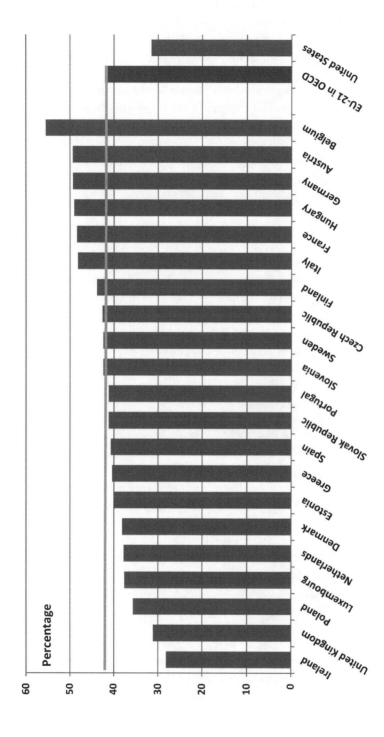

Figure 6.7 The Labor Tax Wedge
Source: OECD, Labor Force Statistics

Source: OECD

sufficient revenues. They have the added advantage to the authorities by not being transparent to the workers, since they are largely paid by employers

During the Eurozone crisis, for example, Hungary, Greece, Slovakia, Spain and Portugal all increased these taxes and thus the labor tax wedge. Bulgaria did the same in 2015. Yet recent analysis suggests that the labor tax wedge is particularly detrimental in Eastern European economies, where workers may choose opportunities in the shadow economy or emigrate in search of better jobs. In these countries a reduction of the tax wedge by 1 percentage point increases employment rate by up to 0.7 percentage points.[34]

The European Commission has started advancing this reform for job creation in its country-specific recommendations for the European Semester: "A priority for many Member States is to alleviate labor taxation in order to increase incentives to work and to reduce the relatively high cost of labor, in particular for low-skilled workers. While several Member States have taken or started to take tax measures in response to the last year's recommendations in this area (Austria, Belgium, Italy, France, Latvia, Hungary and the Netherlands), progress has been limited overall."[35]

European Commissioner Siim Kallas summarized the Commission's analysis: "Reducing excessive tax wedges in a budget-neutral way could bring big gains in employment, and boost competitiveness and growth in the euro area. In fact, our simulations indicate that a joint tax shift from labor to consumption by European countries could add €65 billion to output and create around 1.4 million jobs."[36] With the Eurozone crisis largely in the past, countries are starting to take his advice. In 2015, Romania and the United Kingdom substantially lowered the labor tax wedge, while Finland announced such plans for 2016.

LABOR REGULATION REFORMS

Europe has an old tradition of strong trade unions that pursue collective bargaining with the employers' association. The character, organization and extension of trade unions and collective bargaining have varied greatly from country to country. In general, labor market practices have changed greatly since 1980.

One trend has been significant deregulation of labor markets. The outstanding example is the United Kingdom, where highly restrictive trade union practices led to frequent wildcat strikes and especially in "the winter of discontent" in 1978-9. In the 1980s, many of these aggressive practices were prohibited. Ireland pursued similar deregulation but more quietly.

Another pattern has been a more moderate deregulation of the labor market accomplished through trilateral compromises between government, trade unions and employers. One cherished example is the Danish "Flexicurity," combining a flexible labor market and social security for workers. Unlike in many other EU countries, Danish employers can hire and fire workers with ease. About one quarter of all Danish workers change job every year. The government prides itself of offering social security through high unemployment benefits and getting people back to work soon through an active labor market policy.[37] Yet, this model has drawbacks. Denmark has low unemployment, but not as low as Germany or the United Kingdom, while the fiscal cost of unemployment benefits and especially active labor market measures is rather high.

In 2003, German Chancellor Gerhard Schröder began a series of labor market and welfare reforms—known as Agenda 2010—which reorganized the welfare state. They included the combination of unemployment and welfare benefits, drastic cuts for the long-term unemployed, the deregulation of temporary work and the creation of short-term jobs, essentially limited part-time work that integrated first-time workers and chronically-unemployed workers into the job market. As a result of these reforms, Germany enjoys the lowest unemployment rate since World War II, and the lowest in Europe. Its labor market has expanded to 42 million people, attracting young workers from across Europe as well as immigrants from other countries.

The biggest concern is Southern Europe, where labor markets are highly regulated and inert, leading to great benefits to those who already have jobs at the cost of very high unemployment, especially among the youth. For years, Greece and Spain have stood out for having the highest unemployment, 25 and 22 percent of the active labor force, respectively in October 2015.[38] Economists consider Southern European labor markets unfriendly to job creation. Former IMF Chief Economist Olivier Blanchard has authored a number of studies on labor market rigidities in France, and Harvard University Professor Alberto Alesina has written similar studies in the case of Italy.[39]

If regulation of the employment relation is too rigid, it lowers labor force participation, increases unemployment, and forces workers into the informal economy.[40] These rigidities have been particularly pronounced in Southern Europe, and resulted in high rates of unemployment, particularly among the youth, during the Eurozone crisis. In Greece and Spain, as much as half of the youth of working age was unemployed in 2014.[41] Many chose to emigrate, whereas others swelled the ranks of the informal economy. Fortunately, governments have responded by reforming certain aspects of labor regulation.

These reforms were inspired by the success of Germany in reinvigorating its labor market a decade earlier. The Eurozone crisis provided an opportunity for finance ministers to require reforms from other ministries that would have not happened in normal times. Prior to the crisis, some European governments had sufficient resources to pay generous unemployment benefits. That privilege was rapidly cut with overall unemployment in the Eurozone increasing to 12.6 percent by January 2014.[42] Many Eurozone countries initiated labor market reforms, with various degrees of boldness. These reforms commonly included reductions in severance pay for regular contracts and some simplification of individual or collective dismissal procedures. By the summer of 2014 this was already done with changes in the labor code in Greece and Portugal. Italy tried too, but with little success.

Following Germany's example, Portugal started a job creation reform already in 2009, when the socialist government was still in power. The reform comprised a substantial easing of job protection on regular contracts through a simplification of dismissal procedures. This was followed up by reductions in severance payments for regular contracts and a narrower definition of unfair dismissal. In 2011 and 2012, Finance Minister Vitor Gaspar introduced further reforms, which facilitated firing and hiring. Individual dismissals for economic reasons no longer had to be based on seniority but could be based on worker capability. The obligation to transfer an employee to another suitable position was eliminated. Severance pay was reduced from 30 to 20 days per year of tenure (with a 12-month ceiling instead of a 3-month floor) and a further reduction to 15 days occurred in December 2013. In May 2011, the Portuguese government froze temporarily both the minimum wage and administrative extensions of sector-level collective agreements. The authorities also lowered the threshold above which firm-level bargaining was possible from 500 to 150 workers, which reduced sector-level bargaining and provided additional flexibility. The reform also reduced the disincentives to work by lowering the ceiling on monthly unemployment benefits to €1,048, introducing a 10 percent benefit reduction after six months and reducing the maximum duration.

During the Eurozone crisis, Spain lost nearly 3 million jobs, and its unemployment swelled to 4.3 million people. The construction industry alone lost about 1.8 million jobs.[43] The government responded with a significant labor reform in July 2012, giving priority to collective bargaining agreements at the firm level over those at the sector or regional level. In addition, firms can now opt out more easily from a collective agreement and pursue internal flexibility measures. Employers can introduce unilaterally changes in working conditions (wages, working hours, work schedules) whenever there are objective economic, technical, or production reasons. In the absence of an agreement with workers' representatives, an employer willing to opt out may now unilaterally refer the matter to arbitration by a public tripartite body. Dismissal rules were also changed. The new law specifies that a dismissal is justified if the company faces a persistent decline (over three consecutive quarters) in revenues. The business does not have to prove any longer that the dismissal is essential for the future profitability of the firm. Spain reduced monetary compensation for unfair dismissal to 33 days' wages per year of seniority up to a maximum of 24 months, compared to the previous severance pay of 45 days up to a maximum of 42 months' wages. The 2012 reform removed a worker's right to interim wages between the effective date of dismissal and the final court ruling.[44]

Greece had the most onerous labor market regulations. In 2010 Greek lawmakers started reforms by reducing overtime pay and earnings of part-time employees in an attempt to increase flexibility in the labor market. As it became evident that the fiscal consolidation program in 2011 was derailed, the technocratic Lucas Papademos government made further attempts to deregulate the labor market. It reduced the minimum wage by 22 percent (32 percent for new labor market entrants), decentralized the wage bargaining system (giving seniority to individual contracts over the wage floors agreed on in national and occupational pay agreements), abolished the life-tenure rule in large parts of the public sector, and committed to cuts in public sector employment by 150,000 by.[45]

In Italy, caretaker Prime Minister Mario Monti also tried to achieve more flexibility in hiring young workers and to make it easier for small businesses to adjust their workforce. The goal was to enable companies with more than 15 workers to dismiss employees with open-ended contracts for economic reasons, without facing the prospect of a labor court ordering the company to rehire previous employees. This would limit situations where older employees were protected while younger workers could not find entry to the labor market, even after finishing their education.

The International Monetary Fund recommended moving away from using a variety of temporary labor contracts to a single more flexible contract with phased-in protection that increases with tenure to boost labor force participation.[46] Italian participation rates were low, especially among women—at 50 percent compared to 65 percent in the rest of the European Union. The Monti government proposed to decrease the incentives to hire workers on fixed-term contracts. The cooling-off period between two fixed-term contracts would be extended, and the fiscal incentive for some types of fixed-term contracts reduced. In particular, employers would have to pay higher social contributions on most fixed-term contracts, which could be reimbursed when these were converted into permanent ones (the so-called "stabilization bonus").

The Italian Parliament, however, watered down Monti's proposals. Under the final legislation, court-ordered rehiring remains possible and widely applied. "The labor market reform was under expectations," said Tito Boeri, an economist at Bocconi University in Milan. "It didn't do things it could do. It took very long to negotiate, and at the end brought very modest reforms." Prime Minister Monti was also "very timid" about liberalizing the guilds that serve as entry barriers for most professions.[47]

Substantial progress has been made in the four South European countries, but their labor markets remain the most inert and all maintain high unemployment even if it has fallen. More deregulation is needed.

CONCLUSIONS: JOB CREATING POLICIES NEED TO PROCEED

Few policies can do more to improve Europe's economic growth and welfare than policies creating more jobs. Many policy changes are needed. Variations are great and various European countries have managed in different regards.

Southern Europe needs to expand both high school education and vocational training to enhance their competitiveness. Vocational training through apprenticeship in the old German fashion has proven highly valuable in modern manufacturing and services, where vocational skills are valued highly by the market. In addition, apprentice ships offer a cure against youth unemployment. Other countries should follow the examples of Germany and Austria.

Another important policy is to increase the participation of women in the labor force, which varies dramatically. Much can be done to attract women to the labor force. One part of the solution is equal rights for men and women, and another part is childcare and flexible work arrangements. The Scandinavian countries have been most successful in engaging women in the labor force, though a drawback is that this has taken place at considerable fiscal cost.

Europe needs immigration. Even with record immigration inflows—about a million immigrants in 2014 and 1.5 million in 2015—the continent faces demographic shortfalls. At the current pace, Europe will lose 10-12 million workers by 2040. It is good but does not suffice to increase intra-Europe labor mobility. The continent's greatest immediate challenge is how to receive the large wave of mainly Syrian refugees. The most scary scenario is that European inability to handle large inflows of refugees leads to the breakup of the of the Schengen zone of passport-free travel. A study by the Bertelsman foundation has assessed that such a breakup could cost as much as 10 percent of annual EU GDP over a decade.[48]

Europe has considerable experience of absorbing immigrants. A few lessons are that social benefits need to be exportable and earned benefits should be transportable. Undue regulations of professions should be eliminated, and the necessary regulations should be transparent. Germany offers a laudable example of a move from temporary "guest workers" to the attraction of skilled immigrants. Ireland that used to be the main emigration country in Europe, has arguably adopted the best policy for immigrants: tolerance, limited regulations, welcoming skilled immigrants and foreign direct investment, low taxes and limited but vital social benefits.

Taxation of labor and especially the labor tax wedges are far too great. Because of excessive taxes on labor, Europe gets too few members of the labor force, who work less than they would really like to. It also divert people to work in the informal sector and outside of their specialization, which dissuades them from investing in their human capital. Europe's very high taxation of labor heeds to be reduced.

Finally, most of Europe's labor markets remain far too regulated and inert. This is particularly true of Southern Europe, which has led to low economic growth and high unemployment. After the global financial crisis, these countries have carried out some liberalization, but much more is needed. The positive examples are the highly liberalized labor markets of the United Kingdom and Ireland, and Denmark and Germany that have tried to combine increased flexibility with the maintenance of substantial social support. All these countries have succeeded in keeping low unemployment.

Taken together, these changes to create more jobs would make Europe more competitive globally.

7

Cutting Red Tape

European institutions generate excessive red tape. Examples abound: In 2013, the European Commission proposed legislation to ban refillable jugs for olive oil to prevent restaurants from switching virgin oil for cheap alternatives. The proposal was abandoned after widespread ridicule.[1] In 2012, another legislative proposal called for banning hairdressers from wearing high-heels and jewelry. It, too, was scrapped.[2]

However much EU institutions are ridiculed for their strange regulations, it is primarily up to the national governments to regulate business and ensure that their regulation is competitive. Individual European countries have made steps to improve the environment for doing business. Half of the 25 countries in the world where it is easiest to do business are European Union members, according to the latest World Bank's Doing Business survey.[3] The twelve are: Denmark (3), United Kingdom (6), Sweden (8), Finland (10), Germany (15), Estonia (16), Ireland (17), Lithuania (20), Austria (21), Latvia (22), Portugal (23), and Poland (25). Malta is the lowest ranked EU country, at 80 (of 189 economies). Five Asian economies rank in the top-25 (Singapore, Hong Kong, Korea, Malaysia and Taiwan), as well as Australia and New Zealand (figure 7.1).

In this, European governments can learn from each other. If the regulation that is most amenable to doing business throughout Europe is adopted in each country, the European Union will be second to none in the world in cutting red tape. All European countries could make starting a business as easy as it is in Lithuania, with just two procedures and about half a percent of annual GDP per capita in administrative costs; and adopt Lithuania's property registration procedures—finished in two days and at trivial cost. European countries could also learn from Ireland's tax administration, Austria's customs operations and court procedures for enforcing commercial contracts; and take on Finland's insolvency legislation and implement it in practice. Then Europe will be ahead of both the United States (ranked 7th) and its top Asian competitors as a place to do business.

To increase its competitiveness in the ease of doing business, Europe can adopt objective indicators of progress: for example, how long it takes to abide by a particular business regulation, how much it costs, and how many different documents the business needs to provide. In other words, simple time-and-motion studies that have been used extensively by businesses to improve their own efficiency.[4] The current focus of the European Commission on targeting subjective indicators like

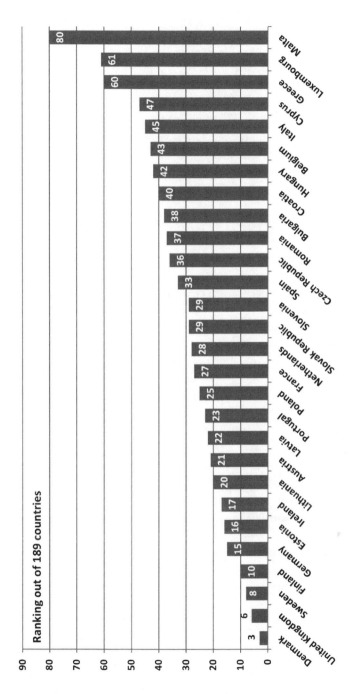

Figure 7.1 Doing Business Ranking, 2016
Note: Lowest is best, scale from 1-189
Source: Doing Business, June 2015

reducing the overall burden of regulation or some notional cost to businesses are easily manipulated, as there is no straight-forward way to measure what is achieved. The same applies to the "one in, one out" rule, which is easily circumvented as more cumbersome regulations are placed instead of older ones.

Another method of cutting red tape is to stem the flow of new regulations, something that the Juncker Commission is already doing, and to introduce sunset clauses in regulatory proposals, for example, expiring after fifteen years. In this way, antiquated regulation will naturally end to the benefit of simpler rules. Australia has been the pioneer in regulatory reform by including "sunset" provisions in all new regulations starting from 1996, with the regulation automatically expiring after a certain period unless renewed by Parliament.[5] Sweden has a "guillotine" approach for regulatory reform, in which hundreds of obsolete regulations are cancelled after the government periodically requires regulatory agencies to register all essential regulations.

As European red-tape cutting measures get grounded in objective indicators, the European Commission may consider doing annual country reports on progress in reducing administrative barriers to business. These reports can approximate the European Semester reports on fiscal discipline and structural reforms, which the Commission prepares for all European Union countries each spring.

This chapter is organized in five sections. Section one describes the current European Union initiatives in cutting red tape. Section two reviews the current measures used by the European institutions to benchmark regulatory burdens. Section 3 details individual European countries' efforts to improve the environment for doing business. Section 4 proposes specific guides to ease the burden on business, which can be adopted by the European Commission. Section five concludes.

EU INITIATIVES

Many initiatives have been made to cut red tape in Europe. Successive strategies, working groups, and committees have designed goals to reduce burdensome regulation. The Lisbon Strategy was an action plan devised in 2000 to make the European Union "the most competitive and dynamic knowledge-based economy in the world capable of sustainable economic growth with more and better jobs and greater social cohesion."[6] By 2009, it was considered a failure.[7]

In November 2006, the European Commission proposed another strategy to reduce the unnecessary administrative burden on businesses. This "Action Program for Reducing Administrative Burdens in the EU," established a working group and set the target to reduce administrative burdens to businesses by 25 percent by 2012. Led by Edmund Stoiber, former prime minister of the state of Bavaria in Germany, the committee published a report, which outlined examples of implementation of EU legislation in the least burdensome way across Europe.[8] The report also claimed that the 25 percent red-tape-reduction goal of the Stoiber committee was surpassed and that its recommendations could lead to savings for businesses of €41 billion annually. Neither claim can be objectively verified.

In December 2012, the European Commission decided it needed to do more and launched the "Regulatory Fitness and Performance Program (REFIT)," aimed at eliminating unnecessary regulatory burdens and ensuring that the body of EU legislation remains friendly to businesses. It is unclear how this program aims to cut red tape, as its outputs are impact assessments, procedural evaluations, and stakeholder consultations, in other words—more bureaucracy.

In December 2014, the new European Commission, led by former Prime Minister of Luxembourg Jean-Claude Juncker unveiled a fourth initiative, the Better Regulation plan, to prune business-unfriendly proposals for legislation before they reach the European Parliament. Commission Vice President Frans Timmermans was tasked with cutting red tape. "We are listening to the concerns of citizens and businesses who worry that Brussels and its institutions don't always deliver rules they can understand or apply," he stated. "We must be honest about what works and what doesn't."[9] The first step of Commissioner Timmermans was to cut 80 planned European directives for 2015, and leave only 23 draft laws, as compared to an average annual rate of 130 new pieces of legislation over the previous five years.[10] A good first step is to reduce bureaucratic waste.

The main reason for the increased EU urgency to cut red tape is the threat of British exit from the European Union. Prime Minister David Cameron has frequently described Brussels as a "huge" bureaucracy that "needed to be scaled back."[11] British corporate leaders have complained of heavy regulation and started publishing an annual report on the most egregious red tape burdening businesses.[12] Graeme MacDonald, the CEO of construction equipment maker JCB, one of Britain's largest manufacturing companies, argues: "What is needed is a lot less red tape . . . Some of it is costly for us and, quite frankly, ridiculous. Whether that means renegotiating or exiting [the EU], I don't think it can carry on as it is. It's a burden . . . It's easier selling to North America than to Europe sometimes."[13]

CURRENT EUROPEAN COMMISSION MEASURES

The European Union has adopted various tools to address the quality and cost to businesses of its legislation. In March 2002, it adopted the "better regulation package," which, introduced widespread consultation and the use of impact assessments of new legislation. Since then, more than 1,150 impact assessments have been completed. The impact assessment guidelines have been updated three times, in 2005, 2009 and 2013. In 2006, an Impact Assessment Board, a task force composed of commission officials, was created. Since 2010, the European Commission has also performed ex post evaluations on major pieces of legislation.

Impact assessments are, however, not based on quantifiable indicators. They create a quality check in the process of adopting new rules, but rarely address the substance of new legislation. Their cost is frequently higher than their possible benefits,[14] partly because the number of requests for specific impact analyses of European regulation has risen dramatically. In addition to the regular impact analyses of social, economic, and environmental dimensions, a series of additional assessments have been carried out with regard to the impact on: the internal market and the four fundamental freedoms, subsidiarity and proportionality, EU fundamental rights, small businesses, and the EU's global competitiveness. Policy making in Brussels is increasingly constrained by recommendations of various "high-level" groups.[15] Instead of building its own expertise and analyses, in the past European institutions have focused on ad hoc initiatives led by former politicians.

Realizing the inadequacy of this approach, the European Commission decided to look at entire areas of law and assess its fitness for purpose. In 2012, the "regulatory fitness" (REFIT) process was started, allegedly to identify areas for cutting red tape.[16] In reality, however, REFIT is another bureaucratic step, which adds a procedural check without addressing the substance of business regulation.[17]

As a first step towards implementing REFIT, the Impact Assessment Board was renamed Regulatory Scrutiny Board, and its composition was changed in 2014. Rather than having nine rotating experts working in various parts of the European bureaucracy, the new board has four permanent members and two independent members, one of whom has an academic background. The new board was formed in response to requests from businesses to secure independent scrutiny of impact assessments, and it is a positive step towards building own expertise. The "RegWatch" group, formed by the regulatory oversight agencies in the Netherlands, Germany, the UK, the Czech Republic and Sweden have advocated a completely independent board, which may be the next logical step.

Under REFIT, the European Commission engages with businesses directly to seek their views on excessive regulatory burdens. One such platform is the identification of the Top 10 most burdensome EU laws. The results from the first round of consultations in 2012 showed that businesses see the biggest difficulties and costs stemming from legislation on chemicals, value added tax, product safety, the recognition of professional qualifications, data protection, waste, the labor market, recording equipment for road transport, public procurement and the customs code.[18]

As a result of these findings, in February 2013 the European Commission replaced the product safety directive by a regulation on consumer product safety, which includes a simpler set of rules for businesses. It is expected that such simplifications in the ease of doing business will lead to an increase of 1.4 percent in Europe's GDP, equivalent to €150 billion,[19] though there is no rigorous analysis to verify this claim. Still, rescinding cumbersome regulation constitutes progress over previous attempts to amend such regulation.

The Juncker Commission is intent to slow the pace of new legislation and to simplify the existing laws. Its 2015 work program focuses extensively on REFIT actions: consolidation of three Directives in the area of information and consultation of workers including the general Framework Directive and Directives on collective redundancies and on transfers of undertakings; evaluation of the Framework Directive and 23 related directives on occupational health and safety; evaluation of the Directives on part-time work and on fixed-term work and on an employer's obligation to inform employees of the conditions applicable to the contract or employment relationship. The merging of seven Company Law Directives into one document is also foreseen for the purpose of increasing transparency, as is the evaluation of legislation regarding equal treatment in social security.[20]

Over time, REFIT may focus more on addressing specific regulatory issues that businesses face. At present, the concept of "burdensome" regulation is imprecise and not easily quantifiable. Is this qualification linked to costs, to administrative formalities, or to the complexity of the wording? Is excessive red tape defined by expressed business views that legislation is an irritant in their everyday operations? Or are regulatory burdens evaluated as measures of Europe's global competitiveness? REFIT, like the previous red-tape cutting exercises pursued by European institutions, has yet to find sound academic backing, like the time-and-motion studies that underlie more rigorous assessments of the costs of regulation.[21] Such backing will clarify the focus of cutting red tape in Europe.

MAKING IT EASIER TO OPEN A NEW FIRM

It is not only the United Kingdom, which insists on the ease of doing business in Europe. Several other governments have worked to reduce the burden of regulation. In Germany, the second Merkel government introduced a "bureaucracy brake" in 2015. This initiative obliges every ministry that aspires to create new regulatory burdens for the economy to dismantle a corresponding amount of business regulations elsewhere. This "one in, one out" principle is applied to stem bureaucratic excesses. In total, the reform is supposed to save the German economy €744 million in administrative costs per year. The Czech Republic, Denmark, the Netherlands, Lithuania and Portugal are also applying the "one in, one out" rule.

Some EU member states have gone further, and most of all Denmark that has mandated digital communication with businesses to reduce regulatory costs. From 2015, all letters to businesses are sent digitally and all regulatory reporting systems are available online through one single website. Cross-border initiatives on reducing red-tape have also emerged: Austria, the Czech Republic and Germany have eliminated administrative obstacles that local small businesses face when they expand their activities to the other side of the border in the neighboring regions of Upper Austria, South Bohemia and Bavaria. Finally, the Tory party in the United Kingdom has proposed applying a "one in, two out" principle in business regulation.[22]

A number of European countries, mostly in Eastern and Southern Europe, have used the World Bank's Doing Business indicators as one guide to cutting red tape. These include Lithuania and Poland, but also Greece, Portugal and Sweden.[23] The focus is typically on how to make entry of new firms easier, and how to improve access to financing and the speed of commercial litigation in case businesses enter disputes with their suppliers or competitors.

Since the Eurozone crisis started, a dozen European countries have made it significantly easier to start a new firm. A constant flow of start-ups into the economy adds new jobs and services. It also increases competition, encouraging existing firms to improve productivity to maintain their market presence. In Finland, a high firm entry rate explains almost all the productivity peaks since 1985. At that time

Finnish labor productivity lagged behind Sweden and the United States, but within two decades Finland raised productivity to 35 percent above the level in Sweden and 16 percent above that in the United States.[24]

Studies on Germany have shown that regions with a higher concentration of new firms had higher growth rates and greater labor productivity.[25] These findings have spurred further reductions in red tape at the federal level. In 2007, Germany implemented an electronic registration and online publication system, doing away with the need to publish a notice of incorporation in the official gazette. In 2009, it reduced the minimum capital requirement to a symbolic €1 (figure 7.2). In 2010, the German government increased the efficiency of communication between notaries and the commercial registry and eliminated the requirement to publish a notice of incorporation in a newspaper.

To reduce the burden on European start-ups, governments revise the laws and regulations related to starting a business as well as their implementation and enforcement. This approach is consistent with the findings of a recent World Bank study highlighting the importance, in promoting the formalization of firms, of not only making the start-up process easier but also simplifying the enforcement of rules. The indicators measure the implicit administrative requirements that entrepreneurs face, such as having to get a company seal made.[26]

European countries have continuously streamlined entry procedures, often by combining multiple registrations. Besides reducing its paid-in minimum capital requirement in 2009, Poland consolidated its application for business registration with those for tax, social security, and statistics registration. During the same year Slovenia combined tax registration with company registration, both online, and the next year it introduced other online services. More recently Slovakia improved its processes for obtaining trading licenses, income tax registration and health insurance registration at its one-stop shop. In 2012, Croatia and Greece introduced new types of limited liability companies with no minimum capital and simpler and less costly incorporation processes.

Greece, Italy, Portugal and Spain—the economies most adversely affected by the Eurozone crisis—have been leaders in cutting red tape recently. In 2014, Greece made starting a business easier by lowering the cost of registration. It facilitated property transfer by reducing the tax and eliminating the requirement for a municipal tax clearance certificate. In 2015 it simplified the enforcement of contracts by introducing an electronic filing system for business disputes. Italy followed suit. In 2013, it reduced the minimum capital requirement for opening a new company, while a year later Spain eased business registration by introducing an electronic system that links several public agencies.

FACILITATING PROPERTY TRANSFERS

Looking at other measures on cutting red tape, getting electricity is easy in Germany, which ranks third in the world behind only South Korea and Taiwan. Sweden, at number 7, is close behind. Registering property is easy in Lithuania (2), Estonia

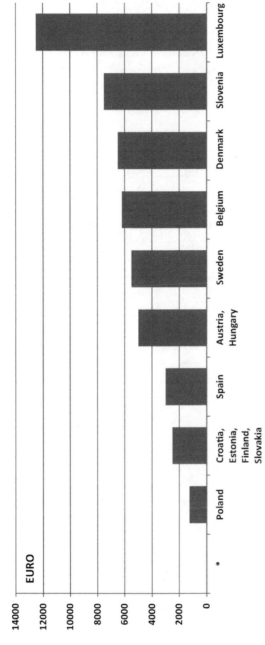

Figure 7.2 Mandated Start-up Capital across Europe

* The following countries have no mandated start-up capital: Bulgaria, Cyprus, Czech Republic, France, Germany, Greece, Ireland, Italy, Latvia, Lithuania, Malta, Netherlands, Portugal, Romania, UK

Source: The World Bank, 2015

(4), Slovakia (5), and Denmark (9), but it is one of the hardest tasks for a new business in Greece, which ranks near the bottom at 144. It takes on average 21 days to register a property in Greece—and ten administrative procedures to complete the registration process. Dealing with construction permits is easy in Denmark (ranked #5 globally), but particularly challenging in Cyprus (145). Achieving such a permit in Cyprus requires 8 procedures and takes 617 days.[27]

Improvement on each of these indicators supports economic growth. Academic evidence suggests that property owners with registered titles are more likely to invest.[28] They also have a better chance of getting credit because they can use their property as collateral. For governments, having reliable, up-to-date information in cadasters and land registries is also essential to correctly assess and collect taxes.

In Europe, computerizing the property transfer process is the easiest way to reduce processing times and enhance efficiency. Going electronic also makes it easier to identify errors and overlapping titles, improving title security. Denmark implemented an efficient and reliable electronic registration system over the past 5 years. In 2009, the government started to modernize its land registry, progressively digitizing its records—more than 80 million documents. Once digitization was complete, the land registry introduced electronic lodgment of property transfers. By 2011, it was accepting property transfer applications only online. The information technology system allows rapid screening of all applications. Implementation of the new system has cut the time required to transfer property in Denmark from 42 days to only 4 (Table 7.1).

The Danish system was designed to respond to the needs of a range of stakeholders, from business start-ups to banks. With online access to a single land registry, businesses can transfer property on their own, with no need for intermediaries. They can also get information on any property. And to facilitate access to credit as well as information, the Danish financial sector created a central hub allowing banks and the land registry to share land registration data.

The United Kingdom is another European country that has made great improvements in property registration. One of the first European territories to have land registration, the United Kingdom had compiled enormous volume of records spanning two centuries. In 1997, the land registry began scanning these historical land records— 272 volumes containing a mix of handwritten and typed pages made from parchment, waxed linen or paper along with printed documents. In three years the total number of titles registered in the database had reached 15 million, while the total number of stored deeds, kept on 80 miles of shelving, was estimated at almost 100 million.

The next major step was the Land Registration Act of 2002, which introduced online registration for the transfer of property. The first internet service was launched in 2005, allowing any applicant to obtain information on any property by entering the identification data. Then it became possible to electronically update the land register in cases not affecting ownership. Finally, in 2010, it became possible to actually transfer property online using electronic signatures.

In January 2013, the British government of Prime Minister David Cameron gave itself 400 days to transform 25 major services—including land registration—by

Table 7.1 Time Required To Transfer Property, 2015

Country	Time (days)
Portugal	1
Lithuania	2
Netherlands	3
Denmark	4
Cyprus	9
Bulgaria	11
Spain	13
Sweden	14
Malta	15
Italy	16
Slovak Republic	16
Hungary	17
Latvia	17
Estonia	18
Romania	19
Greece	20
Austria	21
United Kingdom	21
Luxembourg	27
Czech Republic	31
Finland	32
Ireland	32
Poland	33
Germany	39
France	49
Slovenia	50
Belgium	56
Croatia	62

Source: World Bank (2015)

making them simpler, clearer and faster to use. Some 76 percent of substantive applications were submitted electronically in 2014, and today about 24 million titles are registered. Additional reductions in red tape are planned in the future. During the Queen's speech at the opening of Parliament in 2014, Queen Elizabeth

II announced a new infrastructure bill to "help make the United Kingdom the most attractive place to start, finance and grow a business"— by delivering full digital services by the land registry.[29]

MAKING LITIGATION POSSIBLE

A third area of rapidly improving public services for businesses is the speeding up of commercial litigation. In 2013, Portugal adopted a new code of civil procedure designed to reduce a court backlog, streamline court procedures, and speed up the resolution of commercial disputes. The same year, Spain made resolving insolvency easier by introducing new rules for out-of-court restructuring as well as provisions for prepackaged reorganizations, similar to the rules in the United States.

In 2015, Latvia adopted a new law consolidating provisions that regulate commercial arbitration. Previously, arbitration had been regulated by a few provisions scattered across different legislative instruments and therefore was rarely used. Latvia also adopted a comprehensive new law on business mediation. This law introduces incentives for parties to attempt mediation, including a partial refund of state fees if mediation is successfully completed. Having all substantial and procedural provisions regulating commercial arbitration or mediation in one source makes these mechanisms more accessible, especially for new businesses that do not have extensive experience in resolving legal disputes.

If European countries learn from each other's successful efforts in cutting red tape and combine their knowledge to create a business-friendly environment, the European Union can leap over both the United States (ranked 7th) and its top Asian competitors as a place to do business.

All European countries could make starting a business as easy as it is in Lithuania, with just two procedures and about half a percent of annual GDP per capita in administrative costs; and adopt Lithuania's property registration procedures— finished in two days and at trivial cost (table 7.2). European countries could also learn from Ireland's tax administration, Austria's customs operations and court procedures for enforcing commercial contracts; Denmark's administration of construction permits; and take on Finland's insolvency legislation and implement it in practice. European countries can also adopt Germany's procedures for new businesses or factories getting access to electricity and the United Kingdom's protections of investor rights.

By taking neighboring best practices in business regulation and spreading them across the European Union, politicians can greatly enhance Europe's competitiveness.

A PROPOSED GUIDE FOR REGULATORY REFORM

Several indices gauge the ease of the business environment globally. The most prominent among those are the World Bank's Doing Business rating, already mentioned in the previous section. The two others that are used often are the World Economic

Table 7.2 Best and Worst in Red Tape in Europe, 2015

Indicator	Best Country	Worst Country
Starting a Business	Lithuania (8)	Malta (132)
Licenses	Denmark (5)	Cyprus (145)
Electricity Hook-up	Germany (3)	Romania (133)
Property registration	Lithuania (2)	Greece (144)
Getting Credit	Romania (7)	Luxembourg (167)
Investor Protection	UK (4)	Luxembourg (132)
Paying Taxes	Ireland (6)	Italy (137)
Trading across Borders	Austria (1)	Cyprus (43)
Enforcing Contracts	Lithuania (3)	Cyprus (143)
Resolving Insolvency	Finland (1)	Lithuania (70)

Source: World Bank (2015)

Forum's Global Competitiveness Index, and the Index of Economic Freedom by the Heritage Foundation. All three include the 28 European Union economies in their annual rankings and all can be used by both national governments and the European Commission to guide their reforms on the ease of doing business.

The World Bank's Doing Business rating tracks regulations applied to companies operating in the largest business city of each economy. Its 11 dimensions cover starting a business, construction permits, getting electricity, registering property, getting credit, protecting investors, paying taxes, trading across borders, enforcing contracts, hiring and firing of workers, and closing a business. The data collection and analysis is based on rigorous academic research, published in top economics journals.[30] The sample spans 189 countries and starts in 2002.

The World Economic Forum's Global Competitiveness Index rates institutions, policies, and factors that determine a country's level of productivity. Among its indicators are measures of infrastructure development; goods, labor, and financial markets; and innovation. The analysis is based on qualitative surveys of large businesses. The sample spans 148 countries and starts in 2004.

The Index of Economic Freedom by the Heritage Foundation analyzes a country's commitment to rule of law, size of government, regulatory efficiency, and market openness. The index captures economic freedom through 10 dimensions, including the protection of property rights; corruption; business, labor, and monetary policy; trade; and finance. The sample spans 186 countries and starts in 1995.

These global rankings can be used to compare progress on cutting red tape among European economies, as well as with other countries. In the period 2009-2015 only two European economies—Germany and Poland—have improved their global standing across all three rankings.[31] Perhaps not coincidentally, these two European countries weathered the Eurozone crisis and their economies grew during this period. Three European economies (France, Hungary and Slovakia) slipped in all rankings during 2009-2015.

Using already-established global indicators to track reforms is convenient to measure the improvements made both by individual European countries, as well as due to European Union initiatives.

This analysis of national legislation on business activity is relevant also for rules that are imposed by Europe but implemented by the member states. Work carried out by the Stoiber committee has shown that 32 percent of the red tape felt by businesses in Europe are caused by the decisions of some countries that go beyond the requirements of EU legislation.[32] An evaluation of the EU public procurement rules showed that the typical duration of a procurement procedure from the dispatch of a contract notice to its award varied between 77 days in Latvia and 241 days in Malta. Different countries applied the same rule differently, which led to Latvia being three times as efficient as Malta. Constructing simple country-level indicators on public procurement, using a time-and-motion study, would pick up these inefficiencies.

Another example is the administration of taxes. A quarter of European countries mandate electronic invoicing and inter-company billing: all Nordic and Baltic countries, as well as the Netherlands and the Czech Republic. Due to the large number of bills sent from one company to another, and from businesses to governments, using the same rule across all of Europe would eliminate €18.8 billion a year in mailing and logistics costs to businesses. The European Commission adopted this idea for simplifying VAT invoicing requirements, and it took effect in 2013.[33] Its implementation in Bulgaria fell on the ministry of finance, and was one of the cases where the business community felt immediate benefit.[34] Since then, Bulgaria has gone further and has made compulsory all tax reporting by large businesses. This also saves processing costs in the tax administration, estimated at €30 million a year.

At present, Europe has zeroed in on cutting red tape, with the palpable progress primarily at the national level. European-wide initiatives have lacked actionable and objective indicators to evaluate progress. As a result, several initiatives have identified select areas for reducing administrative burdens, but they have not amounted to consistent efforts. Introducing rigorous methodology will make it easier for European politicians to evaluate the results of their attempts.

CONCLUSIONS: EUROPE CAN CUT MORE RED TAPE

Europe is pretty advanced in establishing relevant and non-intrusive state regulation. Denmark stands out as a leader in sensible state regulation, but the differences between EU countries are great and much more can be done. The Juncker Commission has made cutting red tape a priority, which is a laudable ambition. The first successful initiatives in this respect have significantly cut the flow of new EU regulations, and have attempted to simplify existing regulation, especially in areas, which businesses have identified as particularly burdensome.

What remains to be done is to base future regulatory reforms on time-and-motion studies of specific burdensome procedures, for example, in public procurement or obtaining a construction license. Such studies will make uniform the reform efforts at the national and European level, and ease the verification of reform progress. Various European countries have used similar methodologies in their independent regulatory agencies, for example ACTAL in the Netherlands.

European institutions can also introduce sunset clauses in regulatory proposals, for example with a fifteen-year expiration period. In this way, antiquated regulation will naturally fall out, in favor of simpler rules. Australia has the pioneer in regulatory reform by including "sunset" provisions in all new regulations starting from 1996, with the regulation automatically expiring after a certain period unless renewed by Parliament. Sweden has a "guillotine" approach for regulatory reform, in which hundreds of obsolete regulations are cancelled after the government periodically requires regulatory agencies to register all essential regulations.

For Europe to maintain and in some cases regain global competitiveness, cutting red tape should be a consistent year-after-year process. Eventually, reporting on progress may be institutionalized within a country scorecard similar to the European Semester, the annual exercise in fiscal discipline and structural reforms. Each European country can be benchmarked relative to its peers and its performance can be judged relative to objective indicators. This will remove the need to convene ad hoc working groups and committees, and will add transparency to the administrative simplification efforts. The great divergence between difference European countries shows, however, that most of the efforts have to be made at the national level.

The main take-away from this chapter is that Europe has all the knowledge and experience it needs to be the world's most hospitable place to do business. Individual European states have gone far in improving their administrative procedures and legal requirements for running businesses. All it takes is to put these efforts together and make progress uniform across the union.

8

Developing a Single Energy Market

"I want the energy that underpins our economy to be resilient, reliable, secure and increasingly renewable and sustainable. This is about Europe acting together, for the long term," says Commission President Jean-Claude Juncker.[1] In the second half of the 20th century energy played an outsized role in the European economy. Europe is highly dependent on imports of energy, importing 53 percent of the energy it consumes. In 2013, energy comprised no less than 24 percent of Europe's total imports,[2] costing no less than €400 billion.[3]

Therefore security of energy supplies is a major concern. Much of Europe's energy imports come from Russia. Some European countries—such as Finland, Estonia, Bulgaria, and Slovakia—depend nearly 100 percent on Russian gas supplies. Others, such as Greece and the Czech Republic, receive three-quarters of their gas supplies from Russia. The dependence on Russian energy has been growing in Western Europe as well. The Nord Stream pipeline, constructed in 2011–12, brings gas from Russia to Germany and constitutes about 30 percent of Germany's gas supplies. Gas from Nord Stream also reaches France and the Netherlands.[4]

Russian energy exports to Europe are often used as instruments of foreign policy. One example is the now cancelled South Stream pipeline, a project that aimed to bring Russian gas to Central Europe and Italy, bypassing Ukraine. This project would increase the share of Russian gas supplies to Austria and Italy considerably. As a first step, Russia undermined the rival pipeline project Nabucco by buying Turkmen gas and redirecting it to Russian pipelines. As a second step, in 2014 Russia's Gazprom signed bilateral contracts with governments and companies alongside the route of the pipeline and started construction.

Another issue is to enhance efficiency through well-functioning markets. Energy policy has all along been central for the evolution of the European Union. Its precursor was the European Coal and Steel Community, whose treaty was ratified in 1952. It aimed at "the establishment of a common market" for coal and steel between the six founding members,[5] to achieve "economic expansion, growth of employment and a rising standard of living" (Article 2) as well as "orderly supply," "equal access," and the "lowest prices" (Article 3).[6]

The EU has successfully maintained unified markets for coal and oil, but the markets for electricity and natural gas remain fragmented and stymied. The central question today is whether the European Commission will succeed in its long-standing ambition to create well-functioning markets for these two commodities. The Commission and consumer interests form one side in this battle. Large national energy companies that prefer the old oligopolistic arrangements form the opposing side, while national governments are torn between these forces.

Other energy issues are energy saving, control of pollution and the development of new sources of energy. The current European Commission has made the formation of an energy union its prime goal. It tries to combine all these five laudable objectives. The fundamental step is to secure supplies in all types of energy (oil, gas, electricity). Another aim is an integrated and competitive energy market, a third is energy efficiency, a fourth is reducing carbon emissions and the fifth is innovation in the European energy sector.[7]

Section one presents the current state of the European energy market, while section two contrasts the American energy revolution with European passivity. Section three lays out the EU's attempt at developing a single energy market, through adopting the third energy package in 2009. Section four discusses the current proposed European energy union. Section five adds the theme of energy saving and pollution control. Section six illuminates a major challenge to the energy union, the proposed gas pipeline Nord Stream 2. Section seven concludes.

THE EUROPEAN ENERGY MARKET TODAY

Europe's energy production is falling steadily because old conventional sources of energy have been exhausted, while many new energy technologies are not cherished. From 2003 to 2013, the EU's production of primary energy fell by 15 percent, but its consumption contracted almost as much by 12 percent.[8]

A mismatch prevails between the kinds of energy Europe produces and what it consumes. Of the primary energy the European Union produces nuclear energy accounts for 29 percent, coal for 20 percent, natural gas for 17 percent, and biomass and waste for 15 percent. Crude oil accounts for only 9 percent,[9] but for 37 percent of the EU's primary energy consumption, natural gas for 23 percent, coal 17 percent, nuclear energy provided 12 percent, hydropower 5 percent, and renewables 7 percent.[10]

The energy mix differs substantially between countries. Some countries depend greatly on nuclear energy, accounting for most of the electricity needs of France, Belgium and Sweden and about one-third in the Bulgaria and the Czech Republic, while many countries have no nuclear energy. By contrast, Poland relies primarily on coal, providing over half of its electricity needs and Italy depends 90 percent on oil and natural gas. Denmark is the leader in renewable energy, obtaining one-fifth of its electricity from wind energy.

In recent decades, Europe's imports of oil have not caused any particular problems, while imports of natural gas have been problematic because it has largely been provided by just four countries (Russia, Norway, Algeria and Qatar), and until recently entirely through pipelines. Russia's Gazprom supplied 39 percent of EU natural gas imports in 2013, while Norway's Statoil came second with 30 percent.

Liquefied natural gas (LNG) has provided a stable share of about one-tenth since 2010, with Qatar being the main supplier.[11] Until LNG imports started, Europe did not have any real market for natural gas, which was reflected in great discrepancy in prices across European countries. For example, household prices in Portugal and Sweden and three times higher than in Hungary and Romania, and gas prices for industry in Finland and twice as high as in Belgium.

Supply security is a major concern, because Europe has experienced repeated cuts in its energy imports. In 1973, the Organization of Arab Petroleum Exporting Countries (OAPEC) reduced oil supplies to the United Kingdom and the Netherlands, Europe's main oil hub and oil prices rose sharply.[12] In January 2006 and 2009, Russia's Gazprom cut its gas transit through Ukraine hurting 16 European countries. Several of these countries, for example Bulgaria, had no alternative supplies, storage or interconnectors.[13]

Another European worry is the high cost of its energy. The European Commission has noted: "Wholesale electricity prices in Europe are 30 percent higher, and wholesale gas prices over 100 percent higher than in the US."[14] Natural gas currently costs three times as much in Europe as in the US. Even so, these numbers do not include the high European energy taxes. Gas-intensive European industry has been relocating factories to North America. Among those most affected are industries such as steel and chemicals, because they use natural gas as a raw material and power source.[15]

The energy sector is characterized by long cycles, as one source of fuel expands at the cost of another. Today, renewable sources of energy, such as solar and wind energy, are slowly taking over from carbon fuels. Repeatedly, in the 1880s, after World War I, after World War II, and at the end of the 1970s, people feared that the world would run out of oil.[16] But then one or two decades of low energy prices ensued, prompting demands for energy efficiency and innovation, often best accomplished by small, new private enterprises.

The origin of Europe's inefficient production and trade of energy is that most European countries opted for nationalization of the sector after World War II. They consolidated their fragmented energy companies into national champions with near monopoly of one kind of energy. Nationalization bred British Coal and British Gas in the United Kingdom, Gaz de France, Electricité de France, and Total for oil in France, ENEL for electricity and ENI for oil and gas in Italy. The oil market, however, remained dominated by the "Seven Sisters," large private oil majors like Exxon, Gulf Oil, Chevron, Mobil, Texaco, British Petroleum and Royal Dutch Shell, which managed to fend off most threats of nationalization.[17] The big national energy companies comprise a major lobbying force in the sector today.

Electrical grids and pipelines were considered natural monopolies in Europe, and standard price theory teaches that natural monopolies should be regulated to preclude high monopolistic prices. Given far-reaching regulations, state ownership of electricity companies appeared natural or even desirable.

As in so many spheres, the election of Margaret Thatcher as Britain's Prime Minister in 1979 brought about a change. She questioned state monopolies, calling for their breakup and privatization. She identified the Central Electricity Generating Board as a major hub of inefficiency and costly conflicts with its trade unions. Her government divided power generation into three different competing companies and allowed independent power companies to compete in the open market.[18]

Gradually, one European country after the other has adopted parts of the new British model. In Germany, deregulation of the electricity market took place in 1998. The country's largest power conglomerates, RWE and E.ON, were forced to give up their assets in the former German Democratic Republic to prevent them from dominating the German power market. As a result, other companies entered the power market, for example Sweden's Vattenfall, which now produces 13 percent of Germany's electricity.

Most countries have carried out some privatizations in the energy sector, but usually merely minority shares of their national companies. In many European countries, one single national champion continues to dominate, notably in France and Italy, while a few major companies compete in Germany and Scandinavia. Eastern Europe has taken the British example most whole-heartedly, and in many countries the distribution network is fully private, while generation is mostly in private hands.

THE ENERGY REVOLUTION IN THE LAST DECADE

In the 2000s, the American energy industry went through a rapid change, as several new technologies came to fore. After years of decline, US oil production rose by 72 percent from 2008 to 2014, once again making the US the biggest producer of liquid fuels in the world matching Saudi Arabia and Russia. In parallel, US production of natural gas rose by 28 percent, rendering the country self-sufficient in natural gas.[19] The abundance of gas drove down domestic US natural gas prices to a fraction of their previous level.

The new technologies were an outgrowth of the new information technology. Quick processing of vast amounts of data enhanced the probability of successful geophysical exploration. Horizontal drilling expanded the commercially viable reserves of existing findings.[20] Hydraulic fracking took off, opening up large volumes of nonconventional oil and gas. Drilling could go deeper than before, not least off shore. Suddenly, the potential global reserves of natural gas increased 3-5 times.

Meanwhile, renewable forms of energy developed and their production costs fell rapidly, rendering solar and wind energy commercially competitive. Small and medium-sized new companies have propelled novel technologies. They have remodeled the energy sector, leading to the rise of a variety of trading and service energy firms. Small startups in California and China spearheaded solar energy. Start-up US companies pioneered fracking. The Danish company Vestas became the global leader in wind energy. Qatar in the Persian Gulf spearheaded the production of liquefied natural gas (LNG).

Europe, by contrast, has not changed in its energy policy much since the Eurozone crisis hit in 2008. The shale gas and tight oil revolution passed Europe by. By 2016, no European country has started producing shale gas, while several countries, such as France, Bulgaria and the Czech Republic, have prohibited its production.

Before the global financial crisis, Germany and Spain had been the world leaders in solar energy because of heavily-subsidized "green tariffs," but the crisis rendered these subsidies unaffordable.[21] Instead the United States and China rose as the new leaders in solar energy. In wind energy, Denmark and its star company Vestas were the global leaders in the first decade of the 21st century, but for a few years wind energy as such fell behind and did not become competitive, with Vestas almost going bankrupt.[22]

Nuclear energy looked set to expand in Europe once again as a clean technology, but in March 2011 a major meltdown occurred in the Fukushima nuclear power station in Japan. Two months later, Germany's Chancellor Angela Merkel declared that Germany would close all its many nuclear plants by 2022.[23] Having to bear the cost of tens of billions of euro from such closures, Germany's utilities found their market capitalization halved and have since had to divest other generation capacity to pay off their debts.

Only the LNG revolution has had a great and positive impact also on Europe, providing Europe with a lucrative alternative source of natural gas. LNG has transformed natural gas into a commodity and rendered Europe less dependent on piped gas from Gazprom. The supply of LNG grew quickly, mostly from Qatar, to roughly one-tenth of Europe's natural gas imports, but then leveled off. Still, LNG has made the market more competitive, and LNG prices cap the prices of piped gas in Europe. Even so these prices remain three times higher than the domestic American natural gas prices because of the high costs of liquefaction, transportation and regasification.

THE THIRD EU ENERGY PACKAGE OF 2009: AN ATTEMPT AT MARKETIZATION

European energy market is evolving in a protracted battle. The big electricity and gas companies form a conservative alliance, defending their vertical integration and national or regional monopolies. Their opponents are consumers and European institutions, favoring open, competitive markets to the benefit of economic efficiency. The positions of European governments vary, but the big energy companies tend to win the support of their governments.

The European Commission has led the charge to form a common energy market in Europe. From 1996 until 2009, the EU adopted three different "energy packages" to develop gas and electricity markets.[24] The idea was to transform these monopolistic networks into open markets. The vertically integrated companies that produced, transported, stored and distributed gas or electricity were supposed to be forced to separate these activities.

The first EU energy package of 1996 laid the ground for a competitive internal energy market. Pricing was supposed to become objective, transparent and non-discriminatory, but still regulated nationally. In 2003, a second similar energy package was adopted. It went further, setting deadlines for the liberalization of electricity and gas markets by July 2004 for industrial customers and July 2007 for households. It also mandated the establishment of independent regulatory authorities and insisted on non-discriminatory third party access to transmission and distribution. But none of these two packages had significant impact.

In 2007, the European Commission responded by proposing a third energy package, which was much more far-reaching in its demands for unbundling energy companies and opening markets. Its adoption was prompted by Russia's cut of gas supplies to 16 European countries for two weeks in January 2009. In July 2009, the European Parliament and the Council of the European Union adopted this package, to be implemented by January 2015.

The third energy package made the unbundling of supply and production from networks compulsory, offering three alternative models, between which EU member countries could choose. The first most rigorous model called for full ownership unbundling, separating generation and transmission into companies with different owners. The second model allowed energy companies to retain their ownership of transmission networks, but they had to transfer their operation to an independent system operator. A third model offered a middle way, permitting energy companies to maintain ownership of their transmission networks, but these independent transmission operators had to be legally independent joint stock companies. These rules would also apply also to foreign companies operating in EU countries, notably Gazprom, the dominant gas supplier that owned the gas pipelines in several European countries.

To safeguard a well-functioning internal energy market with an effective regulatory framework, the EU established an Agency for the Cooperation of Energy Regulators to monitor and coordinate energy regulation in the internal energy market.[25] Energy was to flow freely, unhindered by territorial restrictions. The regulators, however, remained national.

The third energy package has instigated the construction of LNG facilities, multiple interconnectors of gas pipelines and large storage facilities. One effect is that Gazprom has divested its gas pipelines in all the three Baltic states. Some EU governments are yet to implement the third energy package, ranging from Bulgaria to France.

Unlike the two previous energy packages, the third energy package has had real impact. A shortcoming, however, is that it avoided the issue of ownership of energy companies, reflecting the resistance of big state companies. The ownership of subsoil assets and the right to utilize natural resources are left to national legislation. Innovation and technical development are ignored.

THE EUROPEAN ENERGY UNION
OF 2015: ANOTHER ATTEMPT AT MARKETIZATION

In February 2015, the European Commission took a step further and proposed an energy union. European Commission President Jean-Claude Juncker declared that the free movement of energy would become a fifth freedom of the EU, in addition to the free movement of goods, services, people and capital.

The European Commission called for a strategy of five related goals, namely energy security, market integration, energy efficiency, decarbonization, and research, innovation and competitiveness.[26] First of all, the energy union called for "strict enforcement of existing energy and related legislation."[27] The Commission's major concern was: "Today, the European Union has energy rules set at the European level, but in practice it has 28 national regulatory frameworks. This cannot continue. An integrated energy market is needed to create more competition, lead to greater market efficiency through better use of energy generation facilities across the EU and to produce affordable prices for consumers."[28] In addition, wasteful energy subsidies had to be cut.

President Juncker also stated that "6 EU Member States are dependent on one single external supplier for all their gas imports."[29] These countries were Bulgaria, Estonia, Finland, Latvia, Lithuania, and Slovakia, whose sole supplier was Russia, and all but Finland had suffered multiple politically motivated supply cuts. The fragmentation of the electricity market was even worse: "12 Member States do not meet the EU's minimum interconnection target—that at least 10 percent of installed electricity production capacity be able to 'cross borders'."[30] The EU introduced a normative target: "A specific minimum interconnection target has been set for electricity at 10 percent of installed electricity production capacity of the Member States, which should be achieved by 2020."[31]

If achieved as planned, the energy union may create an all-European market with market-oriented prices for all kinds of energy. The EU can assist with financing for the development of the necessary infrastructure with links, interconnectors and storage, allowing all members security of supply. The construction of LNG facilities in the Baltics and the Balkans is an important complement. One of the first energy projects for funding under the Juncker Plan is the completion of an underground power line between France and Spain that doubles their interconnection capacity to 2.8GW.

Three omissions in the energy union leave room for future work: addressing the production of conventional energy, the ownership of energy assets, and the current hi-tech revolution in renewable energy. The energy union documents acknowledge the need for a "new strategy for Research and Innovation" if "Europe's Energy Union is to be the world number one in renewable energies," but it does not offer any solution. We discuss how Europe can respond to the US hi-tech challenge in Chapter 9.

ENERGY SAVING AND POLLUTION CONTROL

In the late 1970s, the skyrocketing costs of oil imports turned energy saving into a major topic. Many feared the world was running out of energy resources, prompting calls for sustainable development. In the 1990s, environmental concerns continued to grow but they changed nature. The new worry was climate change. The UN climate conference in Kyoto in December 1997 adopted the so-called Kyoto protocol. Eventually 192 countries joined the Kyoto Protocol, committing themselves to reduce their emissions of carbon dioxide and other greenhouse gases.[32] The EU pledged to reduce its average emission of greenhouse gases in 2008-12 by 8 percent below their level of 1990.[33]

The EU has been highly successful in cutting its greenhouse gas emissions. Between 1990 and 2013, these emissions declined by 19 percent, although the EU GDP grew by 45 percent.[34] In Kyoto, the EU had committed to cut its greenhouse gas emission by 20 percent by 2020 from the 1990 level. The novelty was "cap and trade," large-scale international trading of pollution permits. Governments became entitled to sell tradable permits to the right to generate a given quantity of pollution. High polluters who exceeded their ceiling would have to buy more permits, while low polluters would receive extra revenue from selling their surplus permits. The European Emission Trading System covers more than 11,000 power stations, industrial plants and airlines in 31 countries, but only 45 percent of the EU's greenhouse gas emissions.[35]

The alternative to emissions trading is carbon taxation, that is, a tax that is levied on energy sources in relation to their carbon content. About 40 countries have introduced carbon taxes. They include several EU countries, notably, Denmark, Finland, Germany, Ireland, Italy, the Netherlands, Norway, Slovenia, Sweden, Switzerland, and the United Kingdom.[36] Economists tend to prefer a carbon tax over emission permit trade because a carbon tax is more transparent and predictable for both enterprises and the tax authorities, and transaction costs are lower. The payment of a carbon tax is more difficult to escape. The Kyoto Protocol lapsed in 2012 and the prices of the emission permits have fluctuated and collapsed to a very low level, rendering pollution financially advantageous to enterprises. As early as 1995, energy taxes accounted for 2.5 percent of GDP in Europe. In 2015, energy taxes accounted for 2.3 percent of Europe's GDP.[37]

In December 2015, the United Nations held the 21st session on its Framework Convention of Climate Change in Paris. The aim was to adopt a new agreement on the reduction of emission of greenhouse gases to replace the Kyoto Protocol. The Paris Agreement was adopted with consensus, but its commitments were voluntary, neither requiring ratification nor imposing legal requirements. Each country presented its own targets. The European Commission's long-standing proposal was that the EU would set itself a target of reducing emissions to 40 percent below 1990 levels by 2030.[38] The Paris Agreement takes no stand on cap-and-trade versus carbon tax or regulation.[39]

Regardless of what other countries do, the EU policy on reduction of the emission of greenhouse gases is clear and embraced by a broad European consensus. The question is what the best means is to achieve the desired goals. Given the shortcomings of the current Emissions Trading System with limited coverage and low and unpredictable prices of emission permits, it seems desirable to switch to a carbon tax, which could be national but harmonized over the EU in the same way as the value-added tax has been.

NORD STREAM 2: A CHALLENGE TO EUROPE'S SINGLE MARKET

Soon after President Juncker's announcement on the energy union, Gazprom together with the five large European corporations BASF, E.ON, ENGIE, OMV and Royal Dutch Shell offered a direct challenge to the European Commission's vision for Europe. In June 2015, these corporations announced their intention to build a new large gas pipeline to Europe, Nord Stream 2 from Russia to Germany through the Baltic Sea, and in September 2015 they signed a memorandum of understanding to do so.[40]

"In my perspective, Nord Stream does not help diversification, nor would it reduce Europe's energy dependence," says European Council President Donald Tusk. He notes that the proposed pipeline would heighten instability in Europe by cutting the gas transit fees that add €2 billion a year to Ukraine's national budget.[41]

Nord Stream 2 appears a direct threat to Europe's energy union. To begin with, Europe is saturated with gas, whose demand falls steadily, as Europe saves energy. From 2004 to 2014, consumption of natural gas in the European Union fell by 21 percent.[42] Norwegian Statoil alone has been able to replace the falling production in the Netherlands and the United Kingdom.

Second, only about half of the Gazprom's pipeline capacity for transit to Europe is utilized. That is also true of the project's predecessor Nord Stream 1. Why build more when a surplus already exists? The likely explanation is that joint corporate interests in Russia and Germany aspire to monopolize Russian gas transit and eliminate transit through Ukraine. Matteo Renzi, Italy's prime minister, together with the heads of all Eastern European countries but Bulgaria, warns of losing ground towards the energy union. In a sign of how important the issue has become in Europe, Angela Merkel, Germany's chancellor, has distanced her government from the issue, arguing: "I have made clear, along with others, that this is first of all an economic project. There are private investors for this project."[43]

Third, the energy union aims at the diversification of transportation routes and supplies, while Nord Stream 2 would concentrate 90 percent of Russia's current gas supplies to Europe to one pipeline. Energy Commissioner Arias Cañete has concluded that Nord Stream 2 would "increase Europe's dependence on one supplier" and "increase Europe's dependence on one route."[44]

Fourth, the aim of the EU third energy package is the unbundling of transportation and supply to create an European market for all kinds of energy so that "consumers in one Member State should be able to make informed choices and buy their energy freely and simply from a company in another Member State."[45] However Nord Stream 2 will be composed legally, its aim is to give several large corporations control of the gas market at the heart of Europe. This will hurt European consumers with higher prices, worse service and less supply security.

Fifth, Gazprom is no ordinary corporation. In Eastern Europe, it has been used as a tool for Russia's geopolitical goals, cutting supplies or raising prices whenever the Kremlin objects to a government. Its aim with Nord Stream 2 is to ensure closer cooperation between Germany and Russia and weaken the EU's energy union. This is why nine countries, led by Poland and Slovakia, are petitioning to block the pipeline due to their belief that the EU's most powerful member state Germany has put its own economic needs ahead of their energy security. "Nord Stream 2 would be, above all, detrimental in geopolitical terms, for the purpose of exerting more political pressure and applying blackmail on the EU, its eastern member states and its eastern neighbors," said Jacek Saryusz-Wolski, a Polish member of the European Parliament.[46]

Nord Stream 1, inaugurated in 2011, met similar strong opposition from Eastern Europe, which saw it as a way for the Kremlin to control EU gas supply. Then Polish Foreign Minister Radosław Sikorski compared it to the 1939 Molotov-Ribbentrop Pact, through which Nazi Germany and the Soviet Union agreed to divide Poland between them. It was eventually pushed through with the strong support of former German chancellor Gerhard Schröder, who signed the deal to build the pipe in his last few days in office. Mr Schröder was subsequently appointed chairman of the board of the company that runs Nord Stream.[47]

Finally, Gazprom's recent deals have been riddled with reports of alleged corruption.[48] Some of its managers have faced corruption charges in Switzerland in 2014.[49] A 2015 report by Russia's watchdog Accounting Chamber found that 21 percent of the revenues on sales of natural gas exported by state companies—primarily Gazprom—were deposited to offshore accounts. In 2014 alone, the estimated diversion was close to $100 billion.[50]

With all these considerations, the European Commission has taken a firm stand against Nord Stream's expansion. Commission Vice President Maros Sefcovic has warned that "the Nord Stream 2 project . . . may mean complete cutoffs of supplies of gas from Russia to Europe via Ukraine and Slovakia."[51] Energy Commissioner Arias Cañete concluded that "the Nord Stream 2 project cannot ever become a project of common [EU] interest."[52]

After the European Council meeting on December 18, 2015, President Donald Tusk stated with reference to Nord Stream 2: "What we have agreed is that any new infrastructure should be fully in line with Energy Union objectives, such as reduction of energy dependence and diversification of suppliers, sources and routes. Not to mention the obvious obligation that all projects have to comply with all EU laws, including the third Energy Package."[53]

TOWARDS ENERGY SECURITY AND EFFICIENCY

The evolution of the European single market for energy has proceeded slowly, because the European Commission has encountered significant resistance from several large member states and from the old national energy champions. The Juncker Commission has taken important steps to gain momentum towards achieving the energy union. With the third energy package of 2009 and the energy union of 2015 the European Commission has insisted on open markets with consumer choice and open transmission networks. This aim requires adequate infrastructure to allow energy to be transported in any direction the market demands. The challenge of the EU is to prove itself sufficiently strong to attain these goals.

So far, progress towards the stated common goals has not penetrated energy policy. Many European politicians want to support a particular kind of energy, offering state subsidies and preferential tariffs or prohibitions on arbitrary grounds. The task of European governments is to ascertain energy security through multiple sources of competitive supply. Beyond basic demands for energy security, governments may allow consumers to choose after having included all costs, including external costs for pollution.

Since the 1980s, Europe has been the world leader in energy savings and pollution control through high energy taxes and regulation. Europe's new commitments in the Paris Agreement of December 2015 are welcome, though the best way of achieving them appears to be through national carbon taxes rather than through pollution permit trade.

Over time, Europe needs to abandon its tolerance of state-owned energy companies. They should be privatized as in Britain, which stands out as the most liberalized and diversified and also successful energy market with low prices and secure supplies.

European states should open the access to natural resources to private entrepreneurs. In the US natural resources are predominantly privately owned, and whoever happens to own the land above owns the resources underneath. Therefore, landowners are happy to support oil or gas production on their land, since they stand to benefit. In Europe, by contrast, the state owns all resources under ground, depriving private landowners of the incentive to promote energy production. Resource rents can be properly taxed, which remains a national issue.

Most energy innovation in the world appears to be taking place in the US, leaving Europe behind, as Europeans tend to treat the energy sector as the old economy, while much of it is a hi-tech industry in the US. The absence of shale gas development is only one example. Opponents of shale gas development have utilized the restrictive nature of European politics to achieve the prohibition of shale gas development in several countries. Although Poland allowed exploration for shale gas, it imposed significant regulation and taxation. Poland, which was second only to Russia with 148 trillion cubic feet of initially estimated shale gas reserves, has seen Exxon Mobil, France's Total, Chevron and Marathon Oil back away from exploration since energy prices started falling.[54]

The opening of the European energy markets is going at the same time as further opening of the US energy sector. At the end of 2015, President Obama allowed for the first time for forty years exports of crude oil. American exports of LNG have also undergone a gradual liberalization. Both facilitate the evolution of the European energy market and lower the prices of European energy imports. The conclusion of the Transatlantic Trade and Investment Partnership could provide a further additional impetus for the creation of a single energy market in Europe.

9

Catching-Up in Innovation

Until World War I Europe was as innovative and entrepreneurial as the United States, but the two world wars and the interwar period were devastating in many ways. The cost in human life and material destruction was enormous. The wars expanded the role of the state in a harmful fashion, leading to far-reaching nationalization, wartime regulation of prices and markets, and very high marginal taxes. Europe still has to reduce the size of the state. Higher education suffered from totalitarian ideologies. Until 1933, about one-third of the Nobel Prize winners in sciences were Germans, while after 1945 a corresponding share were Americans, who were often European émigrés.

This chapter aims to explore what went wrong and how Europe can catch up. Section one reviews how innovative Europe used to be, and has actually continued to be. Section two surveys measures of Europe having fallen behind in innovation. Then follows six sections on what needs to be cured: a single market for hi-tech, venture capital, less rigid laws, better university education, more effective business research and development.

EUROPE USED TO BE INNOVATIVE

When Britain's industrial revolution spread to Europe after 1848, new business ventures blossomed. Successful start-ups from this period include ThyssenKrupp, a German steel group, L'Oréal, a French beauty empire, the Møller-Maersk Group, a Danish shipping giant, and Škoda, a Czech bicycles and later car producer. In fashion, the Louis Vuitton house was founded in 1854 in Paris. Also in the 1850s, Abraham Ganz established an iron foundry in Buda, Hungary's capital. Consequently, the Ganz factory started building steam-locomotives, pumps and the railway carriages as the main products. Its innovative engineers built the first electric railway.

This entrepreneurial fervor lasted well into the 1930s. In 1910, Ermenegildo Zegna founded an Italian luxury fashion house for men's clothing and accessories in Trivero, Italy. Within two decades, it became the largest menswear brand in the world. Coco Chanel first developed her famous fragrance in 1921. During the 1920s and 1930s Parfums Chanel thrived. In Italy, Guccio Gucci established his business in the early 1920s. As an immigrant in Paris and then London, Gucci made a living working in luxurious hotels. Inspired by the elegance he witnessed in the Savoy

Hotel in London, on his return to Italy he decided to merge this style of living with the exclusive skills of his native Tuscan artisans.[1] The LEGO Group, maker of the "toy of the 20th century," was founded in 1932 by Ole Kirk Kristians in the village of Billund, Denmark.

Innovation was not limited to the business community. Research at European universities brought about the development of whole new sectors. In Prague, Jaroslav Heyrovský discovered a method for analyzing small quantities of substances, and since 1924 it has successfully been applied in creating solutions containing multiple compounds in the food, construction, and chemical industries. The Nobel Prize in Chemistry 1959 was awarded to Heyrovsky for his discovery and development of the polarographic methods of analysis. In London, Alexander Fleming, a professor at St Mary's Hospital Medical School, discovered in 1928 that certain mold can killed other bacteria. Fleming and his collaborators isolated the bacterium-killing substance produced by the mold: penicillin. For his innovation Professor Fleming was awarded the 1945 Nobel Prize for Medicine.

But after World War II, Europe did not fully regain its innovation energy. The devastation made Europeans risk-averse. The large European market that had been closely linked before World War was fragmented by trade barriers and restrictions to financial flows. Many top researchers had moved to the United States to escape persecution.

Nowadays Europe has to play catch-up in many hi-tech fields with America and parts of Asia. According to *Forbes*, only eleven of the world's most-innovative 100 tech companies in 2015 were based in Europe.[2] Reuters assesses that only 17 of the top-100 global innovators in any industry are European companies.[3] The Massachusetts Institute of Technology considers that only 6 of the world's 50 smartest companies are European.[4]

European companies are global leaders in some technology sectors, for example, aerospace, car manufacturing, pharmaceuticals, chemicals and fashion, and they dominate the emerging field of biotechnology because of the continent's lead in biofuel. The German electrical grid sources 28 percent of its power from renewables, twice as much as the United States. Some established companies continue to innovate and adopt new technologies—Philips (the Netherlands) with LED lighting and ThyssenKrupp (Germany) with magnetic elevators, H&M (Sweden) with affordable fashion designs, and Generali (Italy) by using fitness data to more precisely calculate insurance rates for customers. Some start-ups, such as Shazam (UK), which allows instant music and movie discovery, or Spotify (Sweden), which allows music streaming, have redefined their sectors.

Fashion has become an acknowledged European success, with Italian fashion houses like Versace, established in 1972, Armani in 1975, and Dolce & Gabbana in 1985. Spanish Zara founded in 1975 has been described as "the most innovative and devastating clothing retailer in the world,"[5] dominating the apparel and shoe sectors. The European fashion industry harbors 800,000 companies employing 4.8 million people with sales of €560 billion in 2015. Fashion exports account for

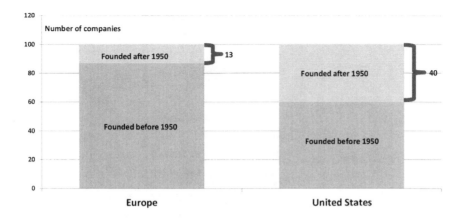

Figure 9.1 Age Structure of Largest Companies in Europe and the US, 2014
Note: The Financial Times 500 ranks companies by their market capitalisation. In the graph, the 100 largest European as well as U.S.companies are included.
Source: Financial Times 500, http://www.ft.com/intl/cms/s/0/988051be-fdee-11e3-bd0e-00144feab7de.html#axzz3gd4tLq3H

10.2 percent of overall EU exports. Europe's fashion industry accounts for three-quarters of all global brands, more than in any other industry.

European companies tend to be comparatively old. Among the largest 100 companies in Europe and the US, respectively, only 13 of the European companies had been founded after 1950 to compare with 40 of the American ones (figure 9.1).

HOW EUROPE IS LAGGING BEHIND

At present European companies trail their competitors in innovation in many ways. The American and Asian superior performance in innovation is evident in patent registration (figure 9.2). In 2014, filings from the US, Japan and China accounted for 53 percent of the 274,000 new patents in Europe, according to the European Patent Office (EPO). China climbed most in the rankings, with an 18 percent year-on-year increase in patent filings. The telecoms company Huawei reflects Chinese companies' attempt to catch up: it filed 49 percent more patents than in 2013, making it the fifth most active applicant.

Only one European company made it into the top five for patents: Philips. Other European companies with numerous patents include Siemens, BASF, Bosch and Ericsson. Filings from Germany accounted for 11 percent of total filings with the European Patent Office, followed by France (5 percent), the Netherlands (3 percent), the UK, Sweden and Italy (2 percent each).

The most relevant measure of innovation might be patent applications to the World Intellectual Property Organization (WIPO) by country (figure 9.3). The US ranks high above the European average, but six European countries rank above the US, namely Luxembourg, Sweden, Finland, Germany, Denmark, and the

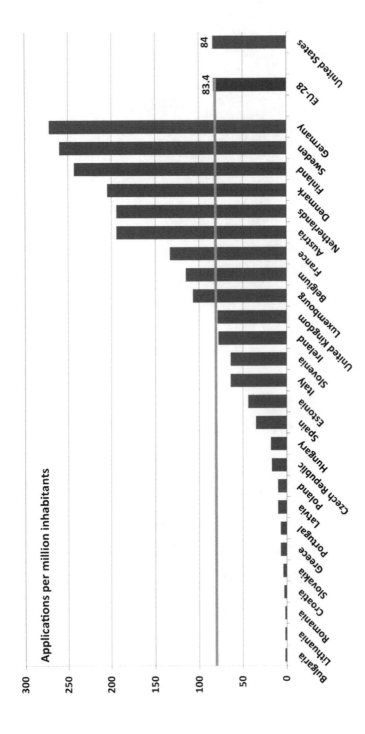

Figure 9.2 Global Patent Applications

Note: No data for Cyprus and Malta

Source: Eurostat, Patent statistics, http://ec.europa.eu/eurostat/statistics-explained/index.php/Patent_statistics

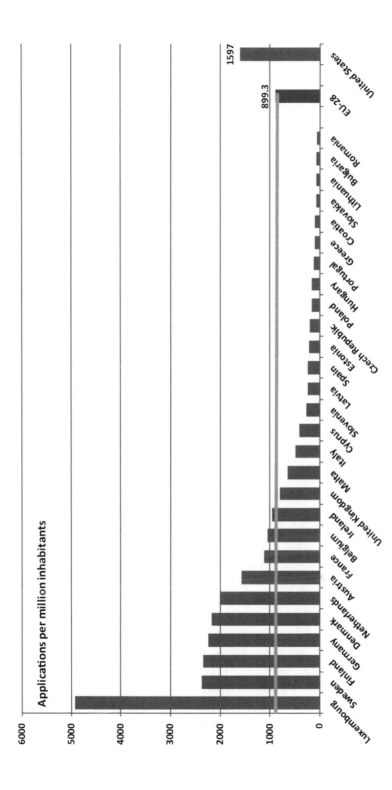

Figure 9.3 Patent applications to the WIPO, 2013

Source: WIPO database for patent data, http://ipstats.wipo.int/ipstatv2/index.htm?tab=patent and Eurostat for population, http://ec.europa.eu/eurostat/web/population-demography-migration-projections/population-data/database

Netherlands. This suggests that Europe has a great potential for catch-up if it learns from its best performers.

The European Commission has such an aspiration, to raise the share of high-tech manufacturing GDP from 15.6 percent to 20 percent by 2020.[6] What changes are needed to catch up with the United States and Asia? To answer this question the reasons for falling behind need to be understood first.

A general problem is the high taxation of entrepreneurship that is general and we have discussed it at length in Chapter 3. On specific distortion is that owners of start-ups are keen to sell their creations early on because they cannot get much money in the form of income, only as capital gain when they sell. This helps old companies and family foundations with cheap funding.

One reason is small market size and national regulations. For an upstart software company Europe is still 28 separate markets. A new social media site in Sweden has just 10 million potential users unless it translates its content to other languages. Due to differences in culture across European countries, it would need a new interface, a different marketing strategy, and probably other advertisers to appeal to a larger European customer base. That would mean dealing with new regulations and multiple tax schemes.

A second reason is the shortage of venture finance in Europe. Silicon Valley and Route 128 near Boston combine a deep talent pool of researchers with easy access to start-up and venture financing. This combination attracts entrepreneurs in new tech businesses, but also companies that provide them with management consulting or infrastructure support. Asian high-tech hubs, such as Singapore, Taiwan, and Bangalore, also have financial and human capital. Israel offers similar advantages in its high-tech incubators near Haifa and Tel Aviv.

In contrast, Europe's financial services are not directed towards start-ups. European venture capital fund-raising was $4 billion in 2014, only about one-tenth of that in the United States.[7] New European regulations have further narrowed the base of potential investors. The European investment hubs are not co-located with financial companies.[8] Start-ups may find early-stage financial backing of up to $500,000, and later-stage support of more than $10 million, thanks to various EU-wide or national government schemes, but Europe has not found a happy way of channeling state money into innovations. Europe's tech companies regularly struggle to land investment needed to bridge the early and mature stages.

A third obstacle to innovation is rigid legislation. In countries, such as France and Germany, hiring and firing employees can be complicated, making rapid expansion difficult and risky. The problem is most pronounced in the tech sector, with its high job mobility and fast-growing competitors. This makes it difficult to attract entrepreneurs and highly-skilled professionals from outside the European Union. It also discourages venture capitalists from investing in European countries with burdensome labor regulation.[9] Rigidities in tax and insolvency regulation further frustrate would-be entrepreneurs.

A fourth problem is that the best university education in Europe lags behind that in the United States and parts of Asia. There are two leading rankings of global

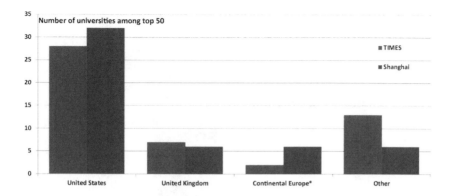

Figure 9.4 Top-ranking universities, 2014

Note: the Shanghai ranking uses four variables with different weights: quality of education (weight 10%), quality of faculty (weight 40%), research output (40%) and per capita performance (10%). The Times ranking uses five categories of variables: industry income (2.5%), international diversity (5%), teaching (30.5%), research (30%) and citation impact (32.5%).

Source: Times: https://www.timeshighereducation.co.uk/world-university-rankings/2015/world-ranking#/; Shanghai: http://www.universityrankings.ch/results/Shanghai/2014?ranking=Shanghai&year=2014&region=&q=&s=50

universities, the Shanghai ranking and the *Times Higher Education Supplement* ranking. They differ somewhat in methodology. The Shanghai list focuses on the quality of faculty and research output, whereas the Times list awards roughly equal weight to teaching, research and citations. Averaging of the two lists, 30 of the 50 top universities are located in the US, 6-7 in the United Kingdom, but only 4 in other EU states (Figure 9.4).[10]

No continental EU university breaks into the top-20 list—France's École normale supérieure is the highest ranked at 23rd. The few good universities are located in Denmark, France, Germany and Sweden. Eastern and Southern Europe are far behind. The top Southern European University is University of Barcelona ranked 166th, while the top Eastern European University is Charles University in Prague ranked 279th.

Total research and development spending varies greatly in Europe. On average, European countries only spend 1.5 percent of GDP, compared with 2.8 percent of GDP in the US, but the Northern European countries expend about as much as the US. Finland, Sweden and Denmark use even more funds than the US, and Germany and Austria about as much. Three of the new EU members spend more than the EU average, namely Slovenia, the Czech Republic and Estonia, but most of the Eastern and Southern European countries do little for R&D (figure 9.5).

The final reason for Europe's lag in innovation is that European companies have fewer incentives to develop in-house research capabilities. When universities lack significant research potential, industries and large companies can turn to their in-house researchers for developing new technologies. This is happening in some European countries. For example, business makes up 35 percent of 250,000

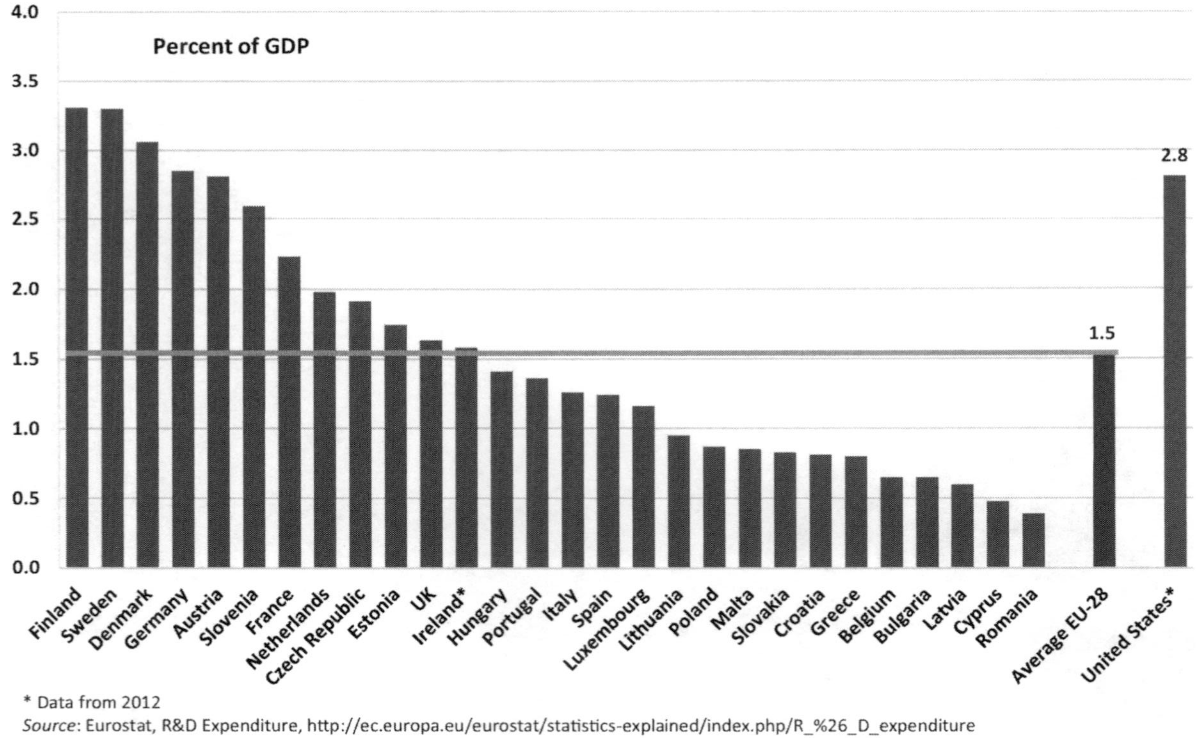
Percent of GDP
4.0
3.5
3.0
2.5
2.0
1.5
1.0
0.5
0.0
2.8
1.5
Finland
Sweden
Denmark
Germany
Austria
Slovenia
France
Netherlands
Czech Republic
Estonia
UK
Ireland*
Hungary
Portugal
Italy
Spain
Luxembourg
Lithuania
Poland
Malta
Slovakia
Croatia
Greece
Belgium
Bulgaria
Latvia
Cyprus
Romania
Average EU-28
United States*
* Data from 2012
Source: Eurostat, R&D Expenditure, http://ec.europa.eu/eurostat/statistics-explained/index.php/R_%26_D_expenditure

Figure 9.5 Total R & D Spending, 2013

* Data from 2012

Source: Eurostat, R&D Expenditure, http://ec.europa.eu/eurostat/statistics-explained/index.php/R_%26_D_expenditure

researchers in the United Kingdom, and spends €29 billion a year on R&D.[11] German and French companies also spend significantly on R&D, €54 and €31 billion, in 2013, respectively. The highest expenditure on innovation by businesses as a share of GDP is in Finland (2.36 percent of GDP in 2012) and Sweden (2.22 percent). But Eastern and Southern Europe lag behind, even Italy and Estonia. Slovenia is the exception, thanks to its innovative pharmaceutical companies (figure 9.6)

Measures can be taken in all five directions to improve Europe's competitiveness in hi-tech. The remainder of this chapter suggests ways in which this can be achieved.

CREATING A SINGLE MARKET FOR INNOVATIVE PRODUCTS

Except for Germany, France and the United Kingdom, Europe's innovation champions are relatively small economies. For innovation to increase Europe's economic potential, a single market for hi-tech products is required.

Many small European countries compete for hosting outsourcing for established US hi-tech companies like HP, IBM, Microsoft and Oracle. They provide local engineers with well-paid jobs but contributes little to domestic innovation. Yet even in small economies successful hi-tech start-ups exist. In Bulgaria, Telerik, a business which began in a dorm room, was bought by US company Progress Software for $263mn in 2014. Telerik offers a.Net toolbox, a mobile development platform, and Sitefinity, a content management system. It had a network of developers that reached 1.4 million. But, as in Telerik's case, such companies are usually acquired by larger American companies early on. Their innovation potential is not only tapped by their new owners, but often diverted from Europe.

The lack of a single European digital market retards innovation. Europe does not have a common patent agency, but each country has its own national patent office. In the healthcare sector national regulations impede innovation. EU legislation provides common rules for the quality, safety and efficacy of healthcare products, which are supposed to be traded on a single EU market. Healthcare expenditures, however, are largely financed by national healthcare systems, which assess and regulate the prices and reimbursement of healthcare products for public funding. These rules are not European but set by national agencies. Currently there are about 50 health technology assessment agencies in Europe, because some countries do not have national but regional agencies, which leads to great regulatory fragmentation. These regulations need to be standardized to create a single European market for healthcare products.

This regulatory fragmentation is a major obstacle to innovation in Europe. Pharmaceuticals and medical devices comprise about 20 percent of healthcare costs, and these industries account for more than 25 percent of all European private R&D investments in recent years. The pharmaceutical industry has the highest R&D intensity of all sectors in Europe: R&D accounted for 15 percent of the net sales in 2015. The sector includes 40 large pharmaceutical companies, mostly in

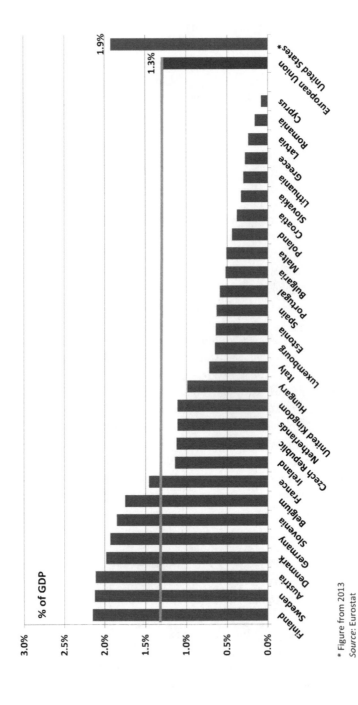

Figure 9.6 R&D Expenditure by Business, 2012

* Figure from 2013

Source: Eurostat

France and Germany, and about 2,000 small and medium-sized healthcare biotechnology companies spread around Europe. A recent study estimated the cost for submitting an application for a single assessment agency at approximately €100,000. The European cost for a new healthcare product is significantly higher given the number of agencies involved. Delays that affect companies' decisions to innovate are also linked to patent duration, the period of time during which companies can recover their R&D investments.[12]

Electricity markets are similarly fragmented, as discussed in Chapter 8. This affects the use of spread of new technologies, for example, electrical cars. Electrical vehicles cannot be recharged when the electricity providers cannot identify the driver as a registered end-user. This occurs when travelling across different European countries or in Italy even across regions within a country. The same is true of using mobile phones in different European states, which may not have access and pay for a service. The possibility to roam across Europe with a single SIM card is already agreed—for mid-2017, and a similar arrangement is needed for electric cars.

Chapter 5 discussed other fragmented markets in great need of integration, the digital market and the capital market. Fragmented markets retard investment and innovation. They hold Europe back as entrepreneurs seek to take advantage of opportunities available elsewhere by new technologies, big data, and cloud computing. Reducing EU cross-border barriers would enable consumers and businesses to access goods and services in other markets, regardless of where they live, more easily and less expensively. Reforms could also provide greater scale and incentives to help EU start-ups grow and compete globally.

One important step would be to make superfast broadband available across the European Union, so that services can be delivered seamlessly across national borders. The European Commission estimates that €200 billion is needed to achieve this task, which can be shared by union, national and private business investment. Individual European states have gone far in this respect, with Eastern Europe moving ahead of some richer European countries.[13]

Politicians need to allocate more spectrum for mobile technology. Few EU states have offered even half of the spectrum required by business, and some countries are experiencing shortfalls of up to 70 percent. Governments can free up spectrum from current allocation, where it is often no longer needed, such as television and military applications, and reallocate it for mobile use.[14] There are enormous spectrum requirements for 5G networks, where the UK is most advanced in Europe.

Better networks can benefit many sectors. Mobile health monitoring could save European citizens 330 million visits to a doctor every year. New mobile technology has helped teachers reach over 40 million European students with online courses and tests. But such services require guaranteed network quality.[15] The key is not just speed but high security.

Regulatory barriers persist. Currently, even simple e-commerce cross-border transactions face obstacles in various European countries, preventing shoppers to log on, find, and pay lower prices with a few clicks, and then receive goods through the mail. The European Union can reduce market fragmentation by applying cross-sector regulation for data security, consumer protection, and privacy. Competition policy should ensure that there is no discrimination by type of business for any digital service.

European competition policy for telecommunications should reflect the abilities of current technology. Consolidation can create stronger, healthier companies, and the big synergies realized in mobile-operator mergers can lead to more investment in technology. This type of consolidation does not mean higher prices, as is often feared. When four mobile companies merged into three in Austria in 2013, prices on a per-unit basis for consumers fell by 40 percent.[16] The European competition authority has since approved similar deals in Germany and Ireland.

THE NEED FOR VENTURE CAPITAL

Some European start-ups manage to attract significant investor interest. TomTom, a Dutch company which once made watches and basic GPS devices, has attracted over a half billion euro in financing since 2013 and it has more than 4,000 employees, selling high-tech software products in 41 countries. Overall, however, "European venture capital lacks scale, lacks diversification and lacks geographical reach," European Commissioner for Financial Markets Jonathan Hill says. Around 90 percent of all EU venture capital is concentrated in eight countries: the U.K., Germany, France, Sweden, the Netherlands, Finland, Belgium and Spain.[17]

Some US venture capital has entered Europe, but not much. In 2014, Google announced that its venture capital unit had started a $125 million fund to back tech companies in Europe. A number of established US private equity funds also have dedicated capacity to invest in European start-ups, though their targets are limited. Despite its name, Google Ventures Europe is focusing on UK companies: 5 out of 6 investments were UK-based companies.[18]

Access to long-term financing is limited. Pension funds make up 14 percent of private VC limited partners in Europe, compared with 29 percent in the United States.[19] To attract institutional investors like pension funds accustomed to investments of €50 million or more, the European capital market has to feature opportunities across European borders. Common EU standards—like those in the recent Prospectus Directive described above—would make it easier for venture fund managers to look across national lines.

That repeat entrepreneurs are less common in Europe and that European VCs lack experience explain much of the difference in performance between Europe and the US. Serial entrepreneurs account for only about 15 percent of venture capital deals done in Europe, but 35 percent of deals done in the US. Yet a recent study finds that previously unsuccessful entrepreneurs have at least as high a chance of getting financing for a new venture in Europe as in the US—hence there is no evidence for a "stigma of failure" in Europe.[20] The remaining difference in performance is explained by heavier regulatory regime sin Europe and larger up-front costs to investing in start-ups and hi-tech growth companies.

In addition to private investors, governments across Europe have designed financing schemes for hi-tech entrants, especially after 2007, when the private equity market dried up. Nearly 40 percent of all venture funds invested in Europe in 2014 came from state-backed sources, up from just 14 percent in 2007.[21] At the European level, the European Union has started providing venture funding for innovation, through the Horizon 2020 program and through giving money to national venture fund initiatives. The main source of venture capital in Europe is the European Investment Fund (EIF), financed by the European Union. In the past decade, the EIF has invested €3.8 billion into 260 venture funds. In recent years, it has developed country and regional funds for hi-tech start-ups.

The UK government has launched the British Business Bank, which is bringing existing government initiatives together and deploys £1 billion of additional capital to finance start-ups. The bank runs an Angel Co-investment Fund, as well as 15 Enterprise Capital Funds with £500 million of venture capital for hi-tech businesses. With $167 million in EU funds to distribute, the Dutch Venture Initiative is the largest country-specific contributor. There are regional funds as well, for example the Baltic Investment Fund.

The substitution of public for private investment in hi-tech has yet to produce the desired results. Venture capital in Europe has delivered remarkably low returns of just 2.1 percent a year in the period 1990-2014, making it the worst investment class outside Japan. In contrast, American venture capital has managed around 13 percent a year.[22] This poor performance requires further investigation. In part, European funds have lower returns because they sell companies too early, missing out on larger returns that come from placing longer-lasting bets.

TOO RIGID LAWS

"We have labor laws designed for workers in large corporations, they don't work for startups," says Niklas Zennström, a founder of Skype who now runs a European venture fund.[23] This is true of both tax laws and labor market regulations. Laws in several EU countries make it hard to pay staff with stock options, a standard practice in hi-tech startups. The cost of paying out large severance packages (six months of severance pay is typical even for very recent hires in Southern Europe) can be a huge cost for a new company. Big severance packages also make it more difficult for start-ups to recruit professional managers, who prefer to stay with established corporations

One improvement is the EU introduction of a start-up visa in March 2011. It awards the right to work to "prospective entrepreneurs," who are able to set up their company and look for funding prior to initiating the official visa application procedure. The start-up visa, initially valid for 12 months, is part of Europe's effort to attract hi-tech entrepreneurs.

A variety of specific European regulations impede innovation. Road vehicle automation can promote user safety and energy efficiency as well as alleviate traffic congestion, and it is critical for the competitiveness of the European automotive industry. Car manufacturers are in a worldwide race towards vehicle automation and connectivity with new players from the IT sector (Google, Apple and Tesla), as automated driving has a huge market potential, but the current legal framework predominantly prohibits automated driving in Europe. In most European countries, the driver still has to be present and be able to take over the steering wheel at any time. In 2015, France, Finland and the Netherlands adopted the necessary legal framework to enable the testing of automated cars on public roads. Germany and Sweden introduced special exemption procedures to allow testing on their roads. Yet a common European framework facilitating automated driving is still missing.

Rigid regulation also hurts European innovation in nanotechnology, which exploits higher strength, lighter weight, increased control of light spectrum, or greater chemical reactivity. Nanotechnology provides new opportunities in sectors such as health, energy, water, construction, consumer goods and clean technologies and offers 300,000-400,000 jobs in Europe.[24] But multiple and inconsistent definitions of "nanomaterial" hamper the development of this sector in the European Union. The same material could be considered a nanomaterial under the regulation of one country but not in another. As a result, businesses move innovation to countries with more flexible regulation, for example, to the United Kingdom and the Netherlands, and avoid certifying or selling their products to other European markets. This significantly diminishes the return to their R&D investment.

THE IMPORTANCE OF GOOD UNIVERSITY EDUCATION

Stanford University, at the heart of Silicon Valley, gave birth to leading hi-tech companies such as Hewlett-Packard and Applied Technologies. These companies have used their proximity to top university researchers to discover and apply new technologies. Based on this experience, Michael Porter from Harvard Business School proposed a new method of creating regional innovation centers—around a top research university. He observed that geographic concentrations of interconnected companies and specialized suppliers gave start-ups productivity and cost advantages.[25]

Boston's Route 128 offers a similar story. It has generated significant startup activity and venture capital investments, around top universities like Harvard and MIT. Bill Gates and Mark Zuckerberg were both Harvard students. Silicon Valley and Route 128 look alike: a mix of large and small tech firms, world-class universities, and venture capital. Start-up entrepreneurs understand that collaborating and competing at the same time leads to success.

Cambridge University displays many similarities with the clusters around Stanford and Harvard/MIT. Although Cambridge University is not private, it has a great traditional autonomy. During its long existence, it has accumulated substantial assets and it charges high tuition fees, allowing it to rely on the state for only about two-fifths of its funding. Its academic reputation draws the world's top students. And the city's bustling intellectual life—thanks to the university—keeps it an attractive destination for bright and ambitious entrepreneurs. It has attempted to replicate the success of Silicon Valley and Route 128, and probably more than any other university in Europe it has managed to do so.

The UK, Sweden, France and Germany have a number of excellent universities, but hardly anyone generates the same entrepreneurial activity as their American counterparts. How successful are these universities in delivering spin-offs? Are cross-disciplinary programs being taught? Is entrepreneurship promoted among students? Is an incubator or accelerator hosted on campus? Does the institution attract risk capital? Are students given opportunities, as part of their studies, to pursue internships or training in hi-tech industry? Are innovators entitled to hold on to the intellectual capital they creat? In most cases, the answer is no.

This pattern is historically predicated. It takes many years to develop a great university and hardly less to breed the combination of a great university and outstanding innovation. After World War II, the US was the undisputed leader in university education. Many European top scientists fled Europe before and during the war and brought their research to the US and their exodus continues because top US university salaries are far higher than European university remuneration that is often capped. European universities have made no impressive come back.

The picture varies a lot with our choice of measurement, but the completion of higher education for the age cohort of 25-34 appears most relevant. In 2015, Europe fell into two large categories divided between north and south with Ireland leading the successful north, and the south headed by Italy. In 16 EU countries 35-50 percent of the young have completed higher education, and nine surpass the US. In the remaining 12 only 20-30 percent of the youth had completed higher education. This group includes Germany and Austria (figure 6.4), but these two countries have extensive vocational training, which may be considered specialized higher education. Secondary education in many European countries is geared towards social studies and humanities and away from hard sciences. The result is a small cohort of students interested in innovation. To escape from this trap, governments are investing heavily in rigorous training.

European universities have many handicaps. They lack in independence from the state, which offers them goals that do not necessarily coincide with education of high quality. University appointments and boards are usually subject to political control. European governments do invest in higher education, but with little success as they are competing with the large university endowments that US universities use to attract top talent and incubate start-ups. Harvard, the world's richest university, boasts a $33 billion endowment, followed by Yale with over $20 billion, and Princeton and Stanford, with $15 billion each. Another 60 US universities have endowments in excess of $1 billion, more than any European university. The American and British universities have substantial revenues from high tuition fees, which are rarely allowed in the rest of Europe. State universities usually have strict salary regulation, which set low ceilings for top salaries. In Finland and Sweden, higher education has been used as regional policy to revive depressed regions, which does not lead to elite quality. It takes time to build a university of top quality, finding the right combination of freedom and stimulus.

TOO SPARSE BUSINESS RESEARCH & DEVELOPMENT

In 1999, Western Europeans bought 32 percent of all mobile phones sold, well ahead of the U.S. with 17 percent. It was a European-driven market ruled by a Finnish company, Nokia, and the runner-up was Swedish Ericsson. By the late 2000s, Apple was better than Nokia at design and at building production chains. Not long thereafter, Samsung and Chinese phone makers were production leaders and Google had the dominant operating system. In 2014, Nokia sold itself to Microsoft.

Expenditure on research and development is concentrated to a few northern countries that have larger R&D expenditures than the US. Eurostat collects and disseminates increasingly detailed regional statistics on R&D spending, human capital for research and patents, showing that R&D activity is heavily concentrated in a relatively small number of regional clusters. Eurostat has identified 21 EU regions that have achieved the 3 percent R&D investment as a share of GDP. Nine of these are in Germany, among them Braunschweig, the region with the highest R&D intensity of all, at nearly 9 percent.

The other regions that have exceeded the 3 percent target are in Sweden (four regions out of Sweden's eight), Finland (three regions out of its five), France and Austria (two regions each) and the UK (one region). R&D expenditure exceeded 2 percent of GDP in another 17 European regions. Most of these regions were in Germany (five), France (four), the Czech Republic and the Netherlands (two each), and one each in Belgium, Denmark, Sweden and the UK.

The regions with the lowest R&D intensity are in Eastern Europe. Of the 104 EU regions with R&D intensities below 1 percent of GDP, half were in the east. Romania and Bulgaria do not have a single region with innovation intensity above 1 percent of GDP.[26]

Europe's business R&D spending has risen by just 2 percent between 2007 and 2015, compared to gains of 40 percent in the United States and 60 percent in Asia. At the same time, European countries have increased their R&D allocation to high-cost offshore countries in North America and Asia. The US is the largest generator of business R&D, spending $145 billion in 2015, up 34 percent since 2007. Imported R&D spend to the US, mostly coming from Europe, in 2015 is $53 billion, up 23 percent from 2007.[27] All these numbers show that Europe is not catching up with the US and Asia but falling further behind.

Where business invests heavily in innovation, Europe has gained competitiveness over American and Asian producers. In this beginning of this chapter we described one such sector—fashion. Another sector that has invested in innovation is food and spirits, which European companies, such as Ferrero (maker of Nutella), LMVH (producer of champagnes Dom Perignon and Moët & Chandon), Danone (yoghurts), Parmalat (milk products), Carslberg (the largest beer producer in the world), Unilever (maker of Lipton teas) enter the top-10 list of global companies in terms of sales.

Italy's Ferrero invests nearly 10 percent of its annual revenue of €8.6 billion in R&D. One example of such innovation is the Kinder product series, including Kinder Surprise (also known as "Kinder Eggs"), Kinder Happy Hippo, Kinder Maxi, and Kinder Bueno, all developed in the past two decades on the basis of extensive research in children's tastes. In 2011, Ferrero introduced a line of frozen products called "Gran Soleil," a frozen dessert which has to be shaken, and if left overnight in the freezer, can be eaten as a sorbet. The company received the top innovation award in the food industry for this product in 2012.[28]

Patents are subject to dense clustering at the regional level. The region with the highest number of patents per capita is Noord-Brabant in the Netherlands. It is followed by seven German regions. The other most patent intensive regions are found in Sweden (three) and in Finland and the UK (two each). These correspond closely to the high levels of business R&D expenditures reported above.

One way to address this disparity is by supporting the establishment of hi-tech clusters, a policy favored by many European governments. Bulgaria is one of the eastern European countries that first answered this call. A hi-tech park was opened in December 2015, with WMware, Microsoft, SISCO and HP as partners. The government funded this project. These hi-tech companies are likely to attract a cluster of smaller technology companies and cooperate on developing new products.

Proximity to technology incubators plays a role for technology development in Sweden, Austria and Denmark, and quantity of R&D personnel for France, Italy and Poland. Geographic proximity to other company sites plays an important role for the location choice of foreign investment in R&D in Germany and the UK, while public R&D support via fiscal incentives appears to be important for locations in France and Spain.[29]

CONCLUSIONS: MANY STEPS REQUIRED

Europe is the world's leader in innovation in a number of industries—from fashion and gastronomy to biomedicine and aerospace, but its competitive edge in innovation has been eroded after World War II, with many manufacturing and service industries trailing their American and Asian competitors.

To make Europe catch up with the US in innovation is arguably the most difficult and complex task, which includes many elements. On their own the resolution of none of these tasks will be sufficient. Innovation requires freedom, markets, skills, resources, and a nurturing environment.

To begin with taxation on entrepreneurship must be eased as discussed in Chapter 3. The integration of the European digital market needs to be completed. Many steps need to be taken to stimulate venture financing and encourage venture capitalists to look more carefully at European start-ups and finance them through their early development. Many regulations involving taxation, business regulation and labor markets are too rigid and need to be eased. Innovation requires freedom.

Top-level innovation requires world-class universities, which are largely located in the US and the UK. European continental universities need to catch up. First of all, the goal of developing elite universities must be accepted. Top universities need more independence from the state. The American and British universities have substantial revenues from high tuition fees, which should be allowed in the rest of Europe. Universities need to abandon strict salary regulation and pay top professors according to merits. It takes time to build a university of top quality, finding the right combination of freedom and stimulus. They also need to develop innovative links with start-ups. European universities can and should once again become the centers of innovation they had been in the first decades of the 20th century. Most of Europe spends too little on research and development, which needs a significant boost.

Conclusions:
How Europe Can Be Turned Around

Our conviction is that Europe can grow faster again. If national governments and European institutions implement certain policies, Europe can become as competitive as the United States and Asia, so that it can maintain its high living standards and social welfare state.

Our ambition is to spur policy change, pinpointing key shortcomings and suggesting cures. After seven years of stagnation most Europeans want change. It is not only the tepid economic performance that warrants action. Europe is confronted with several other challenges. In 2015, a major inflow of refugees from North Africa and the Middle East shook the continent. This migration challenge offers an additional impetus for change. In each area, some European countries have good regulatory practices, which can be adopted by the rest of Europe as well.

The aim of this book is to formulate a reform agenda suggesting how the European economy can speed up its anemic growth. Our intention is to bring the attention of policymakers and the informed public to key issues that could make a difference. This list of recommendations may be extended for each European country, but here we focus on common elements for growth. These are our seven top recommendations.

1. EUROPEAN COUNTRIES NEED TO CUT THEIR PUBLIC EXPENDITURES BY 10 PERCENT OF GDP.

Public expenditures in Europe are on average one-tenth of GDP higher than in other highly developed countries. These excess public expenditures go almost entirely to social transfers, which need to be tightened since they distort incentives. Controlling for other conditions, very high public expenditures depress growth.

A level of public expenditures of 35-42 percent of GDP seems optimal for Europe. One-third of Europe already fulfills this criterion (Bulgaria, Estonia, Ireland, Latvia, Lithuania, Romania, Slovakia, Poland and the Czech Republic), and these countries grow faster than the rest. We suggest a European-wide ceiling of public expenditures in peacetime of 42 percent of GDP, much like the Maastricht criteria of maximum 3 percent of annual budget deficits to GDP and the 60 percent of public debt to GDP.

Poorer European countries need to be careful not to expand public expenditures too fast because it can lead to fiscal crisis and high levels of unemployment over a long period. Yet lower public expenditures than 35 percent of GDP appears politically impossible in developed democracies. How should European countries choose within this range? Most EU countries have allowed their public expenses to swell was simply because they could collect the taxes or sell bonds without much consideration of whether it would be beneficial for their economic growth or employment.

2. PENSION REFORM IS THE MOST IMPORTANT MEANS TO REDUCE PUBLIC EXPENDITURES

Public pension spending is far too large in most EU countries, which endangers the countries financial sustainability, drives up taxes, and undermines economic growth, while public pensions are neither just nor secure, since they are usually subject to political tampering. Especially, Greece and Italy have the large public pensions, which have greatly contributed to stalling economic growth in these countries.

EU governments should aim at cutting public pension costs to no more than 8 percent of GDP to limit the fiscal burden; to render most of the public pensions actuarially correct and transparent; to promote solid private pension savings, whether mandatory or voluntary with sound regulation. Apart from a flat subsistence pension, public pensions should be actuarially correct offering pensioners disbursements related to their contributions. Early retirement schemes should be reined in to what is really necessary, and retirement age can rise with life expectancy. Private pension savings, whether mandatory or voluntary, should be encouraged and shielded.

The Dutch pension system appears the example to follow. It combines all the best features. It is secure and affordable, provides high pensions and contributes to sound economic growth. Its first pillar is a public old-age pension financed with a payroll tax in a pay-as-you-go system. It provides all residents with a flat minimum pension amounting to 70 percent of the minimum income, rendering it very stable. Its outstanding feature is the second pillar, a large private occupational pension for both private and public employees financed with 18 percent of employees' earnings, giving the Netherlands the largest private pension funds in Europe far exceeding its GDP. Together with the state pension, the Dutch occupational pensions offer pensioners 70 percent of their prior salary. Since the occupational pensions are agreed through collective bargaining between employers and trade unions, their institutional arrangement is remarkably stable.

An added advantage of the Dutch system is that any resident of the Netherlands earns 2 percent of his or her public and private pensions each year he or she lives in the country, and this pension capital is treated as individual property regardless of country of residence. The Dutch pension system is an example for other EU countries to follow.

3. REDUCE TAXES ON LABOR

Most European countries collect more taxes than is good for economic growth and is necessary for an adequate social welfare system. In 2014, the average European country collected 40.0 percent of GDP in taxes out of total state revenues of 45.2 percent of GDP. As public expenditures decline, taxes on labor should shrink accordingly.[1]

To encourage entrepreneurship and growth, taxes should be few, low and relatively flat. The tax system should combine the aims of minimizing tax evasion and the administrative burden on citizens and enterprises. It should be simple, with few but clear rules, and minimum loopholes. In many European countries most taxpayer already file their returns electronically.

Europe taxes labor most heavily. This is both unjust and inefficient. Personal income tax and payroll tax are the two high taxes that need to be trimmed to encourage participation in the labor force, especially among European women. These taxes hamper innovation and discourage official work, preventing job-seekers from finding their first employment. Marginal income taxes are too high in many European countries. Europe suffers from high tax wedges on labor, which should be reduced. Taxation of labor should be reduced and equalized with the taxation of capital gains. In order to counter excessive inequality of incomes, European countries may consider introducing a luxury tax to encourage the efficient use of financial wealth

West European countries can draw on the new thinking on taxation from Eastern Europe. The Baltic countries, Slovakia, Romania and Bulgaria have only the taxes we have advocated here. All European corporate profit taxes have fallen through tax competition, and their new lower level reaps more revenues. The value-added taxes have been greatly harmonized by the EU. Most East European countries have opted for a low flat income tax that is equal to the corporate profit tax to avoid discrimination against labor.

4. REDUCE THE BURDENS ON LABOR TO COMBAT UNEMPLOYMENT

One of Europe's greatest social ailments is the high unemployment rate persistently exceeding 10 percent of the active labor force. An even greater tragedy is the high youth unemployment especially in Southern Europe. Few policies can do more to improve Europe's economic growth and welfare than policies creating more jobs. Many measures are needed.

In 2015, the European employment rate was 4.3 percentage points less than in the US. Not only do fewer Europeans work, but those who do work on average 4.9 percent less than in the US. If Europe had as large an employment rate as the US, and Europeans worked as long hours as Americans, the addition to the European labor force would be 9.4 percent.

The need to reduce taxes on labor and especially tax wedges has been discussed above. Most of Europe's labor markets remain overregulated, particularly in Southern Europe. These countries have carried out some liberalization, but much more is needed. It should also become easier both to hire and lay off workers, so that employers do not hesitate to hire new workers and instead push their workers to work overtime. The positive examples are the highly liberalized labor markets of the United Kingdom and Ireland, and Denmark and Germany that have tried to combine increased flexibility with the maintenance of substantial social support. All these countries have low unemployment.

Germany and Austria have also kept youth unemployment at bay thanks to a sophisticated policy of apprenticeships, which offer excellent vocational training. Other countries should follow the examples of Germany and Austria. The four Southern European countries need to expand also their high school education to enhance their competitiveness.

The participation of women in the labor force varies dramatically. Many measures can be used to attract women to the labor force. Equal rights for men and women have to be a start, but they need to be supported by childcare and flexible work arrangements. The Scandinavian countries have been most successful in engaging women in the labor force, though a drawback is that this has taken place at considerable fiscal cost.

With its very low birth rates, Europe needs immigration. Increased intra-Europe labor mobility is good but not sufficient. Europe has considerable experience of absorbing immigrants, but it needs to utilize all the lessons various countries have learned. Social benefits need to be exportable and earned benefits should be transportable. Undue regulations of professions should be eliminated, and remaining regulations should be transparent. Germany offers a laudable example of a move from temporary "guest workers" to the attraction of skilled immigrants. Ireland that used to be the main emigration country in Europe, has arguably adopted the best policy for immigrants: tolerance, limited regulations, welcoming skilled immigrants and foreign direct investment, low taxes and limited but vital social benefits.

5. OPEN UP SERVICES AND DIGITAL TRADE

Services account for 70 percent of modern economies, but trade in services across Europe remains fragmented trade and has been surprisingly neglected. It offers the greatest growth potential for Europe. The European Parliamentary Research Service found that the greatest cost of lacking EU cooperation in 2014-19 was the missing digital single market (€340 billion) and single market for consumers and citizens (mainly for services €330 billion).

Only in 2006, the EU adopted its Services Directives, but it contained too many loopholes to be effective. In addition, it encountered great resistance from vested interests, such as regulated professions. The variety of cultures and customs in European countries has ensured that services have been treated as local in nature. The EU Services Directive needs to be both broadened and reinforced. The other under-developed market is the digital market, which is also fragmented. Both should be unified. New technologies and business practices, notably in digital trade, render the old protectionism untenable. The large migration flows within Europe also contributes to this opening.

The EU should reinforce its Services Directive to make it an effective support for the evolution of intra-European service markets. Its coverage should be expanded to nearly all services, and it should set firmer rules for the opening of EU service markets. The European Commission should also pursue its implementation more forcefully. The establishment of service companies in other EU countries should be facilitated and one-stop shops for registration should be instituted throughout Europe. Unnecessary regulation of professions should be reined in through an improved Services Directive.

Much can be achieved through integrated public procurement. Once Europe starts using one single procurement system for municipal, national and cross-national projects, the many services involved in making this procurement successful will also be integrated.

A second line of action would be national policymaking. For example, each country has an interest in reducing its list of regulated profession at the national level and to improve the efficiency of communications services. This is simply a rational national competition policy.

A third line of action lies in the current negotiations with the US about a new TTIP agreement. It would naturally incorporate far-reaching liberalization of service trade and digital trade. It should lead to increased competition on the telecommunications market and presumably to its consolidation. It should certainly lead to an integration of the now completely fragmented digital market. Hopefully, it would also open up most of public procurement for competition. An added advantage is that TTIP would presumably also be accompanied with a stricter legal enforcement than the current Services Directive. Thus, TTIP can be a means for the European Commission to implement what it wanted to accomplish in any case in the service market.

6. COMPLETE THE EUROPEAN ENERGY UNION

The evolution of the European single market for energy has proceeded slowly, because the European Commission has encountered significant resistance from the old national energy champions and several large member states. The Juncker Commission has taken important steps to gain momentum towards achieving an energy union.

With the third energy package of 2009 and the energy union of 2015, the European Commission has insisted on open markets with consumer choice and open transmission networks. This aim requires adequate infrastructure to allow energy to be transported in any direction the market demands. The challenge of the EU is to prove sufficient strength to attain these goals.

Europe needs to abandon its tolerance of state-owned energy companies. They should be privatized as in Britain, which stands out as the most liberalized and diversified and also successful energy market with low prices and secure supplies. European states should also open the access to natural resources to private entrepreneurs. The state owns all resources underground, depriving private landowners of the incentive to promote energy production. Resource rents can be properly taxed, which remains a national issue. Most energy innovation in the world appears to be taking place in the US, leaving Europe behind, as Europeans tend to treat the energy sector as the old economy. The absence of shale gas development is only one example. Opponents of shale gas development have utilized the restrictive nature of European politics to achieve the prohibition of shale gas development in several countries.

The opening of the European energy markets is going at the same time as further opening of the US energy sector. At the end of 2015, the US allowed for the first time for forty years exports of crude oil. American exports of LNG have also undergone a gradual liberalization. Both facilitate the evolution of the European energy market and lower the prices of European energy imports. The conclusion of the TTIP could provide a further additional impetus for the creation of a single energy market in Europe.

7. IMPROVE HIGHER EDUCATION AND CREATE BETTER CONDITIONS FOR INNOVATION

Increasingly, Europe is falling behind in innovation and hi-tech development. This is the greatest and most difficult challenge to Europe, involving many elements. Elite universities are a precondition. They need sufficient autonomy and financing. They must have a reasonable approach to intellectual property rights so that startups can gather around the elite universities. Startups require venture capital that can only be private equity capital. The tax regime and regulatory framework need to be accommodating, and the immigration of talent should be promoted.

Top-level innovation requires world-class universities, which are largely located in the US and the UK. European continental universities need to catch up. First of all, the goal of developing elite universities must be accepted. Top universities need more independence from the state. The American and British universities have substantial revenues from high tuition fees, which should be allowed in the rest of Europe. Universities need to abandon strict salary regulation and pay top professors according to merits. It takes time to build a university of top quality, finding the right combination of freedom and stimulus. They also need to develop innovative links with start-ups. European universities can and should once again become the centers of innovation they had been in the first decades of the 20th century. Most of Europe spends too little on research and development, which needs to be boosted. Specifically, private R&D needs to be stimulated.

Notes

Introduction

1. United Nations (2015). This index is a combination of three factors: Life expectancy at birth, education, and gross national income (GNI) per capita.
2. For example, Åslund (2002), Åslund (2013), Åslund and Djankov, (2014).
3. One of us was the original author of World Bank and International Finance Corporation, *Doing Business in 2015*, Washington, DC: World Bank, 2015. Available: http://www.doingbusiness.org/.
4. E.g. Åslund (1998), Åslund and Dabrowski (2007), Åslund and Dabrowski (2008).
5. Buti, et al. (2008).
6. European Commission (2015a).
7. Sapir (2010) and Sapri (2015).
8. European Parliament (2000).
9. Buti et al. (2008).
10. Anders Åslund, "Europe's Voters Wisely Stick with Frugal Leaders," Bloomberg, September 29, 2013.
11. Djankov (2014).
12. Åslund (2010), Åslund and Dombrovskis (2011).
13. Eurostat, "General government gross debt—annual data,"
http://ec.europa.eu/eurostat/tgm/table.do?tab=table&init=1&language=en&pcode=teina225&plugin=1, (accessed on August 21, 2015)
14. Reinhardt and Rogoff (2009).
15. Gill and Raiser (2012), p. 23.
16. Fölster and Sanandaji, (2014), pp. 77-81 offer a neat summary.
17. Auerbach (2002).
18. Fatas and Mihov (2003).
19. Blanchard and Leigh (2013).
20. Alberto Gallo, "Monetary Anesthetic Ineffective without Structural Policies," *Financial Times*, September 1, 2015, p. 22.
21. Djankov (2014).
22. Bouis and Dulva. (2011).
23. Lindbeck (2012).
24. Balcerowicz (2013), p. 5.
25. Jean-Claude Juncker, et al., "Preparing for Next Steps on better Economic Governance in the Euro Area. Analytical Note," Informal European Council, Brussels, February 12, 2015, pp. 3-4.
26. Claire Jones, "Economists Call on Governments to Take up Recovery Baton," *Financial Times*, December 28, 2015, p. 2.

27. Keynes [1936] (1973), pp. 383-4.

28. Williamson, (1994).

29. Balcerowicz (1994).

30. "The sick man of the euro," *Economist.* June 3, 1999. http://www.economist.com/ node/209559

31. Drazen and Grilli. (1993).

32. Monnet. 1976.

33. Guiso, Sapienza, and Zingales (2014).

34. Eurostat, "Real GDP growth rate—volume," http://ec.europa.eu/eurostat/tgm/table.do?tab=table&init=1&language=en&pcode=tec0 0115&plugin=1. (accessed on January 8, 2016).

35. Eurostat, "Population on 1 January," http://ec.europa.eu/eurostat/tgm/table.do?tab=table&init=1&language=en&pcode=tps0 0001&plugin=1 (accessed on January 8, 2016).

36. Jean-Claude Juncker, et al., "Preparing for Next Steps on better Economic Governance in the Euro Area. Analytical Note," Informal European Council, Brussels, February 12, 2015, p. 7.

37. Rodrik (2011).

38. World Economic Forum, "Which countries have the largest immigrant populations?" http://wef.ch/1PaC6s0 .

39. Carl Bildt, "A Happy New Year for Europe?" Project Syndicate, December 28, 2015.

40. Djankov (2014a).

41. Anders Åslund, "Revisiting the Latvian and Greek Financial Crises: The Benefits of Front-Loading Fiscal Adjustment," CASE Network Studies and Analyses, no. 477, Warsaw, May 2015.

42. Ayar et al. (2016), p. 4.

43. Kagan, (2012), p. 38.

44. Joschka Fischer, "The Return of Geopolitics to Europe," Project Syndicate, November 2, 2015.

45. SIPRI (2015).

46. Quoted in World Economic Forum (2016), p. 10.

47. Joseph S. Nye, "The Danger of a Weak Europe," Project Syndicate, January 6, 2016.

48. Kagan (2012), p. 139.

49. Quoted in Tony Barber, "Estonia Attacks EU's Response to Migrant Crisis and Putin," *Financial Times,* December 7, 2015, p. 2.

50. Most recently, OECD (2015).

51. European Parliamentary Research Service (2014).

52. Gill and Raiser (2012).

53. World Bank and International Finance Corporation, *Doing Business in 2015,* Washington, DC: World Bank, 2015. Available: http://www.doingbusiness.org/

54. E. g. Roxburgh, Mischke (2010).

55. Roxburgh, Mischke (2010), p. 43.

56. Jensen (2011).

57. Directive 2006/123/EC of the European Parliament And of the Council of 12 December 2006 "on services in the internal market," http://eur-lex.europa.eu/legal-content/EN/ TXT/?uri=celex:32006L0123.

58. Jean-Claude Juncker, et al., "Preparing for Next Steps on better Economic Governance in the Euro Area. Analytical Note," Informal European Council, Brussels, February 12, 2015, p. 6.

Chapter 1

1. The current 28 member countries are: Austria, Belgium, Bulgaria, Croatia, Cyprus, the Czech Republic, Denmark, Estonia, Finland, France, Germany, Greece, Hungary, Ireland, Italy, Latvia, Lithuania, Luxembourg, Malta, the Netherlands, Poland, Portugal, Romania, Slovakia, Slovenia, Spain, Sweden and the United Kingdom.
2. Belgium, France, Germany, Italy, Luxembourg, and the Netherlands.
3. European Commission. 1951. *Treaty Establishing the European Coal and Steel Community*, Paris, April 18, 1951. http://www.ab.gov.tr/files/ardb/evt/1_avrupa_birligi/1_3_ant-lasmalar/1_3_1_kurucu_antlasmalar/1951_treaty_establishing_ceca.pdf.
4. European Commission. 1957. "Treaty establishing the European Atomic Energy Community (Euratom)," EUR-Lex, http://eur-lex.europa.eu/legal-content/EN/TXT/?uri=uriserv:xy0024 (Accessed on September 3, 2015).
5. Servan-Schreiber (1968)
6. European Parliament (2000).
7. European Commission, Lisbon Strategy Evaluation Document, February 2, 2010, http://ec.europa.eu/europe2020/pdf/lisbon_strategy_evaluation_en.pdf
8. Lindbeck (1994).
9. These 15 countries are: Austria, Belgium, Denmark, Finland, France, Germany, Greece, Ireland, Italy, Luxembourg, the Netherlands, Portugal, Spain, Sweden and the United Kingdom.
10. Gill and Raiser (2012), p. 2.
11. Juncker and others (2015), p. 6.
12. Alesina and Giavazzi (2006), pp. 3–4.
13. Balcerowicz and others (2013), p. 3.
14. Barro and Sala-i-Martin (2004).
15. Gill and Raiser (2012), p. 14.
16. Aghion and Howitt (2008).
17. European Parliamentary Research Service, "Mapping the Cost of Non-Europe, 2014–19, 2nd edition, Brussels: European Parliament, July 2014.
18. Jaume Marti Romero, "The Remarkable Case of Spanish Immigration," Bruegel, Blogpost, December 8, 2015.
19. Eurostat, "Total fertility rate, 1960–2013 (live births per woman)," http://ec.europa.eu/eurostat/statistics-explained/index.php/File:Total_fertility_rate, 1960 percentE2 percent80 percent932013_(live_births_per_woman)_YB15.png
20. World Economic Forum, "Which countries have the largest immigrant populations?" http://wef.ch/1PaC6s0.
21. Rick Lyman, "Ukrainian Migrants Fleeing Conflict Get a Cool Reception in Europe," *New York Times*, May 30, 2015.
22. Allison Bray, "Migrant crisis growing here as asylum seekers double in 2015," *The Independent*, June 26, 2015.
23. Fölster and Sanandaji (2014).

24. Lindbeck and Snower (1986), pp. 235–239.

25. Prescott (2004).

26. Reid (2009).

27. Eurostat (2015).

28. Eurostat (2015).

29. http://www.oecd.org/pisa/keyfindings/pisa-2012-results-overview.pdf.

30. Kelly (1992), p. 133.

31. La Porta and others (1998).

32. North (1981).

33. For a good example of that literature, see Rodrik, Subramanian and Trebbi (2004).

34. Transparency International (2015).

35. World Bank (2015).

36. Amin and Djankov (2014).

37. Acemoglu, Naidu, Restrepo and Robinson (2015).

Chapter 2

1. Anita Raghavan, "Sweden's Public Downsizing," *Forbes*, July 16, 2009.

2. World Bank (2012).

3. Eurostat, Total General Government Expenditure, http://ec.europa.eu/eurostat/tgm/table.do?tab=table&language=en&pcode=tec00023

4. Eurostat, Total General Government Expenditure, http://ec.europa.eu/eurostat/tgm/table.do?tab=table&language=en&pcode=tec00023

5. OECD statistics.

6. Kornai (1992).

7. Tanzi and Schuknecht (2000).

8. Tanzi (2011).

9. Tanzi (2011), p. 7.

10. Hayek (1960).

11. Tanzi (2011), pp. 74–75.

12. Tanzi and Schuknecht (2000), pp. 8, 15.

13. Tanzi (2011), p. 9.

14. Tanzi and Schuknecht (2000), p. 9.

15. Keynes, [1936] (1973).

16. Tanzi (2011), p. 85.

17. Holton (1986), p. 67.

18. Notably, the Kamprad family of IKEA and the Rausing family of Tetra Pak.

19. Tanzi (2011), pp. 123–124.

20. Erhard (1957).

21. Musgrave (1959).

22. King (2002).

23. Tanzi and Schuknecht (2000), pp. 10–13.

24. Tanzi and Schuknecht, 2000, pp. 16, 20.

25. Tanzi and Schuknecht (2000), pp. 16, 20.

26. His most sophisticated ideological work was Hayek (1960).

27. Friedman's most popular book was the bestseller: Friedman (1980).

28. Åslund (2013).

29. Barro (1989).

30. Kneller, Richard, Michael F. Bleaney, and Norman Gemmell (1999).

31. Hansson and Henrekson (1994).

32. Barro (1997).

33. Afonso and Furceri (2010).

34. Heitger (2001).

35. Bergh and Henrekson (2010), p. 1.

36. Ibid., p. 9.

37. Bergh and Henrekson (2011).

38. Martin Wolf, "The Gold Age of Government," *Financial Times*, July 11, 2000.

39. Peter Wise, "Portugal debates future of welfare state," *Financial Times*, November 26, 2012.

40. Ibid.

41. Hayek (1960).

42. Tanzi and Schuknecht (2000), pp. 24–49.

43. Ibid., p. 28.; Statistics Explained, *Government Expenditures by Function*. Eurostat, May 2015. (Accessed on July 22, 2015).

44. Statistics Explained, *Government Expenditures by Function*. Eurostat, May 2015. (Accessed on July 22, 2015).

45. Ibid.

46. Tanzi and Schuknecht (2000), pp. 47–48.

47. Peter Spiegel, "How Juncker Plans to Unleash Investment in Europe," *Financial Times*, November 25, 2014.

48. Ibid., pp. 33–35. Statistics Explained, *Government Expenditures by Function*. Eurostat, May 2015. Accessed 22 July 2015.

49. OECD, Health Care Indicators, https://data.oecd.org/healthres/health-spending.htm

50. Statistics Explained, *Government Expenditures by Function*. Eurostat, May 2015. Accessed 22 July 2015.

51. Tanzi, 2011, pp. 39–42.

52. World Bank (1994).

53. Tanzi, 2011, pp. 42–43.

54. Tanzi, 2011, pp. 43–45.

55. Kirkegaard (2015).

56. Statistics Explained, *Government Expenditures by Function*. Eurostat, May 2015. Accessed 22 July 2015.

57. Ibid.

58. Tanzi and Schuknecht (2000), pp. 45–47.

59. Eurostat, Government Expenditures by Function, May 2015, http://ec.europa.eu/eurostat/statistics-explained/index.php/Government_expenditure_by_function_percentE2 percent80 percent93_COFOG#General_government_expenditure_by_function.

60. Eurostat, Government Expenditures by Function, May 2015, http://ec.europa.eu/eurostat/statistics-explained/index.php/Government_expenditure_by_function_percentE2 percent80 percent93_COFOG#General_government_expenditure_by_function.

61. Djankov (2014).
62. Tanzi (2007).
63. Grazia Attinasi and Metelli (2016).
64. Coricelli (2007).
65. One of us published a book arguing that Sweden could benefit from cutting its public expenditures at 63.5 percent of GDP in 1996 by half (Åslund, 1998). From 1993-2007, Sweden's public expenditures fell by 21 percent of GDP.

Chapter 3

1. Atkinson, Piketty and Saez (2011).
2. Tanzi (2011), p. 92.
3. Reinhart and Sbrancia (2015).
4. Early examples include Mirrlees and Diamond (1971a,b). For a recent summary, a good read is Slemrod and Gillitzer (2013).
5. Djankov and others (2010).
6. Oliver King, "The Poll Tax Riot 25 Years Ago Was the Day I Woke Up Politically," *The Guardian*, March 31, 2015.
7. World Bank (2015).
8. Djankov (2014).
9. Laar (2014).
10. "Taxation trends in the European Union." *Eurostat: Statistical books.* 2014. <http://ec.europa.eu/taxation_customs/resources/documents/taxation/gen_info/economic_analysis/tax_structures/2014/report.pdf >, p. 231; De Mooij and Nicodème (2008), p. 27.
11. Djankov and others (2010).
12. These numbers include both central government and local government taxes.
13. "Taxation trends in the European Union." *Eurostat: Statistical books.* 2014. <http://ec.europa.eu/taxation_customs/resources/documents/taxation/gen_info/economic_analysis/tax_structures/2014/report.pdf, p. 231>
14. Duncan Robinson and Christian Oliver, "Luxembourg Abandons Attempt to Keep Tax List Secret," *Financial Times*, December 18, 2014.
15. Appel (2011), p. 81.
16. Tanzi (2011), pp. 68, 96.
17. Astrid Lindgren, "Pomperipossa i Monismanien," *Expressen*, March 3, 1976.
18. Tanzi (2011), p. 96.
19. Tanzi (2011), p. 97.
20. For example the standard book, Musgrave (1959).
21. Tanzi (2011), p. 96.
22. Kornai (1992).
23. Laar (2014), p. 81.
24. Laar (2002), p. 271–278.
25. Gorodnichenko et al. (2009).
26. Mitchell (2008), p. 3.
27. Petkova (2012).

28. The most prominent argument for such a cause has been Piketty (2014).

29. "Taxation trends in the European Union." *Eurostat: Statistical books.* 2014. http:// ec.europa.eu/taxation_customs/resources/documents/taxation/gen_info/economic_analysis/tax_structures/2014/report.pdf, p. 189.

30. "Taxation trends in the European Union." *Eurostat: Statistical books.* 2014. <http:// ec.europa.eu/taxation_customs/resources/documents/taxation/gen_info/economic_analysis/tax_structures/2014/report.pdf>, p. 195.

31. Trabandt and Uhlig (2012).

32. European Commission, Taxation and Customs Union, "VAT History in the EU," last updated April 10, 2015. <http://ec.europa.eu/taxation_customs/taxation/vat/how_vat_works/vat_history_en.htm>; Appel, 2011, p. 45.

33. "Taxation trends in the European Union." *Eurostat: Statistical books.* 2014. <http:// ec.europa.eu/taxation_customs/resources/documents/taxation/gen_info/economic_analysis/tax_structures/2014/report.pdf>, p. 179.

34. Tanzi, 2011, p. 98.

35. See Chapter 7 in Djankov (2014).

36. Kuznets (1955).

37. European Commission, "Financial Transaction Tax: Making the Financial Sector Pay Its Fair Share," Press Release, September 28, 2011. http://europa.eu/rapid/press-release_IP-11-1085_en.htm.

38. European Commission, "Financial Transaction Tax: EU Commission sets out the details," Press Release, February 14, 2011. http://ec.europa.eu/ireland/press_office/media_centre/feb2013_en.htm#22

39. Magnus Viberg, "We Tried a Tobin Tax and It Didn't Work," *Financial Times*, April 15, 2013.

40. Carlsson and Rosen (1961).

41. Transparency International (2015).

42. Bergh and Henrekson (2010), pp. 44–50.

43. George Parker and Vanessa Houlder, "George Osborne Urged to Cut Top Tax Rate to 40p," *Financial Times*, June 24, 2015.

44. Margit Feher, Hungary Wants To Launch 30–35 percent "Luxury" Tax, *Wall Street Journal*, July 26, 2013.

Chapter 4

1. European Commission (2012).

2. European Commission (2015a).

3. European Commission (2015a).

4. Liedtke (2006).

5. World Bank (1994), p. 104.

6. World Bank (1994), pp. 166-7.

7. World Bank (1994).

8. Sweden Ministry of Health and Social Affairs (1998).

9. Sundén (1998).

10. European Commission (2009).

11. OECD (2015).

12. Djankov (2014), Chapter 7.
13. See, for example, European Commission (2015b).
14. Rice, Lang, Henley and Melzer (2010), Dave, Rashad and Spasojevic (2008).
15. Maes and Stammen (2011).
16. OECD (2015b).
17. Editorial Note, "Oettinger warnt vor Neuaufflammen der Euro-Krise (Oettinger Warns of a New Flare of the Euro Crisis)" *Die Welt*, January 18, 2015.
18. Djankov (2014b).
19. OECD (2015).
20. Ibid.
21. Bokros (2013), Djankov (2015).
22. Goleniowska (1997).
23. Pensionsmyndigheten (2014), at https://secure.pensionsmyndigheten.se/AllmanPension.html.
24. Miklos (2014).
25. Karam (2010).
26. Bovenberg and Gradus (2015).
27. OECD (2015).
28. Clements (2012) offers an overview of the challenges for this section.
29. Reinhart and Sbrancia (2011).
30. Natali and Stamati (2013).
31. Antonio Argandoña and Javier Díaz-Giménez (2013).
32. Javier Diaz Gimenez and Julian Diaz Saavedra (2014).
33. This is 1 percent of GDP more than in the Netherlands, and one percent of GDP less than the present EU average, which appears a rather moderate target.
34. Ezra (2011), p. 35.
35. European Actuarial & Consulting Services (EURACS). (2016).
36. Tim Ross, "Ministers Prepare Radical Pension Reform," *The Daily Telegraph*, May 31, 2014.

Chapter 5

1. Eurostat (2015).
2. OECD (2015c).
3. European Parliamentary Research Service (2014).
4. European Commission (2006).
5. Monti (2010).
6. Monti (2010).
7. Monteaguado et al. (2012).
8. European Commission, "The economic impact of the services directive: A first assessment following implementation", June 2012.
9. Booth, Persson and Ruparel (2013).
10. Nazarko and Chodakowska (2015).
11. Winston and Yan (2015).
12. Editor's Letter, "David Cameron and EU leaders call for growth plan in Europe: full letter," *The Telegraph*, February 20, 2012.

13. European Commission (2013b).
14. PwC (2011).
15. FIEC (2014).
16. European Commission (2013a).
17. Digital Agenda Scoreboard 2015, accessed November 30, 2015.
18. European Commission (2015).
19. Jim Brundsen, "Brussels Vows to Crack Down on Cross-Border Postal Prices," *Financial Times*, December 22, 2015.
20. Claes and Vergote (2015).
21. ANACOM (2011).
22. Inti Landauro, "France's Antitrust Watchdog Fines 20 Courier Companies $739 Million," *The Wall Street Journal*, December 15. 2015.
23. Ogrokhina (2015).
24. Anushka Asthana, "The Polish plumber who fixed the vote," *The Guardian*, May 28, 2005.
25. "The Princes of Paperwork," *The Economist*, March 21, 2015.
26. Francois (2013).
27. Barefoot and Koncz-Bruner (2012).
28. European Commission (2015e).
29. Briglauer (2014).
30. Christian Oliver and Daniel Thomas, "European telecoms look to Danish deal for signs on consolidation," *Financial Times*, September 10, 2015.
31. See Letter from Jeb Hensarling, Chairman of the House Committee on Financial Services, et al. to President Barack Obama, May 22, 2013; and U.S. Congress, House Committee on Ways and Means, Subcommittee on Trade, Testimony by Greg S. Slater, Director, Trade and Competition Policy, Intel Corporation, on Behalf of the Coalition of Services Industries and the Business Coalition for Transatlantic Trade, "U.S.-EU Trade and Investment Negotiations," 1st sess., May 16, 2013.
32. Thiel (2014).
33. European Commission (2015h).
34. Langfield and Pagano (2015).
35. Data from the Doing Business database, accessed November 30, 2015.
36. Djankov and others (2008).
37. Véron and Wolff (2015).
38. European Commission (2015c).
39. See Chapter 7 in Djankov (2014a).
40. Quentin Peel, "Trichet seeks single EU finance ministry," *Financial Times*, June 2, 2011.
41. European Commission (2015f).
42. European Commission (2015i).

Chapter 6

1. Eurostat. Available at http://ec.europa.eu/eurostat/statistics-explained/index.php/Employment_statistics.
2. Alesina and Giavazzi (2006), p. 44.
3. Börsch-Supan and Wilke (2009).

4. Ark, O'Mahony and Timmer (2008).

5. Bloom, Sadun, and Van Reenen (2012).

6. Rogerson (2008).

7. Josef Schelchshorn, 2015, "SEAT Points Out The Need For More In-Company Practice-Based Training," Madrid, SEAT Press Release, May 20.

8. Aivazova (2013).

9. Eric Westervelt, "The Secret to Germany's Low Youth Unemployment," National Public Radio, Washington DC, April 4, 2012.

10. Gerrit Wiesmann, "Germany Sets Gold Standard for Training," *Financial Times*, July 9, 2012.

11. Vikat (2004).

12. Mills and others (2014).

13. Begall and Mills (2012).

14. Mundell (1961).

15. See Ager and Brückner (2013) and Peri (2012) for recent studies on the topic.

16. Kahanec (2013) and Bertelsmann Stiftung (2014).

17. Alesina et al. (2013).

18. Kahanec (2012).

19. European Commission (2014a).

20. Mansoor and Quillin (2007).

21. Andor (2014).

22. Eurostat (2015).

23. https://ec.europa.eu/eures/public/homepage.

24. Von Borstel (2014).

25. Furthermore, Directive 2013/55/EU (European Council, 2013) amending the 2005/36/EC (European Council, 2005b) Directive on the recognition of professional qualifications has facilitated the recognition procedures and future introduction of a European Professional Card.

26. Baas and Brücker (2011), and Ruist (2014).

27. Nele Obermueller, "Germany opens doors to immigrants to fuel economy," *Washington Times*, September 11, 2014.

28. Anthony Faiola, "The New Land of Opportunity for Immigrants Is Germany," *Washington Post*, July 27, 2014.

29. Reuters, "ECB's Weidmann - cheap money cannot spur sustained growth," September 15, 2015.

30. European Commission (2013b).

31. Dolenc and Laporšek (2010).

32. Nickell and Layard (1999).

33. Nickell (2003).

34. Võrk et al. (2007).

35. European Commission (2014b).

36. Presentation at the Eurogroup conference, July 8, 2014.

37. Denmark, The Official Website of Denmark, "Flexicurity," http://denmark.dk/en/society/welfare/flexicurity/ (accessed on January 6, 2015).

38. Eurostat, "Unemployment rates, seasonally adjusted, October 2015," http://ec.europa. eu/eurostat/statistics-explained/index.php/File:Unemployment_rates,_seasonally_ adjusted,_October_2015.png (accessed on January 6, 2016).

39. See, for example, Olivier Blanchard and Augustin Landier (2002) and Alberto Alesina, Alberto, Michele Battisti and Joseph Zeira (2015).

40. Botero and others (2004).

41. Djankov (2014a).

42. Eurostat (2014).

43. Christoph Pauly, 2015, Back from the Brink: Spain Emerges as Model for Europe, *Der Spiegel*, March 25.

44. OECD (2013).

45. Djankov (2014).

46. IMF (2015).

47. Boeri and Jimeno (2015).

48. "Schengen Collapse Could Cost EU up to 1.4 trillion euros over Decade," Reuters, February 22, 2016.

Chapter 7

1. Bruno Waterfield, "EU drops olive oil jug ban after public outcry," *The Telegraph*, May 23, 2013.

2. Tim Shipman, "High heels to be cut down to size under new EU proposals forcing hairdressers to wear non-slip flat shoes," *Daily Mail*, April 9, 2012.

3. Doing Business, a project started by one of us in 2002, annually ranks economies by ease of doing business. The genesis of the project is described in Djankov (2016).

4. Coase (1937).

5. World Bank (2004), p. xvii.

6. European Commission (2000).

7. EurActiv, "Sweden admits Lisbon Agenda's failure'", June 3, 2009.

8. European Commission, Secretariat-General, "Europe can do better—Report on best practice in Member States to implement EU legislation in the least burdensome way," Warsaw, 15 November 2011.

9. European Commission, "Better Regulation Agenda: Enhancing transparency and scrutiny for better EU law-making," Strasbourg, May 19, 2015.

10. Leo Cendrowicz, "European Commission moves to cut red tape by overhauling rulemaking procedure," *The Independent*, September 25, 2015.

11. Iain Watson, "David Cameron urges European Union to limit red tape," BBC, October 24, 2013; Tom Parfitt, "Cameron slams EU red tape for harming trade—and urges Britain to do business elsewhere," *The Sunday Express*, July 24, 2015.

12. #cutEUredtape, 2014, Cut EU red tape: One year on, London, November.

13. Vincenzo Scarpetta, "Cutting red tape must be at the heart of any EU reform agenda," Open Europe, May 18, 2015.

14. Parliament, 2010, Impact assessments in the EU: room for improvement: 4th report of session 2009-2010, House of Lords. European Union Committee, Stationery Office, London, Great Britain.

15. 'The Evaluation Partnership Limited' (2007).

16. IP/12/1349.

17. Van den Abeele,(2014).

18. Schömann (2015).

19. European Commission (2013c).

20. European Commission (2014c).

21. Coase (1937).

22. Department of Business and Innovation Skills, 2014, "The Ninth Statement of New Regulation," London, December.

23. For a detailed study on Sweden's efforts at cutting red tape, see World Bank (2014).

24. Maliranta and others (2010).

25. Audretsch and Fritsch (2003) and Audretsch and Keilbach (2004).

26. Bruhn and McKenzie (2013).

27. World Bank (2015).

28. Dower and Potamites (2012).

29. Diniz, Meunier, Mortada, Rakhimova and Taras (2015).

30. Djankov and others (2002, 2003, 2007, 2008a,b, 2009, 2010a,b). Botero and others (2004).

31. Bledowski (2014).

32. European Commission, Secretariat-General, "Europe can do better—Report on best practice in Member States to implement EU legislation in the least burdensome way," Warsaw, 15 November 2011.

33. Directive 2010/45/ EU.

34. Djankov (2014).

Chapter 8

1. BBC Europe Desk, "EU Commission approves proposals for single energy market," February 25, 2015.

2. European Commission, "European Union trade in the World," June 2015, http://trade.ec.europa.eu/doclib/docs/2006/september/tradoc_122532.pdf

3. Eurostat, "Production of primary energy, EU-28, 2013," June 5, 2015. http://ec.europa.eu/eurostat/statistics-explained/index.php/File:Production_of_primary_energy,_EU-28,_2013_(percent25_of_total,_based_on_tonnes_of_oil_equivalent)_YB15.png

4. Djankov (2015).

5. Belgium, France, Germany, Italy, Luxembourg, and the Netherlands.

6. *Treaty Establishing the European Coal and Steel Community,* Paris, April 18, 1951. http://www.ab.gov.tr/files/ardb/evt/1_avrupa_birligi/1_3_antlasmalar/1_3_1_kurucu_antlasmalar/1951_treaty_establishing_ceca.pdf.

7. European Commission (2015j), p. 4.

8. BP (2015).

9. Eurostat (2015).

10. BP (2015), p. 41.

11. Eurostat (2015).

12. Yergin (2011), p. 44; and Alhajji (2005).

13. Åslund (2015), p. 76
14. European Commission, "Energy Union: Secure, Sustainable, Competitive, Affordable Energy for Every European," "Press Release, Brussels, February 25, 2015.
15. Michael Birnbaum, "European industry flocks to U.S. to take advantage of cheaper gas," *Washington Post*, April 1, 2013.
16. Yergin (2011), pp. 229-235.
17. Sampson (1975).
18. Yergin (2011), pp. 382-3.
19. BP (2015), pp. 8, 22.
20. Yergin (2011), pp. 17-18.
21. Griff Witte, "Britain Pulls the Plug on Renewable Energy," *Washington Post*, November 21, 2015.
22. Kjetil Malkenes Hovland, "Vestas Chairman Vows to Keep Company Danish," *The Wall Street Journal*, March 30, 2015.
23. Judy Dempsey and Jack Ewing, "Germany, in Reversal, Will Close Nuclear Plants by 2022," *New York Times*, May 30, 2011.
24. All these documents are conveniently collected in Energy Community (2013).
25. European Commission (2015j), p. 9.
26. European Commission (2015j), p. 4.
27. European Commission (2015j), p. 9.
28. European Commission (2015j), p. 3.
29. European Commission, "Energy Union: Secure, Sustainable, Competitive, Affordable Energy for Every European, "Press Release, Brussels, February 25, 2015.
30. European Commission, "Energy Union: Secure, Sustainable, Competitive, Affordable Energy for Every European, "Press Release, Brussels, February 25, 2015.
31. European Commission, "Energy Union Package: A Framework Strategy for a Resilient Energy Union with a Forward-Looking Climate Change Policy," Brussels, 25.2.2015 COM (2015) 80 final, p. 8.
32. United Nations (1997).
33. Norregaard and Reppelin-Hill (2000).
34. European Commission (2015), pp. 6-7.
35. European Commission, "The EU Emissions Trading System," undated. http://ec.europa.eu/clima/policies/ets/index_en.htm (Accessed on January 1, 2016).
36. Andersen (2010); Gaspar et al. 2016.
37. Norregaard and Reppelin-Hill (2000).
38. Eurostat, "Greenhouse Gas Statistics," December 2015. http://ec.europa.eu/eurostat/statistics-explained/index.php/Greenhouse_gas_emission_statistics (Accessed on January 1, 2016).
39. United Nations (2015b).
40. Gazprom, "Nord Stream," http://www.gazprom.com/about/production/projects/pipelines/nord-stream/ (accessed on October 11, 2015). Gazprom, "Gazprom, BASF, E.ON, ENGIE, OMV and Shell sign Shareholders Agreement on Nord Stream II project," September 4, 2015. http://www.gazprom.com/press/news/2015/september/article245837/ (accessed on October 11, 2015).
41. Christian Oliver and Stefan Wagstyl, "Tusk joins Italian premier in attacking Berlin over gas pipeline," *Financial Times*, December 18, 2015.

42. BP (2015).

43. Henry Foy, "Eastern Europe to confront Berlin over new Russian gas pipeline," *Financial Times*, November 29, 2015.

44. European Commission, "Commissioner Arias Cañete at the European Parliament Plenary: opening and concluding remarks," Strasbourg, 7 October 2015, http://europa.eu/rapid/press-release_SPEECH-15-5797_en.htm

45. European Commission, "Energy Union Package: A Framework Strategy for a Resilient Energy Union with a Forward-Looking Climate Change Policy," Brussels, 25.2.2015 COM (2015) 80 final, p. 11.

46. Henry Foy, "Eastern Europe to confront Berlin over new Russian gas pipeline," *Financial Times*, November 29, 2015.

47. Henry Foy, "Eastern Europe to confront Berlin over new Russian gas pipeline," *Financial Times*, November 29, 2015.

48. Boris Nemtsov and Vladimir Milov, "Putin and Gazprom," *Novaya Gazeta*, September 2, 2008. http://en.novayagazeta.ru/politics/8107.html; Stephen Grey, et al., "How Russia Does Business in the Putin Era," Reuters, November 26, 2014, http://www.reuters.com/investigates/special-report/comrade-capitalism-the-kiev-connection/

49. Reuters, "Gazprom managers may face corruption charges in Switzerland," September 2, 2014.

50. Alexander Bikbov, "A Fifth of Gas Revenues Deposited to Off-Shore Accounts," *RBK*, April 23, 2015.

51. "Energy Union is supported by all EU members, Šefčovič says," *The Slovak Spectator*, November 25, 2015, http://spectator.sme.sk/c/20064659/energy-union-is-supported-by-all-eu-members-sefcovic-says.html

52. European Commission, "Commissioner Arias Cañete at the European Parliament Plenary: opening and concluding remarks," Strasbourg, 7 October 2015, http://europa.eu/rapid/press-release_SPEECH-15-5797_en.htm

53. European Council, The President, "Remarks by President Donald Tusk after the European Council Meeting, 18 December 2015," Statement and Remarks 953/15 Brussels, December 18, 2015.

54. Everett Rosenfeld, "European shale dream is dying before it started," CNBC, February 23, 2015.

Chapter 9

1. Gucci's history is presented at http://www.gucci.com/tr/worldofgucci/mosaic/the_house_of_gucci/gucci_history.

2. Ranking available at http://www.forbes.com/innovative-companies/list/#tab:rank. Accessed December 3, 2015.

3. Ranking available at http://top100innovators.stateofinnovation.thomsonreuters.com/. Accessed December 5, 2015.

4. Ranking available at http://www.technologyreview.com/lists/companies/2015/.

5. Marion Hume, "The secrets of Zara's success," *The Telegraph*, June 22, 2011. Retrieved 2015-12-31.

6. European Commission (2015k).

7. Todd Hixon, "The Rebirth of European Venture Capital," *Forbes*, August 10, 2015.

8. For a list of hi-tech hubs in Europe, see http://younginnovator.eu/innovation-hubs/.

9. Bozkaya and Kerr (2009).

10. Times: https://www.timeshighereducation.co.uk/world-university-rankings/2015/world-ranking#/; Shanghai: http://www.universityrankings.ch/results/Shanghai/2014?ranking=Shanghai&year=2014&region=&q=&s=50

11. Department of Business Innovation and Skills (2014).

12. ten Have, Oortwijn, Broos and Nelissen (2013).

13. Ofcom, "European Broadband Scorecard," Brussels, February 5, 2015.

14. Anne Bouverot. "Mobile sector faces spectrum shortfall," *Financial Times*, October 30, 2014.

15. European Commission (2014).

16. Alex Barker and Daniel Thomas, "Austrian takeover is a touchstone for telecoms deal-makers," *Financial Times*, February 23, 2014.

17. Rebecca Christie, "EU Eyes Public Money to Expand Role of Venture Capital Funds," *Bloomberg*, October 20, 2015.

18. Jamie Nimmo, "Google Ventures: Web giant scraps European start-up investment fund after only eighteen months," Independent, December 7, 2015.

19. Preqin, 2015, 2015 Preqin Global Private Equity & Venture Capital, London, September.

20. Axelson and Martinovic (2015).

21. "Innovation by Fiat," *The Economist,* May 17, 2014.

22. EY, 2015, Global venture Capital Trends and Insights, London, October.

23. Boris Veldhuijzen van Zanten, 2015, "Europe, it's time we built our own Silicon Valley," Next Web, August 15.

24. BCC Research, Nanotechnology: A Realistic Market Assessment (2014).

25. Porter (1998).

26. Eurostat (2015).

27. PWC (2015).

28. Sean Farrell, "Thorntons Bought by Ferrero for £112m," *The Guardian.* 22 June 2015.

29. European Commission (2014d).

Conclusions

1. Eurostat (2015).

References

Acemoglu, Daron, Suresh Naidu, Pascual Restrepo and James A. Robinson. 2015. "Democracy Does Cause Growth," NBER Working Paper No. 20004, Cambridge, Massachusetts, March.

Afonso, Antonio, and Davide Furceri. 2010. "Government Size, Composition, Volatility and Economic Growth," *European Journal of Political Economy*, **26**(4), 517–532.

Ager, P. and M. Brückner. 2013. "Cultural Diversity and Economic Growth: Evidence from the US during the Age of Mass Migration," *European Economic Review*, **64**: 76–97.

Alhajji, A.F. 2005. "The oil weapon: past, present, and future." *Oil and Gas Journal* **103**, no. 17 (May).

Argandoña, Antonio, and Javier Díaz-Giménez, 2013, "Distribution and Capitalization in Spanish Pensions," IESE Business School, Barcelona, Spain.

Aghion, Phillippe, and Peter Howitt. 2008. *The Economics of Growth*, Cambridge, MA: MIT Press.

Aivazova, Natalia. 2013. "Role of Apprenticeships in Combating Youth Unemployment in Europe and the US," Policy Brief 13–20, Washington: Peterson Institute for International Economics, August.

Alesina, Alberto, Michele Battisti and Joseph Zeira. 2015. Technology and Labor Regulations: Theory and Evidence, NBER Working Paper No. 20841.

Alesina, Alberto, and Francesco Giavazzi. 2006. *The Future of Europe: Reform or Decline*. Cambridge, MA: MIT Press.

Alesina, A., Harnoss, J. and H. Rapoport, 2013, "Birthplace Diversity and Economic Prosperity", NBER Working Paper 18699.

Amin, Mohammad, and Simeon Djankov, 2014, "Democratic Institutions and Regulatory Reforms," *Journal of Comparative Economics*, 42, 4: 839–1094, December.

ANACOM, 2011, Comparison of pricing—providers of Universal Postal Service in the European Union, Lisbon, Portugal.

Andor, László. 2014. "Labour Mobility in the European Union—The Inconvenient Truth," Lecture at the University of Bristol, Bristol, The United Kingdom, February 10.

Appel, Hillary. 2011. *Tax Policies in Eastern Europe: Globalization, Regional Integration and the Democratic Compromise*. Ann Arbor: University of Michigan Press.

Åslund, Anders. 1998. *Hälften så dyrt, dubbelt så bra (Half As Expensive, Twice As Good)*, Stockholm: Timbro.

Åslund, Anders. 2002. *Building Capitalism: The Transformation of the Former Soviet Bloc*, Cambridge and New York: Cambridge University Press, 2002.

Åslund, Anders. 2010. *The Last Shall Be the First: the East European Financial Crisis, 2008-10*, Washington, DC: Peterson Institute for International Economics.

Åslund, Anders. 2013. *How Capitalism Was Built: The Transformation of Central and Eastern Europe, Russia, the Caucasus, and Central Asia*, 2nd ed. New York: Cambridge University Press.

Åslund, Anders. 2015. *Ukraine: What Went Wrong and How to Fix It*, Washington, DC: Peterson Institute for International Economics.

Åslund, Anders, and Marek Dabrowski, eds. 2007. *Europe After Enlargement*, New York: Cambridge University Press.

Åslund, Anders, and Marek Dabrowski, eds, 2008. *Challenges of Globalization: Imbalances and Growth*, Washington, DC: Peterson Institute for International Economics.

Åslund, Anders, and Simeon Djankov, eds. 2014. *The Great Rebirth: Lessons from the Victory of Capitalism over Communism*, Washington, DC: Peterson Institute for International Economics.

Åslund, Anders, and Valdis Dombrovskis. 2011. *How Latvia Came through the Financial Crisis*, Washington, DC: Peterson Institute for International Economics.

Atkinson, Tony, Thomas Piketty and Emmanuel Saez, 2011, "Top Incomes in the Long Run of History," *Journal of Economic Literature*, **49** (1): 3–71.

Audretsch, David, and Michael Fritsch. 2003. "Linking Entrepreneurship to Growth: The Case of West Germany." *Industry and Innovation* **10** (1): 65–73.

Audretsch, David, and Max Keilbach. 2004. "Entrepreneurship and Regional Growth: An Evolutionary Interpretation." *Journal of Evolutionary Economics* **14** (5): 605–16.

Auerbach, Alan J. 2002. "Is There a Role for Discretionary Fiscal Policy?" NBER Working Paper No. 9306, Cambridge, MA: NBER.

Axelson, Ulf, and Milan Martinovic. 2015. "European Venture Capital: Myths and Facts," Department of Finance, London School of Economics, July.

Ayar, Shekhar, et al. 2016. "The Refugee Surge in Europe: Economic challenges," IMF Staff Discussion Note, SDN/16/02, January 2016.

Baas, T., and H. Bruecker. 2011. "EU Eastern Enlargement: The Benefits from Integration and Free Labour Movement", CESifo DICE Report 2.

Balcerowicz, Leszek. 1994. "Understanding Postcommunist Transitions," *Journal of Democracy*, **5** (4): 75–89.

Balcerowicz, Leszek, et al. 2013. *Economic Growth in the European Union*, Lisbon Council E-Book.

Barefoot, Kevin, and Jennifer Koncz-Bruner. 2012. "A Profile of U.S. Exporters and Importers of Services: Evidence from New Linked Data on International Trade in Services and Operations of Multinational Companies," *Survey of Current Business*, June.

Barro, Robert. 1989. "Economic Growth in a Cross Section of Countries, NBER Working Paper no. 3120.

Barro, Robert. 1997. *Determinants of Economic Growth*, Cambridge, MA: MIT Press.

Barro, Robert J., and Xavier Sala-i-Martin. 2004. *Economic Growth.* Cambridge, MA: MIT Press.

Begall, Katia, and Melinda Mills. 2012. "The Influence of Educational Field, Occupation, and Occupational Sex Segregation on Fertility in the Netherlands," *European Sociology Review*, 29(4): 720-742.

Bergh, Andreas, and Magnus Henrekson. 2010. *Government Size and Implications for Economic Growth*, Washington: American Enterprise Institute.

Bergh, Andreas, and Magnus Henrekson. 2011. "Government Size and Growth: A Survey and Interpretation of the Evidence," *Journal of Economic Surveys*, **25** (5), 872–897.

Bertelsmann Stiftung. 2014. *Harnessing European Labour Mobility*. Gütersloh.

Blanchard, Olivier, and Augustin Landier. 2002. "The Perverse Effects of Partial Labour Market Reform: Fixed-Term Contracts in France," *The Economic Journal*, **112**: F214-F244.

Blanchard, Olivier, and Daniel Leigh. 2013. "Growth Forecast Errors and Fiscal Multipliers." IMF Working Paper 13/01. Washington.

Bledowski, Krzysztof. 2014. "Europe Slips in Rankings for Ease of Doing Business," mimeo, March.

Bloom, Nicholas, Raffaella Sadun, and John Van Reenen. 2012. "Americans Do IT Better: US Multinationals and the Productivity Miracle," *American Economic Review*, **102** (1): 167–201, February.

Böckers, V., J. Haucap and U. Heimeshoff. 2013. "Benefits of an Integrated European Electricity Market: the Role of Competition," Annex IV to Cost of Non-Europe in the Single Market for Energy, Brussels, May.

Boeri, Tito, and Juan Fransisco Jimeno. 2015. "The unbearable divergence of unemployment in Europe", European Central Bank, Sintra Forum.

Booth, Stephen, Mats Persson, and Raoul Ruparel. 2013. "Kick-Starting Growth: How to Reignite the EU Services Sector," Report 05/2013, Open Europe, Berlin.

Börsch-Supan, Axel H. 2012. "Entitlement Reforms in Europe: Policy Mixes in the Current Pension Reform Process," NBER Working Paper No. 18009, Cambridge Massachusetts, April.

Börsch-Supan, A. and C. B. Wilke. 2009. "Zur mittel- und langfristigen Entwicklung der Erwerbstätigkeit in Deutschland." *Zeitschrift für Arbeitsmarktforschung* (42): 29–48.

Botero, Juan C, Simeon Djankov, Rafael Porta, Florencio C. Lopez-De-Silanes, and Andrei Shleifer. 2004. "The Regulation of Labor," *The Quarterly Journal of Economics*, **119** (4): 1339–1382.

Bouis, Romain, and Romain Dulva. 2011. *Raising Potential Growth after the Crisis*. OECD Working Paper No. 835. Paris: Organization for Economic Co-operation and Development.

Bovenberg, Lans, and Raymond Gradus, 2015, "Reforming Occupational Pension Schemes: the Case of the Netherlands," *Journal of Economic Policy Reform*, **18**, 3: 244–257.

Bozkaya, Ant, and William R. Kerr. 2009. "Labor Regulations and European Private Equity," Harvard Business School, Working Paper 08–043, Cambridge, Massachusetts.

Department of Business Innovation and Skills. 2014. Innovation Report 2014: Innovation, Research and Growth, March.

BP. 2015. "BP Statistical Review of World Energy," London, June.

Briglauer, Wolfgang. 2014. 'The Impact of Regulation and Competition on the Adoption of Fiber-Based Broadband Services: Recent Evidence from the European Member States', *Journal of Regulatory Economics*, 46: 51–79.

Bruhn, Miriam, and David McKenzie. 2013. "Entry Regulation and Formalization of Microenterprises in Developing Countries." Policy Research Working Paper 6507, World Bank, Washington, DC.

Buti, Marco, Alessandro Turrini, Paul Van den Noord, and Pietro Biroli. 2008. "Defying the 'Juncker Curse': Can Reformist Governments Be Re-elected?" *European Economy, Economic Papers* 324, May.

Carlsson, Sten, and Jerker Rosen. 1961. *Svensk Historia (Swedish History)*, Third Edition, Stockholm: Scandinavian University Books.

Claes, Anouk, and Wouter Vergote. 2015. "Econometric study on parcel list prices," Université Saint-Louis Bruxelles, Brussels, Belgium, December.

Clements, Benedict, et al. 2012. "The Challenge of Public Pension Reform in Advanced and Emerging Market Economies," Occasional Paper no. 275, International Monetary Fund, Washington, DC.

Coase, Ronald H. 1937. "The Nature of the Firm". *Economica* **4** (16): 386–405.

Coricelli, Fabrizio. 2007. "Design and Implementation of the Stability and Growth Pact: The Perspective of New Member Sates" in Anders Åslund and Marek Dabrowski, eds., *Europe after Enlargement*, New York: Cambridge University Press, pp. 65–84.

De la Fuente, A and R Doménech, 2013, "The Financial Impact of Spanish Pension Reform: A Quick Estimate," *Journal of Pension Economics and Finance*, **12**(1): 111–137.

De Mooij, Ruud, and Gaëtan Nicodème. 2008 ."How Corporate Tax Competition Reduces Personal Tax Revenue," CESifo DICE Report, no. 1.

Dhaval Dave, Inas Rashad and Jasmina Spasojevic. 2008. "The Effects of Retirement on Physical and Mental Health Outcomes," *Southern Economic Journal*, **75**, 2: 497–523 (October).

Diaz Gimenez, Javier, and Julian Diaz Saavedra. 2014. "The Future of Spanish Pensions," ThE Papers 14/03, Department of Economic Theory and Economic History of the University of Granada.

Diniz, Laura, Frédéric Meunier, Haya Mortada, Parvina Rakhimova and Joonas Taras. 2015. *Registering property: The paths of digitization*, World Bank, Washington DC.

Djankov, Simeon. 2014a. *Inside the Euro Crisis: An Insider's Account*, Washington: Peterson Institute for International Economics.

Djankov, Simeon. 2014b. "Bulgaria: The Greatest Vacillations," in Åslund and Djankov (2014), pp. 135–148.

Djankov, Simeon. 2015a. "Hungary under Orbán: Can Central Planning Revive Its Economy?" Policy Brief 15–11, Peterson Institute for International Economics, Washington DC, July.

Djankov, Simeon. 2015b. *Russia's Economy under Putin: From Crony Capitalism to State Capitalism*, Policy Brief 15–18, Peterson Institute for International Economics, Washington DC.

Djankov, Simeon. 2016. "The Doing Business Project: How It Started: Correspondence." *Journal of Economic Perspectives*, **30** (1): 247–248, February.

Djankov, Simeon, Caroline Freund and Cong Pham, 2010. "Trading on Time," *The Review of Economics and Statistics*, **92** (1): 166–173, February.

Djankov, Simeon, Tim Ganser, Caralee McLiesh, Rita Ramalho, and Andrei Shleifer. 2010. "The Effect of Corporate Taxes on Investment and Entrepreneurship," *American Economic Journal: Macroeconomics*, **2**, 3: 31–64.

Djankov, Simeon, Oliver Hart, Caralee McLiesh and Andrei Shleifer, 2008. "Debt Enforcement around the World," *Journal of Political Economy*, University of Chicago Press, **116** (6): 1105–1149.

Djankov, Simeon, Rafael La Porta, Florencio Lopez-De-Silanes and Andrei Shleifer, 2002. "The Regulation of Entry," *The Quarterly Journal of Economics*, **117** (1): 1–37.

Djankov, Simeon, Rafael La Porta, Florencio Lopez-De-Silanes and Andrei Shleifer, 2003. "Courts," *The Quarterly Journal of Economics*, **118** (2): 453–517.

Djankov, Simeon, Rafael La Porta, Florencio Lopez-de-Silanes and Andrei Shleifer, 2008. "The law and economics of self-dealing," *Journal of Financial Economics*, **88** (3): 430–465.

Djankov, Simeon, Caralee McLiesh and Andrei Shleifer. 2007. "Private Credit in 129 Countries," *Journal of Financial Economics*, **84** (2): 299–329.

Dolenc, Primož, and Suzana Laporšek. 2010. The Tax Wedge on Labor and Its Effect on Employment Growth in the European Union, *Prague Economic Papers*, **4**: 344–358.

Dower, Paul, and Elizabeth Potamites. 2012. "Signaling Credit-Worthiness: Land Titles, Banking Practices and Formal Credit in Indonesia." Working Paper 0186, Center for Economic and Financial Research (CEFIR), Moscow.

Drazen, Allen, and Vittorio Grilli. 1993. "The Benefit of Crises for Economic Reforms," *American Economic Review* **83**, 3: 598–607.

Energy Community. 2013. *The Energy Community: Legal Framework*, 3rd ed., Vienna, July.

Erhard, Ludwig. 1957. *Wohlstand fur Alle (Welfare for All)*, Econ-Verlag Düsseldorf.

Euler, Dieter. 2013. "Germany's dual vocational training system: a model for other countries?" A study commissioned by the Bertelsmann Stiftung.

European Actuarial & Consulting Services (EURACS). 2016. The Netherlands Pension Summary, http://euracs.eu/summaries/summary-the-netherlands/ (Accessed on February 21, 2016).

European Commission. 2000. Presidency Conclusions, Lisbon European Council, Lisbon, March 23–24.

European Commission. 2009. "Longer Working Lives through Pension Reform," Brussels, October.

European Commission. 2012. "The 2012 Ageing Report; Economic and budgetary projections for the 27 EU Member States (2010-2060)," [Joint Report prepared by the

European Commission (DG ECFIN) and the Economic Policy Committee (AWG)], Brussels, May.

European Commission. 2013a. 774% difference in phone call prices across the EU, Press Release, Brussels, August 6.

European Commission. 2013b. A Single Market for Growth and Jobs: An Analysis of Progress Made and Remaining Obstacles in the Member States—Contribution to the Annual Growth Survey 2014, COM (2013) 785 final, Brussels, November.

European Commission. 2013c. Commission initiatives to cut red tape and reduce regulatory burdens, memo, Brussels, September 19.

European Commission. 2014a. Memo on Labor Mobility within the European Union, Brussels, September 25.

European Commission. 2014b. 2014 European Semester: Country-Specific Recommendations: Building Growth, Brussels. September.

European Commission. 2014c. Commission work program 2015. A new start, COM(2014) 910 final, December 16, 2014.

European Commission. 2014d. R&D 2013 Survey, Brussels, May.

European Commission. 2014e. Roma Health Report: Health status of the Roma population, Data collection in the Member States of the European Union, Brussels, August.

European Commission. 2015a. "Growing the Silver Economy in Europe," Background paper, Brussels, February 23.

European Commission. 2015b. Council Recommendation on the 2015 National Reform Program of Croatia and delivering a Council opinion on the 2015 Convergence Program of Croatia, Brussels, May.

European Commission. 2015c. "Completing Europe's Economic and Monetary Union", Report by Jean-Claude Juncker in close cooperation with D Tusk, J Dijsselbloem, M Draghi and M Schulz, Brussels, June.

European Commission. 2015d. A Digital Single Market for Europe: Commission sets out 16 initiatives to make it happen, Brussels, May 6.

European Commission. 2015e. "Action Plan on Building a Capital Markets Union", Communication from the Commission to the European Parliament, the Council, the European Economic and Social Committee and the Committee of the Regions, COM (2015) 468/2 Brussels, September 30.

European Commission. 2015f. Capital Markets Union: an Action Plan to boost business funding and investment financing, Brussels, September 30.

European Commission. 2015g. Report on the Eleventh Round of Negotiations for the Transatlantic Trade and Investment Partnership, Miami, 19–23 October.

European Commission. 2015h. Commission launches work on establishing a Capital Markets Union, Brussels, Press Release, 28 January.

European Commission. 2015i. Proposal for a Regulation of the European Parliament and of the Council on the prospectus to be published when securities are offered to the public or admitted to trading, Brussels, November 30.

European Commission. 2015j. Energy Union Package: A Framework Strategy for a Resilient Energy Union with a Forward-Looking Climate Change Policy," Brussels, 25.2.2015 COM 80, February.

European Commission. 2015k. Europe's future is digital, Press Release, Brussels, 14 April.

European Parliament. 2000. "Lisbon European Council 23 And 24 March 2000, Presidency Conclusions," http://www.europarl.europa.eu/summits/lis1_en.htm

European Parliamentary Research Service. 2014. "Mapping the Cost of Non-Europe, 2014-19, 2nd edition, Brussels: European Parliament, July.

Eurostat. 2015. Brussels.

Eurostat. 2015. "Production of Primary Energy, EU-28, 2013," Luxembourg, June 5.

The Evaluation Partnership Limited. 2007. "Evaluation of the Commission's Impact Assessment System—Final report," Brussels.

Ezra, Don. 2011. "The Dutch Pension system," Benefits Quarterly, Fourth Quarter.

Fatas, A., and I. Mihov. 2003. "The Case for Restricting Fiscal Policy Discretion," Quarterly Journal of Economics, 118, 4: 1419–1447.

FIEC (European Construction Industry Federation). 2014. Contractors are pioneers and key contributors to economic growth, Brussels, November.

Fölster, Stefan, and Nima Sanandaji. 2014. Renaissance for Reforms, Stockholm: Timbro.

Friedman, Milton and Rose. 1980. Free to Choose, New York: Hartcourt.

Gill, Indermit S., and Martin Raiser, eds. 2012. Golden Growth: Restoring the Lustre of the European Economic Model, Washington: World Bank.

Gaspar, Vitor, Michael Keen, and Ian Parry, "Climate Change: How to Price Paris," IMFdirect—The IMF Blog, January 11, 2016.

Goleniowska, Stanislawa. 1997. "Delayed Reforms of the Social Policy," in *Economic Scenarios for Poland*. Warsaw: Center for Social and Economic Research, pp. 31–42.

Gorodnichenko, Yuriy, Jorge Martinez-Vazquez and Klara Sabrianova Peter. 2009. "Myth and reality of flat tax reform: Micro estimates of tax evasion and productivity response in Russia," *Journal of Political Economy*, **117**, 504–554.

Grazia Attinasi, Maria, and Luca Metteli. 2016. "Is Fiscal Consolidation Self-Defeating?" European Central Bank Working Paper no. 1883, February.

Guiso, Luigi, Paola Sapienza, and Luigi Zingales. 2014. "Monnet's Error?" Paper Presented to the Fall 2014 Brookings Panel on Economic Activity, September.

Hansson, Pär, and Magnus Henrekson. 1994. "A New Framework for Testing the Effect of Government Spending on Growth and Productivity," *Public Choice*, **81** (3-4) 381–401,

Hayek, Friedrich A. 1960. *The Constitution of Liberty*. London: Routledge & Kegan Paul.

Heckman, J. J. and B. Jacobs. 2010. "Policies to create and destroy human capital in Europe." NBER Working Paper Nr. 15742.

Hedenskog, Jacob, and Robert L. Larsson, 2007, *Russian Leverage on the CIS and the Baltic States*, Sweden Defense Research Agency, Stockholm.

Heitger, Bernhard. 2001. "The Scope of Government and Its Impact on Economic Growth in OECD Countries," Kiel Institute of World Economics, Kiel Working Paper, no. 1034, April.

High Level group on Administrative Burdens, 2014, Cutting Red Tape in Europe: Legacy and Outlook, Final Report, Brussels, October.

#cutEUredtape, 2014, Cut EU red tape: One year on, London, November.

Holton, Richard. 1986. "Industrial Politics in France: Nationalisation under Mitterand," *West European Politics*, **9**, 1.

Houriet-Segard, G. and J.-M. Pasteels. 2012. "Projections of Economically Active Population. A Review of National and International Methodologies." ILO Department of Statistics Working Paper Nr. 4.

International Monetary Fund. 2015. "Italy: Concluding Statement of the 2015 Article IV Mission," Rome, May 18.

Jensen, Bradford. 2011. *Global Trade in Services: Fear, Facts, and Offshoring*, Washington: Peterson Institute for International Economics.

Juncker, Jean-Claude, et al. 2015. "Preparing for Next Steps on better Economic Governance in the Euro Area. Analytical Note," Informal European Council, Brussels, February 12.

Kagan, Robert. 2012. *The World America Made*, New York: Knopf.

Kahanec, Martin. 2013. "Labor Mobility in an Enlarged European Union", in A.F. Constant and K.F. Zimmermann (eds), International Handbook on the Economics of Migration, Cheltenham: Edward Elgar.

Karam, Philippe, et al. 2010. "Macroeconomic Effects of Public Pension Reforms," Working Paper 10/297, International Monetary Fund, Washington, DC.

Kelly, John. 1992. *A Short History of Western Legal Thought*, Clarendon Press, Oxford, the United Kingdom.

Keynes, John Maynard [1936] (1973) *The General Theory of Employment, Interest, and Money*. London: Macmillan.

King, John Edward. 2002. *A History of Post Keynesian Economics since 1936*. Edward Elgar Publishing.

Kinoshita, Yuko, and Fang Guo. 2015. "Nordic Lessons to Raise Female Labor Participation in NE Asia," IMF WP/15/56

Kirkegaard, Jacob. 2015. "The True Levels of Government and Social Expenditures in Advanced Economies," Peterson Institute for International Economics, Policy Brief, 15-4, March.

Kneller, Richard, Michael F. Bleaney, and Norman Gemmell. 1999. "Fiscal Policy and Growth: Evidence from OECD Countries," *Journal of Public Economics*, **74** (2), 171–190.

Kornai, János. 1992. "The Postsocialist Transition and the State: Reflections in Light of Hungarian Fiscal Problems," *American Economic Review* **82** (2): 1–21.

Kuznetz, Simon. 1955. "Economic Growth and Income Inequality," *American Economic Review*, **45**, 1: 1–28.

La Porta, Rafael, Florencio Lopez-de-Silanes, Andrei Shleifer, and Robert Vishny. 1998. "Law and Finance," Journal of Political Economy, **106** (6): 1113–1155.

Laar, Mart. 2002. *Little Country That Could*. London: Centre for Research into Post-Communist Economies.

Laar, Mart. 2014. "Estonia: the Most Radical Reform" in Anders Åslund and Simeon Djankov, eds., *The Great Rebirth: lessons for the Victory of Capitalism over Communism*, Washington: Peterson Institute for International Economics, pp. 271–278.

Langfield, S., and M. Pagano. 2015. "Bank bias in Europe: Effects on systemic risk and growth", Frankfurt: European Central Bank Working Paper No. 1797, May.

Liedtke, Patrick. 2006. From Bismarck's Pension Trap to the New Silver Workers of Tomorrow: Reflections on the New German Pension Problem. *European Papers on the New Welfare*, no. 4. Trieste: The Risk Institute, August.

Lindbeck, Assar. 2012. *Ekonomi är att välja (Economics Is to Choose)*, Stockholm: Albert Bonnier.

Lindbeck, Assar, et al. 1994. *Turning Sweden Around*, Cambridge, MA: MIT Press.

Lindbeck, Assar, and Dennis J. Snower. 1986. "Wage Setting, Unemployment, and Insider-Outsider Relations," *American Economic Review*, Vol. **76**, 2: 235–239 (May).

Maes, Marjan, and Benjamin Stammen. 2011. "The impact of (early) retirement on the subsequent physical and mental health of the retired: a survey among general practitioners in Belgium," Faculty of Economics, HUB Research paper 2011/03, March.

Maliranta, Mika, Petri Rouvinen and Pekka Ylä-Anttila. 2010. "Finland's Path to the Global Productivity Frontier through Creative Destruction." *International Productivity Monitor* 20 (Fall): 68–84.

Mankiw, Gregory, Matthew Weinzierl and Danny Yagan. 2009. "Optimal Taxation in Theory". NBER Working Paper no. 15071.

Mansoor, A. and B. Quillin, 2007, "Migration and Remittances: Eastern Europe and the Former Soviet Union", World Bank, Washington, D.C.

Mills, Melinda, Patrick Präg, Flavia Tsang, Katia Begall, James Derbyshire, Laura Kohle, Céline Miani and Stijn Hoorens. 2014. "Use of Childcare Services in the EU Member States and Progress towards the Barcelona Targets," Brussels, April.

Mirrlees, James, and Peter Diamond. 1971a. "Optimal Taxation and Public Production I: Production Efficiency," *American Economic Review* **61**: 8–27.

Mirrlees, James, and Peter Diamond. 1971b. "Optimal Taxation and Public Production II: Tax Rules," *American Economic Review* 61 (1971): 261–278.

Mitchell, Daniel J. 2008. "The Global Flat Tax Revolution: Lessons for Policy Makers," *Prosperitas*, vol. 8, 1, February.

Monnet, Jean. 1976. *Memoires*, Paris: Fayard.

Monteaguado, J., A. Rutkowski and D. Lorenzani, 2012. The economic impact of the Services Directive: A first assessment following implementation. *European Economy* No. 456.

Monti, Mario. 2010. A New Strategy for the Single Market: At the Service of Europe's Economy and Society, Bocconi University, Milan, Italy, May.

Mundell, Robert. 1961. "A Theory of Optimum Currency Areas," *American Economic Review*, **51**(4): 657–665.

Musgrave, Richard. 1959. *The Theory of Public Finance: A Study in Public Economy*, New York: McGraw-Hill.

Mustilli, Federica, and Jacques Pelkmans. 2013. "Access Barriers to Services Markets: Mapping, Tracing, Understanding and Measuring," Special Report No.77, Centre for European Policy Studies, Brussels, June.

Natali, David, and Furio Stamati. 2013. "Reforming pensions in Europe: a comparative country analysis," Working Paper 2013.08, European Trade Union Institute, Brussels, Belgium.

Nazarko, Joanicjusz, and Ewa Chodakowska. 2015. Measuring Productivity of Construction Industry in Europe with Data Envelopment Analysis, *Procedia Engineering*, 122, Pages 204–212.

Newbery, David, Goran Strbac and Ivan Viehoff. 2015. The benefits of integrating European electricity markets, EPRG Working Paper 1504, Cambridge Working Paper in Economics, Cambridge University, the United Kingdom.

Nickell, S. 2003. "Employment and Taxes." CESifo Working Paper No. 1109.

Nickell, S., Layard, R. 1999. "Labour Market Institutions and Economic Performance," in Ashenfelter, O., Card, D., ed., Handbook of Labor Economics. Amsterdam: North Holland, pp. 3029–3084.

Norregaard, John, and Valerie Reppelin-Hill. 2000. "Controlling Pollution: Using Taxes and Tradable Permits," International Monetary Fund, *Economic Issues* no. 25, December.

North, Douglass C. 1981. Structure and Change in Economic History. New York: Norton.

Ogrokhina. Olena. 2015. Market integration and price convergence in the European Union, *Journal of International Money and Finance*, **56**: 55–74, September.

PwC, London Economics and Ecorys, 2011. Public procurement in Europe: Cost and effectiveness.

Organization for Economic Cooperation and Development (OECD). 2013. The 2012 Labor Market Reform in Spain: A Preliminary Assessment, Paris: OECD.

Organization for Economic Cooperation and Development (OECD). 2015a. *Economic Policy Reforms: Going for Growth*, Paris: OECD.

Organization for Economic Cooperation and Development (OECD). 2015b. *Pensions at a Glance*, Paris: OECD.

Organization for Economic Cooperation and Development (OECD). 2015c. *Trade Statistics*, Paris: OECD.

Peri, G. 2012. "The Effect of Immigration on Productivity: Evidence from US States." *Review of Economics and Statistics*, **94** (1): 348–358.

Petkova, Lyudmila. 2012. "Tax Reform in Personal Income Taxation". *Ministry of Finance* Bulgaria, June. http://www.minfin.bg/document/10885:1

Piketty, Thomas. 2014. *Capital in the Twenty-First Century,* Harvard University Press, Cambridge, Massachusetts.

Porter, Michael E. 1998. *Competitive Advantage,* New York: Free Press.

Prescott, Edward. 2004. "Why Do Americans Work so Much More than Europeans?" Federal Reserve Bank Minneapolis Quarterly Review, 28, October.

PricewaterhouseCoopers 2015. *2015 Global Innovation 1000 Study,*

Arthur ten Have, Wija Oortwijn, Pieter Broos and Emmy Nelissen, 2013, European Cooperation on Health Technology Assessment, Erasmus University, Rotterdam, January.

Reid, T.R. 2009. The Healing of America: A Global Quest for Better, Cheaper, and Fairer Health Care, New York: Penguin.

Reinhardt, Carmen, and Kenneth Rogoff. 2009. *This Time Is Different,* Princeton: Princeton. University Press.

Reinhart, Carmen M. and M. Belen Sbrancia. 2015. "The Liquidation of Government Debt," IMF Working Paper, WP/15/7, January.

Rice, Neil, Iain Lang, William Henley, and David Melzer. 2011. "Common Health Predictors of Early Retirement: Findings from the English Longitudinal Study of Ageing," *Age and Ageing,* **40**, 1: 54–61.

Rodrik, Dani. 2011. *The Globalization Paradox: Democracy and the Future of the World Economy,* New York: Cambridge University Press.

Rodrik, Dani, Arvind Subramanian and Francesco Trebbi, 2004, "Institutions Rule: The Primacy of Institutions over Geography and Integration in Economic Development," *Journal of Economic Growth.* **9**, 2: 131–165.

Rogerson, Richard. 2008. "Structural Transformation and the Deterioration of European Labor Market Outcomes," *Journal of Political Economy,* **116** (2): 235–259.

Roxburgh, Charles, Jan Mischke, et al. 2010. *Beyond Austerity: A path to economic growth and renewal in Europe.* Washington, DC: McKinsey Global Institute

Ruist, J., 2014, "The Fiscal Consequences of Unrestricted Immigration from Romania and Bulgaria," Working Papers in Economics 584, Dept of Economics, University of Gothenburg.

Sampson, Anthony. 1975. *The Seven Sisters: The Great Oil Companies & the World They Shaped,* New York: Viking.

Sapir, André, ed. 2010. *Europe's Economic Priorities 2010-2015: Memos to the New Commission,* Brussels: Bruegel.

Sapir, André, et al. 2015. *EU to DO 2015-2019: Memos to the New EU Leadership.* Brussels: Bruegel.

Schömann, Isabelle. 2015. "EU REFIT machinery 'cutting red tape' at the cost of the acquis communautaire," ETUI Policy Brief N° 5/2015, European Economic, Employment and Social Policy, Brussels, June.

Servan-Schreiber, Jean-Jacques. 1968. *The American Challenge,* New York: Hamilton

Skou Andersen, Mikael. 2010. "Europe's experience with carbon-energy taxation," *Sapiens,* **3**, 2: 48–71.

Slemrod, Joel, and Christian Gillitzer. 2013. *Tax Systems,* Cambridge, Massachusetts: MIT Press.

Springford, John. 2012. How to Build European Services Markets, Center for European Reform, London.

Steinberg, Chad, and Masato Nakane. 2012. "Can Women Save Japan?" IMF Working Paper 12/248. Washington, October.

Stockholm International Peace Research Institute (SIPRI). 2015. "Trends in World Military Expenditure, 2014," SIPR Fact Sheet, April.

Sundén, Annika. 1998. The Swedish NDC Pension Reform, *Annals of Public and Cooperative Economics*, **69**, 4, December.

Sweden Ministry of Health and Social Affairs. 1998. *The Pension Reform in Sweden*, Final Report, June, available at www.pension.gov.se/in percent20English/final.pdf

Tabellini, Guido, and Charles Wyplosz. 2006. "Supply-side Reforms in Europe: Can the Lisbon Strategy be Repaired?" *Swedish Economic Policy Review* 13 (1): 101–156.

Tanzi, Vito. 2007. "Fiscal Policy and Fiscal Rules in the European Union" " in Anders Åslund and Marek Dabrowski, eds., *Europe after Enlargement*, New York: Cambridge University Press, pp. 50–64.

Tanzi, Vito. 2011. *Government Versus Market: The Changing Economic Role of the State*, New York: Cambridge University Press.

Tanzi, Vito, and Ludger Schuknecht. 2000. *Public Spending in the 20th Century*, New York: Cambridge University Press.

Thévenon, O. 2013. "Drivers of Female Labor Force Participation in the OECD", OECD Social, Employment and Migration Working Papers, No. 145, OECD.

Thiel, M., 2014, Fragmentation of wholesale funding markets—an empirical approach to measure country-specific risk premia in banks' bond spreads, ECFIN Economic Brief, Issue 32.

Trabandt, Mathias, and Harald Uhlig. 2012. "How Do Laffer Curves Differ Across Countries?" NBER (17862).

Transparency International. 2015. *Corruption Perceptions Index*. Berlin. Available http://transparency.org/policy_research/surveys_indices/cpi/2015.

United Nations. 1997. "Background on the UNFCCC: The international response to climate change," New York.

United Nations. 2015a. *Human Development Report 2015*, New York: United Nations Development Program.

United Nations. 2015b. "Framework Convention on Climate Change, "Paris Agreement," December 12.

Van Ark, Bart, Mary O'Mahony and Marcel P. Timmer. 2008. The Productivity Gap between Europe and the United States: Trends and Causes, *The Journal of Economic Perspectives*, Vol. 22, No. 1 (Winter), pp. 25–44.

Van den Abeele, Eric. 2014. "The EU's REFIT strategy: a new bureaucracy in the service of competitiveness?" Working Paper 2014.05, European Trade Union Institute, Brussels, Belgium, May.

Véron, Nicolas, and Guntram Wolff. 2015. "Capital Markets Union: A Vision for the Long Term", Bruegel Policy Contribution 2015/05, Brussels, April.

Vidlund, Mika, and Sirkka-Liisa Kivelä. 2012. Annual National Report 2012. Pensions, Health Care and Long-term Care. ASISP—Analytical Support on the Socio-Economic Impacts of Social Protection Reforms; Finland, March.

Von Borstel, S. 2014. "Zahl der Kindergeldanträge aus Ausland unterschätzt," *Die Welt*, April 29.

Võrk, A., R. Leetmaa, A. Paulus, and S. Anspal. 2007. "Tax-benefit Systems in the New Member States and their Impact on Labor Supply and Employment." Policy Paper 29/2007, praxis Center for Policy Studies, Tallinn.

Williamson, John, ed. 1994. *The Political Economy of Policy Reform*. Washington, DC: Institute for International Economics.

Winston, Clifford, and Jia Yan. 2015. "Open Skies: Estimating Travelers' Benefits from Free Trade in Airline Services," *American Economic Journal: Economic Policy*, **7** (2): 370–414.

World Bank. 1994. *Averting the Old Age Crisis: Policies to Protect the Old And Promote Growth*. Oxford: Oxford University Press.

World Bank. 2004. *Doing Business: Understanding Regulation*, Washington DC.

World Bank. 2014. *Sweden's Business Climate: Opportunities for Entrepreneurs through Improved Regulations*, Washington DC.

World Bank. 2015. *Doing Business: Measuring Regulatory Quality and Efficiency*, Washington DC.

World Bank. 2016. *Doing Business in 2016: Measuring Regulatory Quality and Efficiency*, Washington, DC: World Bank.

World Economic Forum. 2016. "Europe: What to Watch out for in 2016-2017." Geneva: World Economic Forum, January.

Daniel Yergin, 2011, *The Quest: Energy, Security, and the Remaking of the Modern World*, New York: Penguin.